teach® yourself

beginner's russian
rachel farmer

For over 60 years, more than
40 million people have learnt over
750 subjects the **teach yourself**
way, with impressive results.

be where you want to be
with **teach yourself**

Dedication
To Peter, Lucy and Catherine

For UK order enquiries: please contact Bookpoint Ltd, 130 Milton Park, Abingdon, Oxon OX14 4SB. Telephone: +44 (0) 1235 827720. Fax: +44 (0) 1235 400454. Lines are open 09.00–18.00, Monday to Saturday, with a 24-hour message answering service. Details about our titles and how to order are available at www.teachyourself.co.uk

For USA order enquiries: please contact McGraw-Hill Customer Services, PO Box 545, Blacklick, OH 43004-0545, USA. Telephone: 1-800-722-4726. Fax: 1-614-755-5645.

For Canada order enquiries: please contact McGraw-Hill Ryerson Ltd, 300 Water St, Whitby, Ontario L1N 9B6, Canada. Telephone: 905 430 5000. Fax: 905 430 5020.

Long renowned as the authoritative source for self-guided learning – with more than 40 million copies sold worldwide – the **teach yourself** series includes over 300 titles in the fields of languages, crafts, hobbies, business, computing and education.

British Library Cataloguing in Publication Data: a catalogue record for this title is available from the British Library.

Library of Congress Catalog Card Number: on file.

First published in UK 1996 by Hodder Arnold, 338 Euston Road, London, NW1 3BH.

First published in US 1996 by Contemporary Books, a Division of the McGraw-Hill Companies, 1 Prudential Plaza, 130 East Randolph Street, Chicago, IL 60601 USA.

This edition published 2003.

The **teach yourself** name is a registered trade mark of Hodder Headline Ltd.

Copyright © 1996, 2003 Rachel Farmer

Typeset by Transet Limited, Coventry, England.
Printed in Great Britain for Hodder Arnold, a division of Hodder Headline, 338 Euston Road, London NW1 3BH, by Cox & Wyman Ltd, Reading, Berkshire.

Hodder Headline's policy is to use papers that are natural, renewable and recyclable products and made from wood grown in sustainable forests. The logging and manufacturing processes are expected to conform to the environmental regulations of the country of origin.

Impression number   10 9 8 7 6 5 4
Year   2009 2008 2007 2006 2005 2004

contents

introduction

Teach Yourself Beginner's Russian is the course to use if you are a complete beginner or have just a smattering of Russian. It is a self-study course, and will help you to speak, understand and read the language sufficiently for you to visit Russia or receive Russian visitors at home.

The course works best with the accompanying recording, but it is not essential. The recorded dialogues and exercises will give you practice in understanding the language and in pronouncing it correctly, and will give you confidence to speak out loud. Each unit contains at least one activity which requires the recording, but the material will always be covered by other activities as well. If you don't have the recording, use the **Pronunciation guide** to help you pronounce the words correctly. Always read the words and dialogues out loud in a strong, clear voice.

How the units work

In Units 1–2 you will learn to read the Russian alphabet, and in Units 3–10 you will learn the basic structures of the language which you will need in different situations. In Unit 11 you will learn to read the handwritten Russian script and to write it if you choose, and in Units 12–20 you will learn how to cope with practical situations in more detail.

Within each unit you will find:

• A list of things you can expect to learn.

• Notes marked ℹ provide some basic background information on Russian customs and way of life relevant to the unit. You should bear in mind that in recent times there have been many changes in Russian life and even in the language as it absorbs many new international words. You may therefore find if you visit Russia that details of everyday life have changed. This is particularly likely to be true with matters relating to the economic state of the country.

- **Key words and phrases** which will be used in the unit. Try to learn them by heart as they will help you with the rest of the unit and will often appear again later in the book. In Units 3–10, while you are getting used to the Russian alphabet, each word will have its pronunciation in English letters next to it. Try not to become dependent on this, but just use it to check any sounds you are not sure of.

- If you have the recording, listen to the dialogue **Диалóг** once or twice to try and get the gist of it. Then use the pause button to break it up into phrases and repeat each phrase out loud to develop your accent. If you only have the book, read the dialogue through several times before you look up the words and say the phrases out loud. As you become more confident, you could cover up part of the dialogue and try to remember what to say.

- All languages work by following certain patterns, and the **Mechanics of the langauge** section shows you examples of the mechanics of constructing Russian. Once you have become used to the patterns you can make up sentences yourself by changing words or their endings.

- The exercises allow you to practise the language which you have just learned in the **Mechanics of the language** section. For some of the exercises you need the recording. It is important to do the exercises and to check your answers in the back of the book so that you are sure you understand the language in one unit before moving on.

- In the later units you may find a short Russian anecdote or joke.

- At the end of Units 3–9 you will find a short revision section entitled **Test yourself**.

- At the end of Unit 20 you will find two **Revision tests**, the first covering Units 1–10 and the second covering Units 12–20.

How to succeed in learning Russian

1 Spend a little bit of time on Russian each day, rather than a marathon session once a week. It is most effective to spend no more than 20–30 minutes at a time.

2 Go back and revise words and language patterns regularly until things which seemed difficult become easier.

3 Say the words and phrases out loud and listen to the recording whenever you can.

4 Take every opportunity to use the language. Try to meet a Russian speaker or join a class to practise with other people.

5 Don't worry if you make mistakes. The most important thing is to communicate, and by jumping in at the deep end and trying things out, you may surprise yourself with how well you can make yourself understood!

Symbols and abbreviations

▶ The recording is needed for the following section.

ℹ Basic background information about Russia and the Russians.

(*m*) masculine   (*n*) neuter   (*f*) feminine   (*pl*) plural
(*sing*) singular

At the back of the book

At the back of the book is a reference section which contains:

• Answers
• Numbers
• A brief summary of Russian language patterns
• An English–Russian vocabulary list
• A Russian–English vocabulary list containing all the words in the course

Pronunciation guide

First, here are a few tips to help you acquire an authentic accent:

1 Listen carefully to the recording or Russian speaker, and whenever possible, repeat words and phrases loudly and clearly.

2 Make a recording of yourself and compare it with the one provided.

3 Ask a Russian speaker to listen to your pronunciation and tell you how to improve it.

4 Practise specific sounds which you find difficult.

5 Make a list of words which give you trouble and practise them.

Russian sounds

Most English speakers can pronounce most Russian sounds without difficulty. What is more, reading Russian is often easier than reading English with its complicated spelling, e.g. *enough*, *plough*, *cough*. In Russian, what you see is more or less what you get, and if you join together the sound of the individual letters you will usually end up with the sound of the whole word. The first two units will take you through the sounds in detail, but here is a reference guide to help you.

Consonants

Б	б	**b**	as in *bag*
В	в	**v**	as in *visitor*
Г	г	**g**	as in *good*
Д	д	**d**	as in *duck*
Ж	ж	**zh**	as in *pleasure*
З	з	**z**	as in *zoo*
К	к	**k**	as in *kiss*
Л	л	**l**	as in *lane*
М	м	**m**	as in *moon*
Н	н	**n**	as in *note*
П	п	**p**	as in *pin*
Р	р	**r**	as in *rabbit*
С	с	**s**	as in *sit*
Т	т	**t**	as in *tennis*
Ф	ф	**f**	as in *funny*
Х	х	**ch**	as in *loch*
Ц	ц	**ts**	as in *cats*
Ч	ч	**ch**	as in *chicken*
Ш	ш	**sh**	as in *ship*
Щ	щ	**shsh**	as in *Spanish sherry*

When you listen to spoken Russian, you may notice that the first six consonants in the list will change their sound if they occur at the end of a word. Don't worry about this, but try to get into the habit of imitating the way that Russians speak.

Б	б	**b**	at the end of a word sounds like **p**
В	в	**v**	at the end of a word sounds like **f**
Г	г	**g**	at the end of a word sounds like **k**
Д	д	**d**	at the end of a word sounds like **t**
Ж	ж	**zh**	at the end of a word sounds like **sh**
З	з	**z**	at the end of a word sounds like **s**

Vowels

If a word has more than one syllable there will be one vowel which is pronounced more strongly than the others. This is called a stressed vowel. When vowels are stressed they are pronounced clearly and strongly. When they are in an unstressed position they are pronounced more weakly. Listen to the recording whenever possible and notice what happens to vowels in different positions as you repeat the words.

А	а	**a**	as in *father*
Е	е	**ye**	as in *yesterday*
Ё	ё	**yo**	as in *yonder*
И	и	**ee**	as in *street*
Й	й	**y**	as in *toy*
О	о	**o**	as in *born*
У	у	**oo**	as in *boot*
	ы		sounds rather like **i** in *ill* (say it by keeping your mouth very slightly open and drawing your tongue back as far as it will go).
Э	э	**e**	as in *leg*
Ю	ю	**yoo**	as in *universe*
Я	я	**ya**	as in *yard*

The soft and hard signs

ь   The soft sign has the effect of softening the preceding consonant, as if adding a soft **y** sound to it.

ъ   The hard sign is rare, is not pronounced, and makes a tiny pause between syllables.

01

the Russian alphabet

In this unit you will learn
- how to read 20 letters of the Russian alphabet
- how to ask where something is
- how to show where something is
- how to thank someone

Before you start

You may think that Russian will be difficult to learn because of its different alphabet, but you will probably be surprised how quickly you can learn to recognize the letters. The Russian alphabet is called the Cyrillic alphabet after the monk, St Cyril, who invented it. In order to follow this course, you will need to know how to read Russian in its printed form, so that is what you will concentrate on for the first two units. Later, in Unit 11, you will have the chance to see how Russian is written by hand. One of the good things about Russian is that words are pronounced more or less as they are written, so in that way it is easier than English with its complicated spellings.

If you have the recording, make sure you have it handy as you'll be using it to practise the pronunciation of the words. Russian has some sounds which will be new to you, but if you listen carefully and repeat the words clearly, you should soon make progress. It might be helpful to record yourself and compare what you sound like with the recording. If you don't have the recording, use the **Pronunciation guide** on page viii.

Remember that it is more effective to study little and often than to try and do a long session every now and then. Your concentration will probably be best in 20-minute bursts.

The Russian alphabet

The Russian alphabet can be divided into four groups of letters: those which look and sound like English letters; 'false friends' which look like English letters but sound different; a group of unfamiliar letters with familiar sounds; and those which are quite unlike English letters.

▶ English look- and sound-alikes

The first group (those which look and sound like their English counterparts) contains five letters:

A a	sounds like	a	in	*father*
T т	sounds like	t	in	*tennis*
O o	sounds like	o	in	*born*
M м	sounds like	m	in	*moon*
К к	sounds like	k	in	*kiss*

With these letters you can already read the following Russian words:

а́том	atom
ма́ма	mum
кот	cat

You will notice that **а́том** and **ма́ма** have an accent over the letter **а́**. This is called a 'stress mark' and is used to show you which syllable to emphasize in words of more than one syllable. In English, if we underlined every stress syllable, it would look like this: *the pi<u>a</u>no pl<u>a</u>yer wants to rec<u>o</u>rd a r<u>e</u>cord.* When you are speaking Russian, put lots of energy into the stressed syllable and pronounce it clearly. The vowels in unstressed syllables are underplayed and do not need to be pronounced so clearly. For example, in the syllable before the stress, **o** will sound like **a** in *father*, and in any other position it will sound like **a** in *again*. You will soon get used to where the stress falls on words which you use often, but to help you, the stress marks will be shown throughout the book.

▶ False friends

The next group of letters contains seven letters:

C	**c**	sounds like	**s**	in	*sit*
P	**p**	sounds like	**r**	in	*rabbit*
E	**e**	sounds like	**ye**	in	*yesterday* (when unstressed, like **yi** or **i**)
B	**в**	sounds like	**v**	in	*visitor*
H	**н**	sounds like	**n**	in	*note*
У	**y**	sounds like	**oo**	in	*boot*
X	**x**	sounds like	**ch**	in	*loch* (Scots)

Reading practice

To practise the 12 letters which you have now met, see if you can read the words in the following exercises. They are mostly international words, so you should recognize them without too much difficulty. When you have done this, listen to them on the recording if you have it, and repeat them. Then try reading them again without looking at the English meaning until you can say them easily.

▶ **1** First, we have five cities. See if you can match them up with their English names.

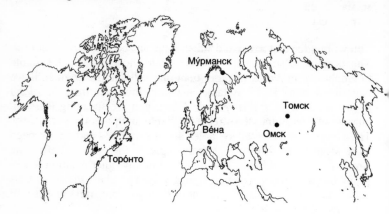

If you decide that **a** is Tomsk, write **a ii**. You can check the answers in the back of your book. Don't forget to say the words out loud.

a Томск   **b** Торóнто   **c** Вéна   **d** Омск   **e** Мýрманск
i *Vienna*   **ii** *Tomsk*   **iii** *Murmansk*   **iv** *Toronto*   **v** *Omsk*

▶ **2** Now try to identify these five Russian names.

a Свéта   **b** Антóн   **c** Вéра   **d** Ромáн   **e** Áнна
i *Anna*   **ii** *Vera*   **iii** *Sveta*   **iv** *Anton*   **v** *Roman*

▶ **3** Imagine you are walking around Moscow and you see the following places signposted. What are they?

a МЕТРÓ

b ТЕÁТР

c РЕСТОРÁН

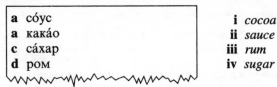

4 A Russian friend gives you a shopping list. What do you need to buy?

a со́ус

a кака́о

c са́хар

d ром

i *cocoa*

ii *sauce*

iii *rum*

iv *sugar*

If you have managed to read these words out loud and have practised them until you are fairly confident, you are ready to move on to another group of letters.

▶ Unfamiliar letters with familiar sounds

The next group of letters contains 13 new letters. To make it easier, you are going to meet only five of them to begin with.

П п sounds like **p** in *pin*

Л л sounds like **l** in *lane*

И и sounds like **ee** in *street*

З з sounds like **z** in *zoo*

Д д sounds like **d** in *duck*

Now see if you can read words containing the 17 letters you have met so far. Remember to say them all out loud, and check your pronunciation with the recording if you have it.

Reading practice

5 These words are to do with sport. Read them and match them up with the pictures below. The English words will appear in the correct order in the answers at the back of the book.

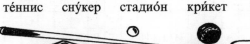

те́ннис   сну́кер   стадио́н   кри́кет

Now match up the remaining words about sport with the English words below.

старт	нокáут	трéнер	рекóрд	атлéтика	спорт	спортсмéн
record	*knockout*	*sport*	*trainer*	*start*	*sportsman*	*athletics*

▶ **6** Next can you identify the names of the nine cities around the world? Draw lines linking the Russian and English names.

a	Минск	i	*Moscow*
b	Москвá	ii	*Samarkand*
c	Амстердáм	iii	*Tokyo*
d	Кúев	iv	*London*
e	Тóкио	v	*Madrid*
f	Лóндон	vi	*Minsk*
g	Одéсса	vii	*Kiev*
h	Мадрúд	viii	*Amsterdam*
i	Самаркáнд	ix	*Odessa*

▶ **7** Match up these four words connected with travel and transport with their English equivalents below

вúза	трáктор	пáспорт	таксú
taxi	*passport*	*tractor*	*visa*

▶ **8** In this grid you will find nine words which refer to occupations or leisure activities. They are written in capital letters. Read them out loud and pronounce them clearly.

Д	И	П	Л	О	М	А	Т					
						У			Д			
						Р			О	Т		
					Х	И	М	И	К	Р		
					С			Т	А			
К	О	С	М	О	Н	А	В	Т		О	К	
	Т							Р	Т			
	У								О			
А	Д	М	И	Н	И	С	Т	Р	А	Т	О	Р
	Е								И			
	Н								С			
	Т					К	А	П	И	Т	А	Н

Here they are again in lower-case letters. You will notice that in their printed form, most Russian capital letters are just bigger versions of lower-case letters. Check their meanings against the list in English, which again is in the wrong order.

дипломáт   турúст   космонáвт   хúмик   студéнт
администрáтор   дóктор   тракторúст   капитáн

administrator   captain   diplomat   doctor   student (male)
tractor driver   tourist   cosmonaut   chemist

▶ **9**   Below is a list of ten Russian names, five for men and five for women. The women's names are the ones ending in -**a**. See if you can read them all out loud, and underline the feminine ones.

Ивáн   Нúна   Алексáндр   Владúмир   Екатерúна
Лúза   Лев   Ирúна   Валентúн   Ларúса

▶ **10**   You overhear a conversation between **Вéра** (Vyera) and **Алексáндр** (Alexander). **Вéра** cannot find her friend, and asks **Алексáндр** if he knows where she is. Listen to the conversation and repeat it. Otherwise, read it out loud. You will hear three unfamiliar words.

где?	pronounced	gdye	*where is?*
вот	pronounced	vot	*there is*
спасúбо	pronounced	spaseeba	*thank you*

Вéра   Алексáндр, где Ирúна?
Алексáндр   Вот Ирúна.
Вéра   Спасúбо, Алексáндр.

▶ **11**   Your next set of words are all to do with science. See if you can read them. Don't look at their meanings in English until you have finished.

áтом   комéта   метеóр   клúмат   механúзм   микроскóп
спýтник   килó   литр   планéта   лунá   киломéтр

kilo   microscope   sputnik   comet   litre   atom   kilometre
planet   mechanism   moon   meteor   climate

▶ 12 Now see if you can recognize these pieces of technical equipment. There is one word in this list which doesn't belong. Underline it, and don't forget to pronounce all the words clearly. Cover up the English version until you have tried to read the Russian.

телеви́зор	*radio*
кассе́та	*printer*
монито́р	*television*
кинока́мера	*cassette*
лимона́д	*cine-camera*
ра́дио	*monitor*
при́нтер	*lemonade*

▶ Unfamiliar letters with familiar sounds – three more!

Once you are confident reading the 17 letters you have met so far, you are ready to learn three more from the group of unfamiliar letters with familiar sounds.

Ф ф sounds like **f** in *funny*

Ю ю sounds like **yoo** in *universe*

Г г sounds like **g** in *good*

Reading practice

▶ 13 Here are some signs which might help you as you walk around a Russian town if you do not have a **план** (plan) *a town plan*. Match them up with their English meanings. Remember that they would not normally have accents to show where the stress is.

stadium park Internet café telephone casino kiosk zoo sauna café institute antiques grocer's (gastronom) *university*

парк ‎ **КИО́СК** ‎ ГАСТРОНО́М

 СТАДИО́Н ‎

сáуна	ТЕЛЕФÓН	ИНСТИТУ́Т	Казинó

интернéт кафé	университéт	антиквариáт

▶ **14** Nina is always getting lost. She supports the football team **Динáмо** (Deen<u>a</u>mo) and she is looking for the stadium. If you have the recording, listen to the conversation and repeat it. If not, try to read it out loud.

Ни́на	Ивáн, где стадиóн?
Ивáн	Стадиóн? Вот стадиóн.
Ни́на	А, вот стадиóн. Спаси́бо Ивáн.

When Nina says «**А**» it is like saying *Aah* in English.

▶ **15** You are visiting friends in their flat (**квартúра** kvart<u>ee</u>ra) in a block of flats (**дом** dom). You hear them mention the following domestic objects as they show you around. Try to read them out loud before looking at the English equivalents to check the meaning.

лáмпа	стул	коридóр	дивáн	ми́ксер	вáза
		тóстер	газ	лифт	

gas	*corridor*	*lamp*	*mixer*	*vase*	*toaster*	*lift*
		sofa (divan)	*chair*			

▶ **16** As you listen carefully to their conversation, you hear the following words and realize they are interested in music.

саксофóн	композúтор	гитáра	пиани́но	орке́стр
соли́ст	óпера	пиани́ст	компáкт-ди́ск	
		хéви металл-рóк		

piano	*opera*	*composer*	*pianist*	*saxophone*
	compact disk	*orchestra*	*guitar*	*soloist*
		heavy metal rock		

▶ **17**   You are in a concert hall when you hear a pianist asking his colleague, the composer, for help in finding something. Repeat the conversation. What has the pianist lost?

Пиани́ст	Влади́мир, где пиани́но?
Компози́тор	Пиани́но? Где, где пиани́но? А, вот пиани́но, Валенти́н!
Пиани́ст	А, вот пиани́но! Спаси́бо.

▶ **18**   Now you are in a restaurant looking at a menu. Work out what is on it and underline the drinks. Read out the whole list as if you were giving your order to the waiter. The menu is below.

Меню́	
омле́т	сала́т
ви́ски	фрукт
ко́фе	мю́сли
котле́та	вино́
пепси-ко́ла	суп министро́не

pepsi-cola   muesli   salad   coffee   wine   minestrone soup
whisky   omelette   cutlet (flat meatball)   fruit

Congratulations! You can now read 20 letters of the Cyrillic alphabet, and you have only 13 more to learn. To test yourself, read back over all the Russian words you have met and say them out loud without looking at the English. Check your pronunciation with the recording if you have them. Then read the English words and see if you can remember them in Russian. Don't worry if you don't get them all exactly right. Then you are ready to move on to Unit 2.

02

the remainder of the alphabet

In this unit you will learn
- how to read the remaining 13 letters of the Russian alphabet
- how to say you don't know
- how to ask who someone is
- how to say 'no'

Before you start

Make sure that you can read and say all the Russian words in Unit 1. Remember to use the recording if you have it, and say each new word out loud to practise your pronunciation.

More letters and sounds

You already know these 20 letters of the Russian alphabet:

- those which look and sound like English letters: **а т о м к**
- the 'false friends' which look like English letters but sound different: **с р е в н у х**
- and the unfamiliar letters with familiar sounds: **п л и з д ф ю г**

▶ Unfamiliar letters with familiar sounds – the last five

There are still five letters to learn in the group of unfamiliar letters with familiar sounds, and we will begin with these.

Б б	sounds like	**b**	in	*bag*
Э э	sounds like	**e**	in	*leg*
Й й	sounds like	**y**	in	*toy*
Ё ё	sounds like	**yo**	in	*yonder*
Я я	sounds like	**ya**	in	*yak* (except in the syllable before the stress, when it sounds like *yi*.)

The letter **я** on its own means *I*, so that is another word to add to your repertoire! To practise these new letters along with those you already know, see if you can read the words in the following exercises. Try to work out what they mean before you look at the English meanings. If you have the recording, listen to the words and repeat them carefully. Remember to emphasize each syllable which has a stress mark. Wherever **ё** appears in a word, that syllable will be stressed. So **ёлка** (y<u>o</u>lka) *a Christmas tree*, will be emphasized on the first syllable.

Reading practice

▶ 1   First try matching up these cities with their English names.

a Берли́н **b** Я́лта **c** Санкт-Петербу́рг **d** Софи́я **e** Бухаре́ст **f** Багда́д

i *Sofia* **ii** *Baghdad* **iii** *Berlin* **iv** *Saint Petersburg* **v** *Bucharest* **vi** *Yalta*

You can check the answers in the back of your book.

▶ 2 All these words are to do with travel and transport. Write the correct letter next to each English word to show that you have understood.

a	стюардéсса	*trolleybus*
b	платфóрма	*airport*
c	экскýрсия	*signal*
d	автóбус	*express*
e	трамвáй	*stewardess*
f	аэропóрт	*Aeroflot*
g	экспрéсс	*platform*
h	сигнáл	*tram*
i	Аэрофлóт	*excursion*
j	троллéйбус	*bus*

▶ 3 If you want to read the sports pages of a Russian newspaper, here are some words which will be useful. Match them up with the English words that follow.

ФУТБÓЛ	ВОЛЕЙБÓЛ	БАДМИНТÓН
МАРАФÓН	ÁРМРЕСТЛИНГ	БОКС
ГИМНÁСТИКА	ПИНГ-ПÓНГ	СÉРФИНГ
ФИНÁЛ	РÉГБИ	ПЭЙНТБÓЛ
ХОККÉЙ	БАСКЕТБÓЛ	БÓДИБИЛДИНГ

*rugby   marathon   boxing   volleyball   football   hockey
basketball   final   surfing   badminton   ping-pong   arm
wrestling   bodybuilding   gymnastics   paintball*

▶ 4 You are visiting your music-loving Russian friends again. This time their conversation is about music, theatre and books, and you hear them mention the following words. Try to read them out loud before looking at the English words to check their meaning.

симфóния   балери́на   поэ́т   актри́са   бестсéллер
актёр   балéт   три́ллер

*best-seller   actress   ballet   symphony   ballerina
thriller   poet   actor*

▶ 5 You pick up a magazine about science, and work out the following words.

> энéргия   киловáтт   атмосфéра   килогрáмм
> электрóника   эксперимéнт
>
> *kilogram   experiment   atmosphere   energy*
> *kilowatt   electronics*

▶ 6 Your friends have an atlas, and you browse through it recognizing these names.

> Амéрика   Мéксика   Áфрика   Пакистáн   Аргентúна
> Áнглия   Россúя   Украúна   Канáда   Úндия
> Австрáлия   Норвéгия
>
> *Argentina   Mexico   Russia   Australia   America   Norway*
> *England   Ukraine   Canada   Pakistan   India   Africa*

▶ 7 You play a game with their little girl, **Лéна** (Lyena). You ask her where certain countries are on a world map and she shows you. Occasionally she doesn't know and then she says: **Я не знáю**   (Ya nye znayoo)   *I don't know.*

Listen to the conversation or read it out loud.

You	Лéна, где Канáда?
Лéна	Канáда? Вот Канáда.
You	Где Россúя?
Лéна	Вот Россúя, и вот Москвá.
You	Где Áнглия?
Лéна	Áнглия? Я не знáю. Где Áнглия?
You	Вот Áнглия, и вот Лóндон.

Did you work out what **и** means?

и   (ee) *and*

▶ The last eight letters and sounds

Once you are happy with those new letters you are ready to move on to learn the remaining eight letters of the Russian alphabet, which are quite unlike English letters. The first five letters of this group make sounds which will be familiar to you, but in English you would need more than one letter to show the whole sound.

Ж ж	sounds like	**zh**	as in	*pleasure*
Ц ц	sounds like	**ts**	as in	*cats*
Ч ч	sounds like	**ch**	as in	*chicken*
Ш ш	sounds like	**sh**	as in	*ship*
Щ щ	sounds like	**shsh**	as in	*Spanish sherry*

The last three letters of the group never occur at the beginning of a word. They are:

ы   sounds rather like **i** in *ill*, but with the tongue further back in the mouth

ь   is a 'soft sign' which adds a soft 'y' sound to the letter before it. Think of how you would pronounce the **p** in *pew*. When you see a Russian word written using English letters in this book, a soft sign will be indicated by an apostrophe '. So for example, the word for computer **компьютер** will be written **komp'yooter**.

ъ   is a 'hard sign'. This is very rare, and makes a tiny pause between syllables.

Now you have met all the letters of the Russian alphabet. The Russian alphabet is shown in its correct order in your **Alphabet guide** on page 66. Remember that Russian spelling and pronunciation are simpler than English, and if you just join together every letter in a word you will come fairly close to pronouncing it correctly. Now have a go at reading some more words in which any letter of the alphabet may appear! Good luck!

Reading practice

▶ **8** Imagine you are walking around the centre of Moscow. You see these signs outside some of the buildings. What are they?

a бар **b** Мелодия **c** Пицца Хат **d** музей **e** цирк **f** банк **g** библиотека **h** Кремль **i** почта **j** Большой театр

▶ **9** Signs outside some other buildings tell you what you can find inside. Match the signs and the English words (overleaf).

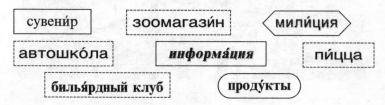

сувенир   зоомагазин   милиция   автошкола   *информация*   пицца   бильярдный клуб   продукты

information   souvenirs   pet shop   pizza   driving school
provisions   militia (police)   billiard club

▶ **10**   Traditional Russian cookery is delicious, and includes such dishes as **борщ** (borshsh) which is beetroot soup, and **щи** (shshee) which is cabbage soup. They are often served with bread **хлеб** (khlyep) and sour cream **сметáна** (smet<u>a</u>na). **Вóдка** (v<u>o</u>tka) vodka is a traditional Russian drink, and **чай** (chai) tea is also frequently drunk, usually without milk. However, many Russians now enjoy Western-style food as well. See if you can match the words with the pictures.

a чúзбургер   **b** банáн   **c** кóфе каппучúно   **d** пúцца сýпер супрúм

▶ **11**   Many words to do with the world of work are also familiar. What are these?

a мéнеджер   **b** факс   **c** брúфинг   **d** мáркетинг
e флóппи диск   **f** бизнесмéн   **g** нóу-хау
h брóкер   **i** уúк-энд   **j** компьютер   **k** нóутбук

▶ **12**   Here is a family portrait. It has been labelled for you. Can you read who everyone is?

бáбушка   кот   дéдушка   мáма   пáпа   сын   дочь

Pointing to the picture and speaking out loud, answer the following questions. (In answer to the first one you would say: «Вот ма́ма».)

Где ма́ма?   Где дочь?
Где сын?   Где де́душка?
Где ба́бушка?   Где кот?
Где па́па?

The children are described in Russian as **сын** (syn) *son* and **дочь** (doch') *daughter*. You could also describe them as **брат** (brat) *brother* and **сестра́** (sistr<u>a</u>) *sister*.

▶ **13** Just as many English words are familiar to Russians, names of many famous Russians are familiar to us. Can you work out who these people are?

Writers		Composers		Political leaders	
a	Че́хов	**d**	Чайко́вский	**g**	Ле́нин
b	Толсто́й	**e**	Рахма́нинов	**h**	Горбачёв
c	Пу́шкин	**f**	Шостако́вич	**i**	Е́льцин
				j	Пу́тин

Writers: i *Pushkin* **ii** *Tolstoy* **iii** *Chekhov*. **Composers: i** *Rachmaninov* **ii** *Tchaikovsky* **iii** *Shostakovich*. **Political leaders: i** *Lenin* **ii** *Yeltsin* **iii** *Gorbachev* **iv** *Putin*

▶ **14** For your last alphabet reading exercise, imagine you have to visit the doctor in Russia. Let's hope it never happens, but if it does here are some words which might prove useful:

a температу́ра   **b** бакте́рия   **c** антибио́тик
d масса́ж   **e** табле́тка   **f** диа́гноз   **g** пеницилли́н
h инфе́кция

Well done! You have managed to read words containing any letter of the Russian alphabet except for the hard sign **ъ**. That is because it is so rare, but just for good luck, here is a word which contains a hard sign: **объе́кт** (ob-y<u>e</u>kt) *object*. So now there is nothing which can surprise you! With every new word, just say each sound in order, emphasizing the stressed syllable, and you should be pronouncing it well enough for a Russian to understand you.

Mechanics of the language

Now that you can pronounce Russian and feel confident with the
sounds, you'll be glad to know that it is a logical language and that
all you need to make up your own sentences is an understanding of
the patterns of the language. Before learning any more words and
phrases, here are some key points on starting to use those patterns.
Russian is very logical, and while some things may seem to be more
complicated than English, some things are definitely easier.

1 'The' and 'a'

The good news is that there are no words in Russian for *the* or *a*. So
студе́нт means either *the student* or *a student*.

2 'To be'

More good news! In Russian the verb *to be* is not used when you are
talking about things happening now. So you do not need to learn to
say *I am, you are, he is* and so on. In English you would say *I am a
businessman*, but in Russian this is simply **Я – бизнесме́н**, literally
I businessman. This may sound like Tarzan speaking, but don't
worry, it is real Russian. So if you hear **Анто́н – студе́нт**, it means
Anton is a student. Note that Russian may use a dash to replace the
verb *to be*.

3 Gender of nouns

A noun is a word that names someone or something: **ме́неджер**
manager, **Лари́са** *Larisa*, **Росси́я** *Russia*, **авто́бус** *bus*, **кот** *cat*,
электро́ника *electronics*. Russian nouns are divided randomly into
three groups called 'gender groups': masculine, feminine and neuter.
Later it will be helpful to know which group a noun belongs to. As
you might expect, **бизнесме́н** *businessman* is masculine and
балери́на *ballerina* is feminine, but even non-living things in
Russian have a gender. The good thing is that you do not have to
memorize which gender each noun has. You can tell simply by
looking at the ending. Here are the most common endings.

Masculine

Most masculine nouns end in a consonant or **-й**. (Look at your
pronunciation guide if you are not sure what a consonant is.) So
стадио́н *stadium*, **чи́збургер** *cheeseburger*, **Ло́ндон** *London*, and
дом *house* or *block of flats* are all masculine. So are **музе́й** *museum*,
and **трамва́й** *tram*.

Feminine

Most feminine nouns end in **-а** or **-я**. So **кассе́та** *cassette*, **Оде́сса** *Odessa*, **А́нглия** *England*, and **эне́ргия** *energy* are all feminine. If you meet a word like **студе́нтка** which ends in **-а**, you know that this must be a female student. A male student, as you know, is **студе́нт**. (There are exceptions to this rule, e.g. **па́па** *Dad* which ends in **-а** but which is masculine because of its meaning.)

Neuter

Most neuter nouns end in **-о** or **-е**. So **метро́** *metro*, **вино́** *wine* and **кафе́** *café* are all neuter.

Soft sign ь

There is also a small group of nouns ending in a soft sign **ь**. These may be either masculine or feminine, and you have to learn which gender they are. **Кремль** (Kryeml') *Kremlin* is masculine and **меда́ль** (med<u>a</u>l') *medal* is feminine. **Дочь** *daughter* is, of course, feminine. Every time you meet a new noun ending in **ь** it will have (*m*) or (*f*) next to it to show you whether it is masculine or feminine.

To summarize:

Masculine nouns end in	**a consonant**	парк
	й	музе́й
	ь	Кремль
Feminine nouns end in	**а**	кассе́та
	я	эне́ргия
	ь	дочь
Neuter nouns end in	**о**	метро́
	е	кафе́

Exercises

▶ **15** Listen to the recording to find out what jobs people do. Match up the numbers and the letters. So if you think Nina is an actress write **a iv**.

a	Ни́на	**i**	бизнесме́н
b	Алекса́ндр	**ii**	поэ́т
c	А́нна	**iii**	администра́тор
d	Влади́мир	**iv**	актри́са
e	Бори́с	**v**	стюарде́сса

16 Look at the following pictures and make up a sentence about each person, using the words in brackets. For example, **Лари́са – студе́нтка** (*Larisa is a student*).

Йгорь   Лари́са   Анто́н   Ната́ша   Бори́с

(тенниси́ст, студе́нтка, футболи́ст, балери́на, тури́ст)

▶ **17** Ната́ша is at a party. She is rather short-sighted so she asks Лари́са for help in spotting her friends. But Лари́са doesn't know them all. In this conversation you will meet two new words:

Кто? (Kto?) *Who?*

Нет (Nyet) *No*

Ната́ша	Лари́са, где Анто́н?
Лари́са	Анто́н? Кто Анто́н?
Ната́ша	Анто́н – студе́нт.
Лари́са	А, вот Анто́н.
Ната́ша	Спаси́бо, Лари́са. Где А́нна?
Лари́са	А́нна? Кто А́нна? Актри́са?
Ната́ша	Нет. А́нна – балери́на.
Лари́са	Балери́на? А, вот А́нна.

18 Read this list of words and decide which are masculine, feminine and neuter. Write (m), (f) or (n) in the brackets at the side to show their gender.

a	а́том	( )	**e**	Аме́рика	( )	**i**	кино́	( )
b	кассе́та	( )	**f**	теа́тр	( )	**j**	дочь	( )
c	сала́т	( )	**g**	трамва́й	( )	**k**	волейбо́л	( )
d	пиани́но	( )	**h**	информа́ция	( )	**l**	вино́	( )

19 These words are grouped according to gender, but there is one word in each group which has the wrong gender. Find the odd one out in each group and underline it.

Masculine	Feminine	Neuter
суп	гита́ра	метро́
Кремль	А́нглия	кафе́
план	меда́ль	ра́дио
па́спорт	во́дка	саксофо́н
сестра́	стадио́н	кака́о
трамва́й	кассе́та	пиани́но

20 You are in a restaurant ordering three items. Can you find them hidden in the string of letters below?

> абресуптономлетхалисалаткуд

Which gender are all three things which you ordered?

21 See if you can decipher these jumbled words using the clues. The first letter of each word is in bold print. They are all feminine.

a тасре**с** (a relative)
b фими**с**оян (orchestral music)
c г**А**нетиран (a country)
d аке**б**итбило (a place for bookworms)
e урме**т**ерпата (this is high if you are feverish)

Did you know that you can already say and read more than 350 words in Russian? When you are confident that you understand everything in these first two units, you are ready to move on to Unit 3.

03

Добрый день!
good day!

In this unit you will learn
- how to say 'hello' and 'goodbye'
- how to greet and address someone
- how to say you don't understand
- how to ask if anyone speaks English

Before you start

It is very important for you to read the **Introduction** to the course. This gives some useful advice on studying alone and how to make the most of the course. If you are working with the recording, keep it handy as you will need it for the **Key words** and **Dialogue** sections. If you don't have the recording, use the **Pronunciation guide** on page viii.

ℹ Russian names

If you have ever seen a Russian play or read a Russian book in English you will have noticed that one Russian person may appear to have many names. Actually, Russians have three names each.

Their first name **имя** (<u>ee</u>mya) is their given name, for example, **Иван** (Eev<u>a</u>n) or **Нина** (N<u>ee</u>na). Then they have a 'patronymic' name, **о́тчество** (<u>o</u>tchestvo). This is formed from their father's first name plus a special ending: **-ович** (<u>o</u>veech) or **-евич** (y<u>e</u>veech) for boys and **-о́вна** (<u>o</u>vna) or **-евна** (y<u>e</u>vna) for girls. Finally they have a family name, **фами́лия** (fam<u>ee</u>liya), which has the same function as our surname. So you would be able to work out that **Влади́мир Ива́нович Козло́в** (Vlad<u>ee</u>mir Eev<u>a</u>novich Kazl<u>o</u>v) had a father called **Иван** (Eev<u>a</u>n), and **Еле́на Алекса́ндровна Попо́ва** (Ily<u>e</u>na Aliks<u>a</u>ndrovna Pap<u>o</u>va) had a father called **Алекса́ндр** (Aliks<u>a</u>ndr). Notice that the man's name has masculine endings (consonants) and the woman's name has feminine endings (**-а**).

имя	<u>ee</u>mya	*given name*
отчество	<u>o</u>tchestvo	*patronymic*
фами́лия	fam<u>ee</u>liya	*family name*

How to address Russians

Adult Russians who are on formal terms may call each other by their first name and patronymic. This is a mark of respect, and young people may address older people in this way, for example, a schoolchild may address a teacher as **Гали́на Миха́йловна** (Gal<u>ee</u>na Mikh<u>a</u>ilovna). In Soviet times, another official form of address was **това́рищ** (tav<u>a</u>rishsh) *comrade*, used either with the surname or on its own to address someone whose name was not known. Nowadays, **това́рищ** has lost popularity and the pre-Revolutionary **господи́н** (gaspad<u>ee</u>n) *sir* and **госпожа́** (gaspazh<u>a</u>) *madam* have reappeared. Sometimes people use the words **мужчи́на** (moozhch<u>ee</u>na) *man* and **же́нщина** (zh<u>e</u>nshsheena) *woman* to address strangers. The phrase *ladies and gentlemen* in Russian is **Да́мы и господа́** (d<u>a</u>my i gaspad<u>a</u>).

Adult Russians who are close friends will call each other by their first name, and children will usually be addressed by their first name. People on first name terms will often use 'diminutive' forms. This is like using Mike for Michael or Annie for Annabel but each Russian name has lots of possible diminutives. For example, **Еле́на** (Ilyena) might be called **Ле́на** (Lyena) for short, **Ле́ночка** (Lyenochka) or **Лену́ся** (Lyinoosya) affectionately, **Лено́к** (Lyinok) jokingly, **Ле́нка** (Lyenka) perhaps by an angry parent, and more rarely but affectionately, **Алёна** (Alyona) and **Алёнушка** (Alyonooshka).

Key words and phrases

Диало́г 1 *Dialogue 1*

До́брое у́тро	Dobroye ootra	*Good morning*
До́брый день	Dobry dyen'	*Good day*
До́брый ве́чер	Dobry vyecher	*Good evening*
Здра́вствуйте	Zdrastvooeetye	*Hello*
До свида́ния	Da sveedanya	*Goodbye*

Диало́г 2 *Dialogue 2*

Меня́ зову́т	Minya zavoot	*I am called*
О́чень прия́тно	Ochen' preeyatna	*Pleased to meet you (lit. very pleasant)*
Как вас зову́т?	Kak vas zavoot?	*What are you called?*
Как дела́?	Kak dyila?	*How are things?*
хорошо́	kharasho	*good, well*

Диало́г 3 *Dialogue 3*

извини́те	eezveeneetye	*excuse me/I'm sorry*
молодо́й челове́к	maladoy chilavyek	*young man*
вы	vy	*you*
нет	nyet	*no*
я	ya	*I*
не	nye	*not*
де́вушка	dyevushka	*young woman/miss*
да	da	*yes*

Диало́г 4 *Dialogue 4*

Я не понима́ю	Ya nye paneemayoo	*I don't understand*
Ме́дленнее, пожа́луйста	Myedlyn-ye-ye, pazhal-sta	*slower, please*
Вы говори́те по-англи́йски?	Vy gavareetye pa-angleesky?	*Do you speak English?*
Я говорю́ по-ру́сски	Ya gavaryoo pa-roosky	*I speak Russian*
пло́хо	plokha	*badly*

Dialogues

Listen to the dialogues on the recording, or read them through several times until you feel comfortable with them. Pretend to be one of the people in each dialogue and try to memorize what they say. Pause the recording and say your part out loud. Then check your pronunciation with the recording or with the pronunciation given in the **Key words and phrases** box. If you are not working with a recording, remember to emphasize the stressed syllables and to underplay the unstressed ones.

▶ Диало́г 1 *Dialogue 1*

In this dialogue people are greeting each other and saying 'goodbye' in Russian at different times of day.

Ви́ктор До́брое у́тро, Ната́ша.
Ната́ша До́брое у́тро, Ви́ктор.

Бори́с До́брый день, А́нна.
А́нна До́брый день, Бори́с.

Све́та До́брый ве́чер, Ле́на.
Ле́на До́брый ве́чер, Све́та.

Ири́на Здра́вствуйте!
Анто́н Здра́вствуйте!

Та́ня До свида́ния, Ива́н.
Ива́н До свида́ния, Та́ня.

Now cover up the text and see if you can remember how to say:
a good morning **b** good evening **c** hello **d** good day **e** goodbye.

▶ Диало́г 2 Dialogue 2

In this dialogue Igor and Alison meet and introduce themselves.

Igor	Alison
До́брый ве́чер. Меня́ зову́т Йгорь.	О́чень прия́тно.
Как вас зову́т?	
	Меня́ зову́т А́лисон.
О́чень прия́тно. Как дела́, А́лисон?	Хорошо́, спаси́бо.

Practise the dialogue, then imagine that you are Alison. Cover up the right-hand side of the dialogue. Say you are pleased to meet Igor and answer his questions. Now cover up the left-hand side and practise Igor's part of the conversation.

▶ Диало́г 3 Dialogue 3

*In connection with an advert about a flat, Volodya has arranged to meet a young man called Sasha and his girlfriend Nastya outside a metro station. (Incidentally, **Воло́дя** is a diminutive of **Влади́мир**, **Са́ша** is a diminutive of **Алекса́ндр** and **На́стя** is a diminutive of **Анаста́сия**.) Read their conversation carefully.*

Воло́дя	Извини́те, молодо́й челове́к, вы Са́ша?
Ми́ша	Нет, я не Са́ша.
Воло́дя	Извини́те. . . . . Де́вушка, вы не На́стя?
Ве́ра	На́стя? Нет, я не На́стя.
Воло́дя	Извини́те, вы Са́ша и На́стя?
Са́ша и На́стя	Да. Вы Воло́дя?
Воло́дя	Да, я Воло́дя. О́чень прия́тно, Са́ша. О́чень прия́тно, На́стя.

Repeat the dialogue, and check that you know how to say *excuse me* or *sorry*, and how to address an unknown young man or woman.

▶ Диало́г 4 Dialogue 4

In the second dialogue in this unit, Alison managed to understand what Igor said to her. Andrew is not quite so lucky and has a few problems understanding a new acquaintance at a party.

Никола́й	Здра́вствуйте.
Andrew	Здра́вствуйте.
Никола́й	Как вас зову́т?
Andrew	Ме́дленнее, пожа́луйста.
Никола́й	Как вас зову́т?

Andrew	Извини́те, я не понима́ю.
Никола́й	Как вас зову́т? Меня́ зову́т Никола́й Петро́вич. Как вас зову́т?
Andrew	А, меня́ зову́т А́ндрю. Вы говори́те по-англи́йски?
Никола́й	Да, я говорю́ по-англи́йски.
Andrew	Oh good! Хорошо́! Я пло́хо понима́ю по-ру́сски.

Practise the dialogue several times until you are happy with the new words.

Mechanics of the language

1 Two ways of saying 'you'

In Russian, as in many languages, there are two different words for *you*. English used to have two words – *you* and *thou* – but now we nearly always use *you*. The two Russian words are **вы** (vy) and **ты** (ty). **Вы** is used whenever you are speaking to more than one person, or to an adult with whom you are on formal or polite terms. **Ты** is used whenever you are speaking informally to one person only. So you would nearly always use **ты** to address a child or a close friend or relation. (Let your Russian friends decide whether to use **вы** or **ты** with you. The younger generation often prefer the less formal **ты** while older people may feel more comfortable using **вы** even when they have known you for years.)

There are also two ways of saying *hello*, depending on whether you call someone **вы** or **ты**. If you are talking to more than one person or formally to one adult, you say **здра́вствуйте** as you have already learned, but if you are talking to a child, close friend or relative, you say **здра́вствуй**, missing off the last two letters. So, if you picked up the phone and heard your Russian boss calling, you might say: **Здра́вствуйте, Влади́мир Ива́нович. Где вы?** *Hello, Vladeemir Eevanovich. Where are you?*

If, on the other hand, it was your long-lost friend, you would say: **Здра́вствуй, Ле́на. Где ты?** *Hello, Lyena. Where are you?*

2 Asking questions

A statement can easily be turned into a question in Russian simply by varying the rise and fall of your voice. If you make a statement in Russian, your voice should fall:

Ива́н – студе́нт. *Ivan is a student.*

If you want to make the statement into a question, your voice should rise:

Ивáн – студéнт? *Is Ivan a student?*

If the question contains a question word, like *who? what? where? why? when? how?* then your voice should rise on the question word itself:

Как делá? *How are things?*

3 To do or not to do

You have already met people saying that they can and can't do things, and you have probably noticed the little word **не** (nye) which means *not*. In Unit 2, little Лéна said **Я не знáю** *I don't know*. In the last dialogue, Andrew said **Я не понимáю** *I don't understand*. Николáй told him: **Я говорю́ по-англи́йски** *I speak English*. So you can work out that:

Я знáю Ya znayoo	means	*I know*
Я понимáю Ya paneemayoo	means	*I understand*
Я говорю́ Ya gavaryoo	means	*I speak*

If you want to say that you can't do any of these things, simply slip **не** *not* between **я** and the word which says what you are doing.

Я не знáю	*I don't know*
Я не понимáю	*I don't understand*
Я не говорю́	*I don't speak*

The action words *to know, to understand, to speak* may be described as verbs. If you want to say that you do any of these things well or badly, slip **хорошó** *well* or **плóхо** *badly* between **я** and the verb.

Я хорошó знáю Áлисон	*I know Alison well*
Я хорошó понимáю Áндрю	*I understand Andrew well*
Я плóхо говорю́ по-рýсски	*I speak Russian badly*

By the end of the course you should be able to say truthfully *I speak Russian well*. Why not try it out now! **Я хорошó говорю́ по-рýсски**.

4 Who's who?

You already know how to say *I* (**я**) and *you* (**ты** or **вы**) in Russian. Now you should be ready to learn *he, she, we* and *they*.

In Russian, *he* is **он** (on). So you could say: **Он – поэт.** *He is a poet.*

She is similar to *he* but has a feminine ending: **она́** (an<u>a</u>). So you could say: **Она́ – балери́на.** *She is a ballerina.*

We is **мы** (my), rhyming with **ты** and **вы**. So you might hear: **Мы – ма́ма и па́па.** *We are Mum and Dad.*

They is **они́** (an<u>ee</u>). So you might say: **Они́ – Са́ша и На́стя.** *They are Sasha and Nastya.*

Now you can refer to anyone in a conversation, even if you don't know what they are called.

я	*I*	**мы**	*we*
ты	*you* (one person, familiar)	**вы**	*you* (more than one person,
он	*he*		or formal acquaintance)
она́	*she*	**они́**	*they*

Exercises

1   Imagine you have to fill in a form for a male Russian friend. Match the names provided with the blanks on the form.

   a   и́мя _____   **i**   Влади́мирович
   b   о́тчество _____   **ii**   Смирно́в
   c   фами́лия _____   **iii**   Бори́с

Now do the same for a female Russian friend.

   a   и́мя _____   **i**   Ни́на
   b   о́тчество _____   **ii**   Горбачёва
   c   фами́лия _____   **iii**   Бори́совна

What is the first name of your male friend's father? And your female friend's father?

2   How would you say 'hello' at these times of day?

   a   9.15
   b   14.45
   c   20.30

3 You meet a Russian who asks you what your name is: **Как вас зовут?** How do you answer: *My name is . . .*?

М——— з——— Stuart.

He says he is pleased to meet you. How does he say that in Russian?

О——— п———.

4 Imagine that you are working in Russia and an old friend and colleague Анна Михайловна calls to see you. What should you say?

a Как вас зовут? **b** Я не понимаю **c** Дéвушка
d До свидáния **e** Здрáвствуйте **f** Извините

5 a You want to attract the attention of the young man serving behind the counter of a crowded shop in St Petersburg. How do you address him?
 b You step on someone's foot. What do you say?
 c You want to ask the girl at the cash-desk a question. How do you address her?
 d You think you recognize a girl called Nina whom you met on the tram yesterday. What do you say to her?

Choose your answers from the suggestions below:

i Дéвушка! **ii** Извините, вы Нина?
iii Молодóй человéк! **iv** Извините!

▶ **6** How do you pronounce these words and phrases?

a Здрáвствуйте	**e** Где Борис?
b Спасибо	**f** Я не знáю
c Я говорю по-английски	**g** Мéдленнее, пожáлуйста
d Хорошó	**h** Извините

What do they all mean?

7 Draw lines to link the matching phrases in Russian and English.

a	Я говорю по-английски.	**i** *I don't know.*
b	Я не понимáю.	**ii** *I understand Russian well.*
c	Я хорошó понимáю по-рýсски.	**iii** *I speak English.*
d	Я не знáю.	**iv** *I understand.*
e	Я понимáю.	**v** *I don't understand.*

8 Which word is missing? Refer to the words in brackets below if you need to.

a Меня ——— Ивáн.

b ——————— ве́чер.
c Я —— понима́ю.
d Вы ——————— по-англи́йски?
e Молодо́й ———————.

(До́брый, челове́к, зову́т, не, говори́те)

9 Using the recording, check that you understand which is the right answer.

a The speaker says **i** good morning **ii** good day **iii** good evening.

b She is called **i** Nina Petrovna **ii** Nina Borisovna **iii** Anna Petrovna.

c She **i** speaks English **ii** doesn't speak English **iii** speaks English well.

10 Match up the questions and answers so that they make sense.

a	Кто он?	**i**	Они́ – ба́бушка и де́душка.
b	Кто ты?	**ii**	Она́ – стюарде́сса.
c	Кто она́?	**iii**	Мы – брат и сестра́.
d	Кто вы?	**iv**	Он – студе́нт.
e	Кто они́?	**v**	Я – космона́вт.

Test yourself

You have arrived at the end of Unit 3. Now you know how to say 'hello' and 'goodbye', find out who people are and exchange greetings. You also know how to cope if you don't understand. How would you:

1 say 'hello'?
2 say 'goodbye'?
3 say 'excuse me'?
4 ask for someone's name?
5 find out if someone speaks English?
6 say you don't understand?

You'll find the answers to this little test at the end of the book. If most of them are correct you are ready to move on to the next unit. If you still need practice, spend some more time revising this unit until you feel confident enough to move on. You should expect to take quite a while over each unit because you are still getting used to the new alphabet, so do not be discouraged if your progress seems slow. Look back to the start of Unit 1 to remind yourself how much you have learned since then! Well done!

04

где банк?
where's the bank?

In this unit you will learn
- how to name some important places in a town
- how to ask and say where things are
- how to describe things that you see
- how to understand a Russian address
- how to count to ten

Before you start

Look back at page 18 to make sure that you can recognize whether a noun is masculine, feminine or neuter. Just to check, write *m*, *f*, or *n* in the brackets following these words: автóбус ( ) óпера ( ) пианúно ( ) метрó ( ) мáма ( ) банк ( ).

🛈 Пассажúрский трáнспорт (passazh<u>ee</u>rsky tr<u>a</u>nsport) *passenger transport*

Passenger transport in Russian cities includes the **автóбус** (avt<u>o</u>boos) *bus*, **трамвáй** (tramv<u>a</u>y) *tram* and **троллéйбус** (trolly<u>ei</u>boos) *trolleybus* and, in some cities, an underground system **метрó** (mitr<u>o</u>). Tickets for the bus, tram and trolleybus services may be bought from the driver and each ticket **талóн** (tal<u>o</u>n) must have holes punched in it when it is used. A ticket **билéт** (beely<u>e</u>t) to the value of a given number of journeys valid up to a given date has to be inserted into an entry barrier to gain access to the metro. The time, date and route of the journey are recorded on the reverse of the ticket.

In Moscow, around 10 million passengers use the metro system with its 160 stations each day.

Маршрýтное таксú (marshr<u>oo</u>tnoye taks<u>ee</u>), a minibus taxi service, follows a fixed route for a fare that costs more than a bus ticket but less than a taxi fare.

Taxis (**таксú**) and private drivers offering unregistered taxi services for a negotiated fare complete the picture of passenger transport in Russian cities.

автóбус, троллейбус, трамвáй и метрó

метрó
билéт

Russian addresses

Russian addresses are written in a different order from most of Europe, starting with the city **го́род** (<u>go</u>rat), then the street **у́лица** (<u>oo</u>leetsa), the number of the block of flats **дом** (dom), the building section number **ко́рпус** (<u>ko</u>rpoos) and finally the flat number **кварти́ра** (kvart<u>ee</u>ra). If a name is included, this will be written after the rest of the address with the surname first. So a typical address **а́дрес** (<u>a</u>dryes) might look like this:

Москва́,
Ботани́ческая у́лица,   (*Botanical street*)
дом 8, ко́рпус 4, кварти́ра 10.

Key words and phrases

Диало́г 1

москви́ч/москви́чка	maskv<u>ee</u>ch/ maskv<u>ee</u>chka	*Muscovite (m, f)*
э́то	<u>e</u>to (*rhymes with letter*)	*it is/is it?*
вон там	von tam	*over there*

Диало́г 2

кинотеа́тр	keenoti<u>a</u>tr	*cinema*
спра́вочное бюро́	spr<u>a</u>vuchnoye byur<u>o</u>	*information office*
Не́ за что!	Ny<u>e</u> za shto!	*Don't mention it!*

Диало́г 3

здесь	zdyes'	*here, around here*
он/она́/оно́	on/on<u>a</u>/an<u>o</u>	*it (m/f/n)*
скажи́те	skazh<u>ee</u>tye	*tell me*
гости́ница	gast<u>ee</u>neetsa	*hotel*

Диало́г 4

како́й э́то го́род?	kak<u>oy</u> <u>e</u>to <u>go</u>rat?	*What sort of city is it?*
како́й/кака́я/како́е	kak-<u>oy</u>/-<u>a</u>ya/-<u>o</u>ye	*what sort of (m/f/n)?*
го́род	<u>go</u>rat	*city/town*
большо́й/больша́я/ большо́е	bol'sh-<u>oy</u>/-<u>a</u>ya/-<u>o</u>ye	*big (m/f/n)*
краси́вый/краси́вая/ краси́вое	kras<u>ee</u>v-y/-aya/-oye	*beautiful (m/f/n)*

Диало́г 5

хоро́ший/хоро́шая/ хоро́шее	khar<u>o</u>sh-y/-aya/-eye	*good (m/f/n)*
там	tam	*there*

Диало́г 6

ма́ленький/ма́ленькая/ ма́ленькое	m<u>a</u>lyen'-ky/-aya/-oye	*little (m/f/n)*

Dialogues

▶ Диало́г 1

Andrew's Russian is getting better every day, and he has gone out to find his way around Moscow. First he needs to change some money.

Andrew	Извини́те, пожа́луйста, э́то банк?
Москви́чка	Нет, э́то по́чта.
Andrew	Где банк?
Москви́чка	Банк вон там.

▶ Диало́г 2

He has read in the paper that there is a good film on at the «Ко́смос» cinema.

Andrew	Молодо́й челове́к, э́то кинотеа́тр «Ко́смос»?
Москви́ч	Нет, э́то кинотеа́тр «Плане́та».
Andrew	Где кинотеа́тр «Ко́смос»?
Москви́ч	Извини́те, я не зна́ю.
Andrew	Где спра́вочное бюро́?
Москви́ч	Вон там.
Andrew	Спаси́бо.
Москви́ч	Не́ за что! До свида́ния.

▶ Диало́г 3

Andrew is feeling hungry, but can't make up his mind whether to eat at a restaurant, hotel or café.

Andrew	Извини́те, где здесь рестора́н?
Москви́ч	Вот он.
Andrew	Скажи́те, пожа́луйста, где здесь гости́ница?
Москви́ч	Вот она́.
Andrew	Спаси́бо. Где здесь кафе́?
Москви́ч	Вот оно́.

▶ Диало́г 4

While he is having lunch, he asks a Muscovite what sort of city Moscow is.

Andrew	Скажи́те, како́й э́то го́род?
Москви́ч	Э́то большо́й, краси́вый го́род.

▶ Диало́г 5

Meanwhile, Volodya asks Sasha and Nastya about the flat in the advert.

Воло́дя   Скажи́те, кака́я э́то кварти́ра?
Са́ша   Э́то больша́я, хоро́шая кварти́ра. Там лифт, телефо́н и краси́вый балко́н.

▶ Диало́г 6

The pianist from Unit 1 has found his piano, but he is disappointed with it, and complains to the composer.

Пиани́ст   Э́то о́чень ма́ленькое пиани́но!
Компози́тор Нет, э́то не ма́ленькое пиани́но. Пиани́но – большо́е, краси́вое.

▶ Numerals 0–10

0	ноль	nol'			
1	оди́н	adeen	6	шесть	shest'
2	два	dva	7	семь	syem'
3	три	tree	8	во́семь	vosyem'
4	четы́ре	chyetirye	9	де́вять	dyevyat'
5	пять	pyat'	10	де́сять	dyesyat'

Number practice

Read all the numbers aloud or listen to the recording and repeat the numbers after you hear them spoken. Try to say the first three numbers without looking, then add another three until you can say them all without looking. If you have a pack of playing cards shuffle the pack and then turn over a card at a time calling out the number, or throw some dice, calling out the score each time. Do this until you can say the numbers up to ten in random order as soon as you see them. Then read these numbers out loud in the right order.

пять де́вять четы́ре два шесть ноль во́семь оди́н де́сять три семь

Now try reciting the numbers from 10 down to 0.

Mechanics of the language

1 Это *This is*

You already know that you do not need a verb *to be* in Russian if you are talking about things happening now. For example, **Антон студéнт** *Anton is a student*. But there is a very useful word in Russian meaning *this is* or *these are*: **э́то**. So, **Э́то телефóн** means *This is a telephone*. You can also use **э́то** as a question word: **Э́то телефóн?** *Is this a telephone?*

Э́то рестора́н?   Нет, э́то не рестора́н. Э́то кафé.

2 Он, она́, оно́ *it*

In English we use *it* to refer to anything we have already mentioned which is not a person, for example, *it (the bus) is late*. In Russian, every time you want to use *it* you must think whether the noun you are referring to is masculine, feminine or neuter. Look back at page 18 to remind yourself how to tell whether a word is masculine, feminine or neuter. You already know that **он** means *he* and **она́** means *she*. **Он** and **она́** also mean *it* when referring to a masculine and feminine noun respectively. **Оно́** is what you use to refer to a neuter noun. Notice that the endings of these words do what you would expect: the masculine **он** ends in a consonant, the feminine **она́** ends in **-a** and the neuter **оно́** ends in **-o**.

Где автóбус?	*Where is the bus?*	Вот он. *(m)*	*There it is.*
Где вáза?	*Where is the vase?*	Вот она́. *(f)*	*There it is.*
Где рáдио?	*Where is the radio?*	Вот оно́. *(n)*	*There it is.*

3 Какóй э́то . . .? *What sort of . . .?*

Just as there are three similar words for *it* in Russian, so there are also three forms of the word meaning *What sort of . . .?* when you are asking about a singular noun. Again you choose which to use by remembering whether the noun you are referring to is masculine, feminine or neuter.

Какóй? means *what sort of?* when it refers to a masculine noun.
Какáя? means *what sort of?* when it refers to a feminine noun.
Какóе? means *what sort of?* when it refers to a neuter noun.

Notice that **какóй** has a typical masculine ending in **-й**, **какáя** has a typical feminine ending in **-я**, and **какóе** has a typical neuter ending in **-е**.

Какóй э́то суп? *What sort of soup is it?* *(m)*
Какáя э́то гитáра? *What sort of guitar is it?* *(f)*
Какóе э́то винó? *What sort of wine is it?* *(n)*

4 Adjectives

When you want to describe a singular noun, possibly in answer to a question like **Какóй э́то суп?** you will need to choose a masculine, feminine or neuter ending for the adjective (or describing word) you want to use. Again this will depend on the gender of the noun to which you are referring. This is called making the adjective 'agree' with the noun. If you want to describe something as beautiful, work out which gender the noun is, and use the correct ending to make the adjective agree.

Masculine	*Feminine*	*Neuter*
Э́то краси́**вый** парк.	Э́то краси́**вая** вáза.	Э́то краси́**вое** рáдио.
It's a beautiful park.	*It's a beautiful vase.*	*It's a beautiful radio.*

Look at the other adjectives in your word list. You will notice that the most common endings are **-ый** *(m)*, **-ая** *(f)* and **-ое** *(n)*. Sometimes, as in **мáленький**, the masculine ending will be spelt **-ий** because of a spelling rule which need not concern us here, (see **Summary of language patterns**). Similarly, the neuter form may sometimes be spelt **-ee** as in **хорóшее**. Finally, any masculine adjective with the last syllable stressed will have the ending **-óй** as in **большóй**. In your word lists from now on, adjectives will appear in singular masculine form only, unless there is anything unusual about them. Don't worry – even if you get the endings wrong you will still be understood!

Exercises

1   Look at the map of part of Moscow and imagine that you are a tourist asking someone where certain places are. So you might ask out loud: **Где здесь парк?** Now imagine what the reply will be and say it aloud: **Вот он.** Carry on until you can say where everything on the map is.

Здесь (zdyes') means *here*, and if you include it in the question, it implies that you do not have a particular park in mind, or you do not know if you are looking in the right area, but you just want to know where there might be a park around here.

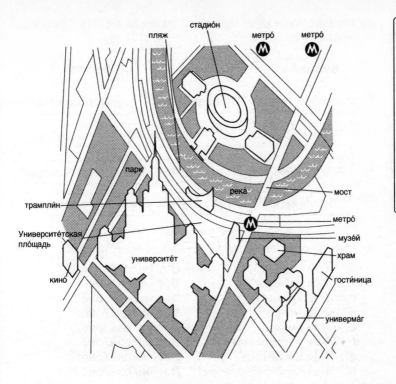

стадио́н
пляж
метро́
метро́
парк
река́
мост
трампли́н
Университе́тская пло́щадь
метро́
музе́й
университе́т
храм
гости́ница
кино́
универма́г

Ключ *Key*		
река́	ryik<u>a</u>	*river*
мост	most	*bridge*
стадио́н	stadee<u>o</u>n	*stadium*
музе́й	moozy<u>ey</u>	*museum*
парк	park	*park*
метро́	mitr<u>o</u>	*metro*
храм	khr<u>a</u>m	*church*
универма́г	oonivermak	*department store*
гости́ница	gast<u>ee</u>nitsa	*hotel*
кино́	keen<u>o</u>	*cinema*
университе́т	ooniversity<u>et</u>	*university*
трампли́н	trampl<u>ee</u>n	*ski jump*
пляж	plyash	*beach*
Университе́тская пло́щадь *(f)*	ooniversity<u>et</u>skaya ploshshad'	*University square*

2 Here are some more signs that you might see. Try to work out what they mean.

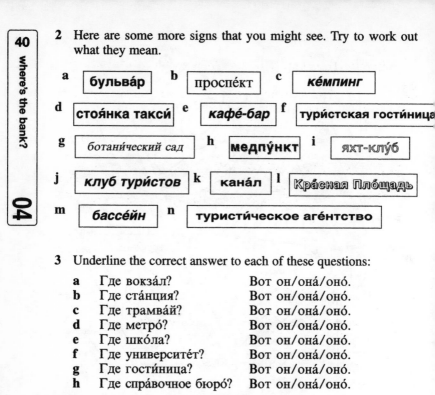

a бульва́р b проспе́кт c ке́мпинг

d стоя́нка такси́ e кафе́-бар f тури́стская гости́ница

g ботани́ческий сад h медпу́нкт i яхт-клу́б

j клуб тури́стов k кана́л l Кра́сная Пло́щадь

m бассе́йн n туристи́ческое аге́нтство

3 Underline the correct answer to each of these questions:

a Где вокза́л?   Вот он/она́/оно́.
b Где ста́нция?   Вот он/она́/оно́.
c Где трамва́й?   Вот он/она́/оно́.
d Где метро́?   Вот он/она́/оно́.
e Где шко́ла?   Вот он/она́/оно́.
f Где университе́т?   Вот он/она́/оно́.
g Где гости́ница?   Вот он/она́/оно́.
h Где спра́вочное бюро́? Вот он/она́/оно́.

4 What are these numbers? Say them out loud.

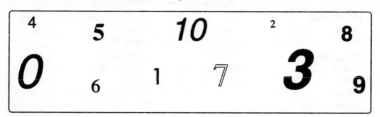

4 5 10 2 8
0 6 1 7 3 9

▶ **5** Listen to the recording and write down the scores of these entirely fictional, amazingly high-scoring international football matches as you hear them. The countries involved are Russia, Italy, Spain, France and England.

Металли́ст (Росси́я) [   ]   Юве́нтус (Ита́лия) [   ]
Реа́л (Испа́ния) [   ]   Дина́мо (Росси́я) [   ]
Нант (Фра́нция) [   ]   Спарта́к (Росси́я) [   ]
А́стон Ви́лла (А́нглия) [   ]   Ла́цио (Ита́лия) [   ]

Ньюка́сл юна́йтед (А́нглия) [   ]   Атле́тик (Испа́ния) [   ]

На́поли (Ита́лия) [   ]   Торпе́до (Росси́я) [   ]

▶ 6 Listen to the recording and fill in the columns to say which number bus, tram or trolleybus people are looking for.

авто́бус   трамва́й   тролле́йбус

a

b

c

d

7 A Russian tourist asks you:

    a   Где спра́вочное бюро́?   *Tell him it's over there.*

    b   Где тролле́йбус?   *Tell him you are sorry, you don't know.*

    c   Э́то библиоте́ка?   *Tell him no, it's the post office.*

    d   Спаси́бо.   *Tell him not to mention it.*

8 Try out a few new adjectives. They are all colours.

кра́сный	kr<u>a</u>sny	*red*
бе́лый	by<u>e</u>ly	*white*
жёлтый	zh<u>o</u>lty	*yellow*
зелёный	zily<u>o</u>ny	*green*
чёрный	ch<u>o</u>rny	*black*

In the box above, each adjective is in its masculine form. Below you have the same adjectives in different forms: masculine, feminine and neuter. They have become separated from their nouns. See if you can match them up.

бе́лая
зелёный
кра́сное
чёрный
жёлтый

вино́
бана́н
табле́тка
кот
сала́т

9 Rearrange the following information into an address, and read it out loud including the numbers.

a кварти́ра 3
b Краснода́р
c ко́рпус 7
d Восто́чная у́лица (*East Street*)
e дом 5

Test yourself

By now you know about the public transport system in Russian cities, you can read a Russian address, and you can request and give information about where places are. You can also give a description of something, and you can count to ten. To test yourself, see if you can unjumble the Russian sentences below to put this conversation into Russian.

Tourist *Excuse me. Where is the park?*
Tour guide *There it is. Over there.*
Tourist *What sort of park is it?*
Tour guide *It is a beautiful big park!*
Tourist *Thank you. Goodbye.*

a Како́й э́то парк? **b** Спаси́бо. До свида́ния. **c** Вот он. Вон там. **d** Извини́те. Где парк? **e** Э́то краси́вый, большо́й парк!

If you managed that and the exercises in this unit, you are now ready to move on. If you need to spend more time on this unit don't worry – there's a lot to absorb. It is best to work slowly and be sure of things before you move on to new information.

05

идйте прямо
go straight ahead

In this unit you will learn
- how to ask for and give directions
- how to ask whether things are available
- how to make plural forms
- how to say whether somewhere is open or closed
- how to count from 10 to 30

Before you start

If you are at all unsure about how to tell whether a noun is masculine, feminine or neuter, go back to page 18 again.

Look back at page 38 and re-read the section on how to choose adjective endings, as you will have the chance to practise this later in this unit.

Revise your numbers 0–10 on page 36, as this will help you to learn the numbers up to 30.

In this unit you will be asking for directions. Remember that in real life, the Russians whom you ask for directions probably won't have read this book, and they may give you rather complicated answers! Don't panic, but just try to pick out the essential words. Remember that you can always ask them to speak more slowly, and in this unit you will also learn how to ask someone to repeat something.

ℹ️ Телефо́н-автома́т (Telef<u>o</u>n-avtam<u>a</u>t) *Pay phone*

To use a public telephone, you will need to buy a **телефонка́рта** (telefonk<u>a</u>rta) *phone card*. When you get through to a home number, if the person you want does not pick up the phone, ask **Cа́ша до́ма?** (S<u>a</u>sha d<u>o</u>ma?) *Is Sasha at home?*

Кио́ск (Ki<u>o</u>sk) *Kiosk*

Kiosks can be found on many city streets in Russia. They sell all manner of goods, including theatre tickets, newspapers, maps, flowers, confectionery and tobacco. Look out for the following signs: **театра́льный** (tiyatr<u>a</u>l'ny) for theatre tickets, **газе́тный** (gaz<u>ye</u>tny) for newspapers and magazines, and **цветы́** (tsvit<u>y</u>) for flowers. Russians love to give and receive flowers, but you should remember to give an odd number of blooms on happy occasions as an even number is associated with sad events. In winter you may see glass cases of flowers for sale on the streets, with candles burning inside to stop the flowers from freezing. **Табáк** (Tabak) means that cigarettes are for sale, and you may see people smoking a version of a cigarette called **папирóса** (papir_o_sa) which has a cardboard mouthpiece.

Key words and phrases

Диалóг 1

как попáсть в…?	kak pap_a_st' v …?	How do I/you get to?
центр	tsentr	the centre
идѝте	eed_ee_tye	go
прямо	pry_a_ma	straight ahead
потóм	pat_o_m	then
налéво	naly_e_va	to the left
крáсный	kr_a_sny	red
плóщадь f	pl_o_shshad'	square
повторѝте	pavtar_ee_tye	repeat

Диалóг 2

Кудá вы идёте?	Kood_a_ vy eedy_o_tye?	Where are you going?
Я идý в …	Ya eed_oo_ v …	I am going to …
далекó	dalyik_o_	far, a long way
недалекó	nidalyik_o_	not far
напрáво	napr_a_va	to the right
интерéсный	intiry_e_sny	interesting

Диалóг 3

закрыт/а/о	zakr_y_t/zakr_y_ta/zakr_y_to	closed
на ремóнт	na rim_o_nt	for repairs
Ой, как жаль!	Oy, kak zhal'!	Oh, what a pity!
галерéя	galiry_e_ya	gallery
открыт/а/о	atkr_y_t/atkr_y_ta/atkr_y_to	open

Диалóг 4

У вас есть …?	Oo vas yest' …	Do you have …?
сувенѝр/сувенѝры	soovin_ee_r/soovin_ee_ry	souvenir/s
матрёшка/матрёшки	matry_o_shka/matry_o_shky	set/s of stacking wooden dolls
конфéта/конфéты	konfy_e_ta/konfy_e_ty	sweet/s
рýсский	r_oo_sky	Russian
америкáнский	amirik_a_nsky	American
кнѝга/кнѝги	kn_ee_ga/kn_ee_gy	book/s
Дом Кнѝги	dom kn_ee_gy	House of the Book (book shop)

Dialogues

▶ Диало́г 1

Andrew is still exploring Moscow. Now he is heading for Red Square and the Kremlin.

А́ндрю Де́вушка, извини́те, как попа́сть в центр?

Де́вушка В центр? Иди́те пря́мо, пото́м нале́во, и там Кра́сная Пло́щадь и Кремль.

А́ндрю Повтори́те, пожа́луйста.

Де́вушка Иди́те пря́мо, пото́м нале́во.

А́ндрю Спаси́бо.

▶ Диало́г 2

Alison is looking for the museum when Igor sees her.

Йгорь Здра́вствуйте, А́лисон. Куда́ вы идёте?

А́лисон Я иду́ в музе́й. Это далеко́?

Йгорь Нет, э́то недалеко́. Иди́те пря́мо, и музе́й напра́во. Музе́й о́чень интере́сный.

А́лисон Спаси́бо. До свида́ния.

▶ Диало́г 3

As Alison sets off, Igor suddenly remembers something.

Йгорь А́лисон, музе́й закры́т. Закры́т на ремо́нт.

А́лисон Ой, как жаль!

Йгорь Но галере́я откры́та. И галере́я о́чень интере́сная.

А́лисон Как попа́сть в галере́ю?

Йгорь Иди́те нале́во, пото́м напра́во, и галере́я пря́мо. Это недалеко́.

▶ Диало́г 4

A tourist called Colin is asking a **киоскёр** *(kioskyor) stall-holder about the souvenirs she is selling.*

Ко́лин У вас есть сувени́ры?

Киоскёр Да. Вот матрёшки и конфе́ты. Здесь кассе́ты и там ру́сская во́дка и ру́сское вино́.

Ко́лин Это ру́сский шокола́д?

Киоскёр Нет, америка́нский. О́чень хоро́ший шокола́д.

Ко́лин А у вас есть кни́ги?

Киоскёр Нет, иди́те в Дом Кни́ги. Это недалеко́.

Ко́лин Где Дом Кни́ги?

Киоскёр Иди́те нале́во, пото́м пря́мо, и Дом Кни́ги напра́во.

▶ Numerals 11–30

11	оди́ннадцать	adeenatsat'	18	восемна́дцать	vasyemnatsat'
12	двена́дцать	dvyenatsat'	19	девятна́дцать	dyevitnatsat'
13	трина́дцать	treenatsat'	20	два́дцать	dvatsat'
14	четы́рнадцать	chyetirnatsat'	21	два́дцать оди́н	dvatsat' adeen
15	пятна́дцать	pitnatsat'	22	два́дцать два	dvatsat' dva
16	шестна́дцать	shesnatsat'	23	два́дцать три	dvatsat' tree
17	семна́дцать	syemnatsat'	30	три́дцать	treetsat'

Number practice

Read all the numbers out loud or listen to the recording and repeat them. You will notice that 11–19 are made up more or less of the numbers 1–9 plus the ending **-надцать** which is a contracted form of **на де́сять** *on ten*. To practise numerals this time, you could add 10 or 20 to the numbers on your playing cards or dice. Or make up sums:

13 + 8 = 21   трина́дцать плюс во́семь – два́дцать оди́н
30 – 11 = 19   три́дцать ми́нус оди́ннадцать – девятна́дцать

Mechanics of the language

1 Как попа́сть в ...? *How do I get to ...?*

To ask how to get somewhere in Russian, simply say **как попа́сть в ...** *How to get to?* and add the place to which you want to go. This simple rule works for masculine and neuter nouns, like **теа́тр** and **кафе́** but for feminine words you should try to remember to change the ending of the noun from **-а** to **-у** and **-я** to **-ю**. (For those people with an interest in grammar, these endings are called *accusative* endings, and you use them after **в** and **на** when movement to a place is indicated.)

Masculine	*Feminine*	*Neuter*
Как попа́сть в теа́тр?	Как попа́сть в библиоте́ку? Как попа́сть в галере́ю?	Как попа́сть в кафе́?

When talking about going to a certain place, occasionally you need to use **на** instead of **в** to mean *to*: for example, **Как попа́сть на стадио́н?** *How do I get to the stadium?* **Как попа́сть на по́чту?** *How do I get to the post office?*

If you meet a new word in the **Key words and phrases** list which needs **на** instead of **в** you will see **(на)** next to it.

2 Куда́?/Где? *Where to?/Where?*

You already know the word **Где?** *Where?* In **Диало́г 2** you met a different word which you use to ask *Where to?* **Куда́?**

Где музе́й? *Where is the museum?*
Куда́ вы идёте? *Where are you going to?*

In the same dialogue, you also met part of the verb *to go*. This refers to going somewhere on foot, not by transport.

я иду́ *I am going*   вы идёте *you are going*

3 Откры́т/закры́т *Open/closed*

Note that these words have different endings depending on the gender of the noun they refer to.

Masculine	*Feminine*	*Neuter*
Медпу́нкт откры́т.	По́чта откры́та.	Спра́вочное бюро́ откры́то.
Бассе́йн закры́т.	Гости́ница закры́та.	Кафе́ закры́то.

4 Plural forms of nouns

To make a plural form in English we usually add -*s*: *rabbit/rabbits*. In Russian, to make the plural forms of masculine nouns you usually add **-ы** unless the spelling rule (see **Summary of language patterns**) makes you use **-и** instead. For feminine plural forms, you remove the last letter (usually **-а** or **-я**) and then add **-ы** or **-и**. You will remember that nouns ending in a soft sign **-ь** may be either masculine or feminine, and these also lose the last letter before adding **-и**.

Masculine	*Feminine*
рестора́н/рестора́ны *restaurant/s*	гости́ница/гости́ницы *hotel/s*
кио́ск/кио́ски *kiosk/s*	библиоте́ка/библиоте́ки *library/libraries*
рубль/рубли́ *rouble/s*	пло́щадь/пло́щади *square/s*

Neuter nouns also lose their last letter before adding **-а** or **-я** to make the plural form, so **у́тро** *morning* becomes **у́тра**. But most of the neuter nouns which you have met so far (бюро́, кака́о, кафе́, кило́, кино́, метро́, пиани́но, ра́дио) do not change their form at all when they become plural. This is because neuter nouns which have been borrowed directly from other languages are exempt from all the usual rules. So you have to try to tell from the context whether there is one piano or many!

Exercises

1 Look at the town plan and its key on pages 50–51. Only new words are shown in English. Make sure you know how to say all the places in Russian. Then sit yourself down with a Russian friend in the window of a café in the left-hand corner and ask whether the places shown on the plan are far away or not, for example:

Гости́ница далеко́?   Да, э́то далеко́.
Институ́т далеко́?   Нет, э́то недалеко́.

2 Now you can try asking your friend for directions. **Как попа́сть в библиоте́ку?** *How do I get to the library?* To begin with, all the places that you ask about are feminine, so you will need to change **-а** to **-у** and **-я** to **-ю**. Underline the correct form of the question.

a Как попа́сть … i … на по́чту? ii … на по́чта?
b Как попа́сть … i … в гости́ница? ii … в гости́ницу?
c Как попа́сть … i … в поликли́ника? ii … в поликли́нику?
d Как попа́сть … i … на фа́брику? ii … на фа́брика?

Now ask for directions to all the places on the town plan, including the masculine and neuter places, remembering that their endings do not change: **Как попа́сть в рестора́н?** *How do I get to the restaurant?* Ask your questions in the order given in the key so that you can check them in the back of the book.

What will your friend say in reply? Make up suitable answers using **иди́те напра́во** *go to the right*, **иди́те нале́во** *go to the left*, and **иди́те пря́мо** *go straight ahead*.

3 Now ask your Russian friend where he or she is going: **Куда́ вы идёте?** *Where are you going?* and supply suitable answers. **Я иду́ в гости́ницу** *I am going to the hotel.*

4 Match up these nouns and adjectives to make sentences. Use one word from each column, for example: **a) И́горь хоро́ший футболи́ст.**

a	И́горь	ру́сская	го́род
b	Ле́на	большо́й	кафе́
c	Хард-Рок	краси́вая	газе́та (*newspaper*)
d	Ло́ндон	америка́нское	футболи́ст
e	Пра́вда	хоро́ший	балери́на

▶ 5 Listen to the conversations and tick the statements which are true.

a Музе́й откры́т.   d Рестора́н закры́т.
b Библиоте́ка закры́та.   e По́чта откры́та.
c Кафе́ откры́то.

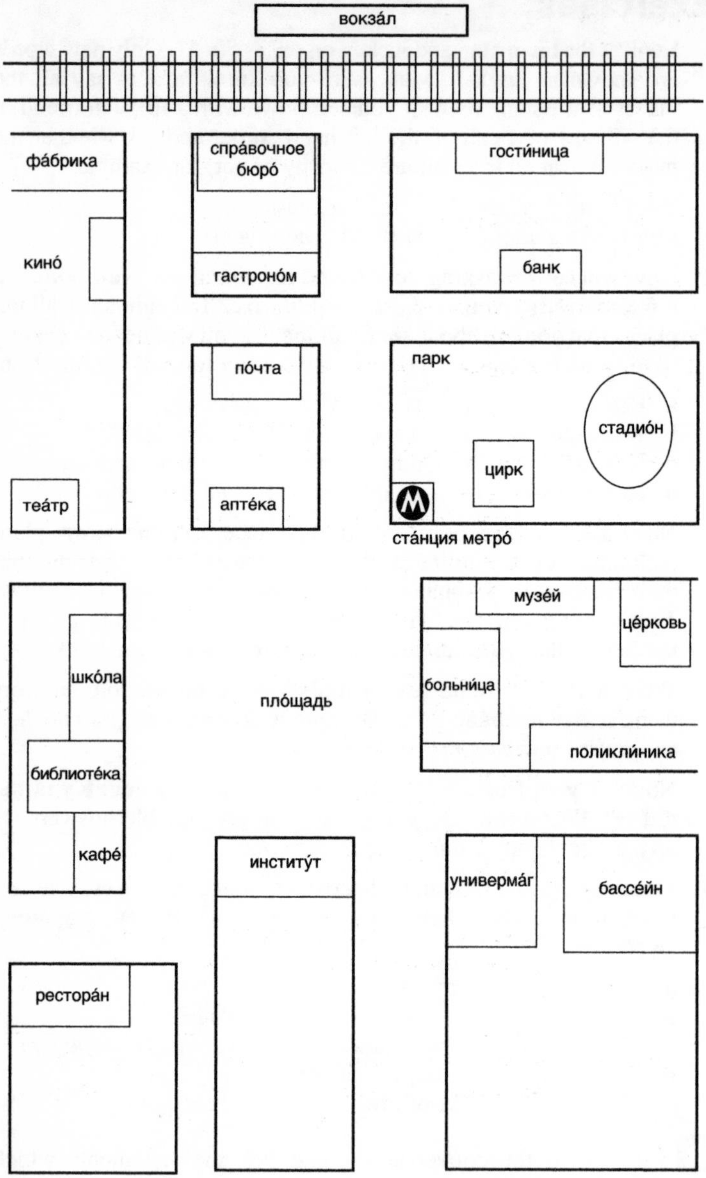

вокза́л

фа́брика

кино́

теа́тр

спра́вочное бюро́

гастроно́м

по́чта

апте́ка

гости́ница

банк

парк

стадио́н

цирк

Ⓜ

ста́нция метро́

шко́ла

библиоте́ка

кафе́

пло́щадь

музе́й

це́рковь

больни́ца

поликли́ника

институ́т

универма́г

бассе́йн

рестора́н

план

Ключ *Key*

1 рестора́н
2 институ́т
3 универма́г
4 бассе́йн
5 кафе́
6 библиоте́ка
7 шко́ла (shkola) *school*
8 пло́щадь (на)
9 поликли́ника
   (polykleenika) *health centre*
10 це́рковь *(f)* (tserkov') *church*
11 больни́ца (bal'neetsa) *hospital*
12 музе́й
13 теа́тр
14 апте́ка (aptyeka) *pharmacy*

15 цирк
16 ста́нция метро́ (на)
   (stantseeya metro)
   metro station
17 по́чта (на)
18 парк
19 стадио́н (на)
20 кино́
21 гастроно́м
22 банк
23 фа́брика (на) (fabreeka) *factory*
24 спра́вочное бюро́
25 гости́ница
26 вокза́л (на) (vakzal)
   train station

6 Match up these questions with suitable answers.

a У вас есть кни́ги?
b У вас есть ко́фе?
c У вас есть табле́тки?
d У вас есть проду́кты?
e У вас есть сувени́ры?
f У вас есть котле́та и сала́т?

i Нет, иди́те в апте́ку.
ii Нет, иди́те в кио́ск.
iii Нет, иди́те в гастроно́м.
iv Нет, иди́те в кафе́.
v Нет, иди́те в рестора́н.
vi Нет, иди́те в библиоте́ку.

7 Read Ivan's shopping list, and wherever he wants more than one of something (e.g. bananas), put a tick. The first one has been done for you.

Гастроно́м	Апте́ка	Таба́к	Кио́ск	Теа́тр
бана́ны ✓	табле́тки	сигаре́ты	цветы́	биле́т
ко́фе		и папиро́сы	конфе́ты	
са́хар				
фру́кты				

8 When you are reasonably confident with your numbers, listen to the recording and jot down the missing numbers from each six-digit phone number **но́мер телефо́на** as it is read out. The numbers will be read in pairs: *17-25-10* **семна́дцать – два́дцать пять – де́сять**.

a 12 – ____ – 1__   **d** 1__ – ____ – 24
b 25 – ____ – __7   **e** ____ – ____ – 12
c 14 – 3__ – ____

If you do not have the recording or if you want more practice, you could make up and jot down some more phone numbers, and read them out clearly.

9 Look at these road signs and see if you can match them up with their captions below. You do not need to understand every word to do this.

a инвали́ды   **g** авто́бусы
b движе́ние пря́мо   **h** движе́ние напра́во
c телефо́н   **i** разводно́й мост
d ке́мпинг   **j** тра́кторы
e гости́ница/моте́ль   **k** движе́ние нале́во
f больни́ца

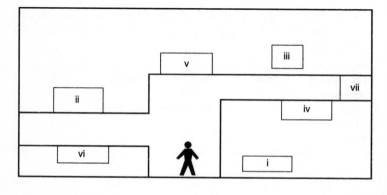

10 You are visiting another town. Read the instructions below to identify the buildings on your new plan. Match up the letters with the numbers.

a Теа́тр пря́мо.
b Иди́те пря́мо, пото́м напра́во и библиоте́ка напра́во.
c Иди́те нале́во, и гастроно́м напра́во.
d Иди́те пря́мо, пото́м напра́во, и вокза́л нале́во.
e Иди́те нале́во, и рестора́н нале́во. Э́то недалеко́.
f Иди́те пря́мо, пото́м напра́во, и гости́ница пря́мо.
g Вот кафе́, напра́во.

Test yourself

Now you should be able to find your way around a Russian town happily understanding numbers up to 30, never rattling a shop door which says **закры́т**, and finding out what is available in shops which are open! Well done! To test yourself, see if you can put the following phrases into Russian. If your memory needs jogging, the answers are written below, but in the wrong order. Good luck!

1 Excuse me, how do I get to the restaurant?
2 Go straight ahead, then to the left and the restaurant is on the right.
3 Is it far? No, it's not far.
4 Is the museum open?
5 Do you have any chocolate?

i Музе́й откры́т?
ii Извини́те, как попа́сть в рестора́н?
iii Э́то далеко́? Нет, э́то недалеко́.
iv У вас есть шокола́д?
v Иди́те пря́мо, пото́м нале́во, и рестора́н напра́во.

How did you manage? If you think you could make yourself understood then you are ready to move on to Unit 6. However, now that you have completed five units, you may decide it would be helpful to look back over everything you have done so far. If nothing else, you may find that things which seemed difficult at the time now seem easier!

06

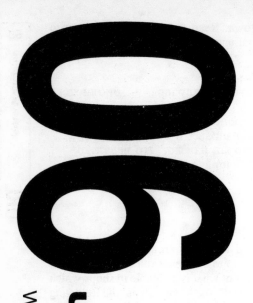

что вы хотите?

what do you want?

In this unit you will learn
- how to say what you want
- how to pay for something in a shop
- how to say that something belongs to you
- how to make plural forms of adjectives
- how to count from 30 to 100

Before you start

You have already spent two units finding your way around a Russian city. In this unit you will learn more things to say when you finally find the shop or café you were looking for. Since you already know lots of words and phrases you could try rehearsing them in your own environment. Be as active in your language learning as possible.

Every time you talk to a friend, colleague, salesperson or waiter in your own language, try to repeat the transaction to yourself in Russian. Wherever you are, try to name what you see around you in Russian. When you are going somewhere, even if it is just down the corridor, pretend to give directions to a visiting Russian. Say telephone numbers, bus numbers and number plates to yourself in Russian.

If there was anything you didn't understand in an earlier unit, look back at it before you go on. It may be clearer now that you understand more.

Revise your numbers 0–30 in the **Numbers** section at the back of the book, as this will make learning the higher numbers much easier.

i Универма́г (Oonivermak) *Department store*

The most famous Russian department store is **ГУМ (Госуда́рственный универса́льный магази́н)** *State department store* in Red Square in Moscow. This used to be centrally run, but since *perestroika* it has been divided up into individual shops which are leased out to leading Russian and Western retailers.

Ры́нок (Rynok) *Market*

If you want to buy fresh vegetables and fruit **о́вощи и фру́кты** (ovashshee ee frookty), milk and dairy produce **молоко́** (malako) and meat and fish **мя́со и ры́ба** (myasa ee ryba) the local markets are a good source of supply, although in the winter months there is inevitably less choice.

Кафе́ (kafeh) *Café*

The waiter **официа́нт** (afitsiant) and waitress **официа́нтка** (afitsiantka) in a café or restaurant may be addressed as **молодо́й челове́к** and **де́вушка**, forms of address which apply to anyone up to about fifty years of age!

Kácca (Kassa) *Cash desk*

In some shops, such as old-fashioned book shops, you may need to pay for your purchases at a cash desk **кácca** (kassa), and then take your receipt **чек** (chek) back to the counter to collect your goods.

Key words and phrases

Диалóг 1

что	shto	*what?*
Что вы хотúте купúть?	Shto vy khateetye koopeet'?	*What do you want to buy?*
подáрок/подáрки	padarak/padarky	*present/presents*
я хочý	ya khachoo	*I want*
балалáйка	balalaika	*balalaika (stringed instrument)*
пойдём	paeedyom	*Let's go*

Диалóг 2

покажúте	pakazheetye	*show (me)*
скóлько стóит?	skol'ka stoeet?	*How much is it?*
Сто пятьдеся́т рублéй	sto pidisyat rooblyei	*150 roubles*
где платúть?	gdye plateet'?	*Where do I pay?*
кácca	kassa	*cash desk*

Диалóг 3

фруктóвый сок	frooktovy sok	*fruit juice*
úли	eely	*or*
официáнтка	afitsiantka	*waitress*
идúте сюдá	eedeetye syooda	*come here*
Что у вас есть?	Shto oo vas yest'?	*What have you got?*
минерáльная водá	miniral'naya vada	*mineral water*
с	s	*with*
с лимóном	s leemonum	*with lemon*
с сáхаром	s sakharum	*with sugar*
с молокóм	s mulakom	*with milk*
сейчáс	seychas	*now, right away*

Диалóг 4

ваш/вáша/ вáше/вáши	vash/vasha/ vashe/vashy	*your (m/f/n/p)*
мой/моя́/моё/мой	moy/maya/mayo mayee	*my (m/f/n/p)*
джаз	dzhaz	*jazz*

Dialogues

▶ Диало́г 1

Peter is visiting Russia on business, but before returning home he goes shopping for presents with a colleague, Anton Pavlovich. Anton Pavlovich speaks some English, but they have agreed to speak only Russian in the morning and English in the afternoon.

Анто́н Па́влович	Что вы хоти́те купи́ть, Пи́тер?
Пи́тер	Сувени́ры и пода́рки.
Анто́н Па́влович	Каки́е сувени́ры и пода́рки?
Пи́тер	Я хочу́ купи́ть кни́ги, матрёшки, шокола́д, во́дку и балала́йку.
Анто́н Па́влович	Хорошо́. Пойдём в Дом Кни́ги.

▶ Диало́г 2

In Дом Кни́ги Peter soon gets into his stride.

Пи́тер	Молодо́й челове́к, у вас есть кни́га «А́нна Каре́нина»?
Молодо́й челове́к	Да.
Пи́тер	Покажи́те, пожа́луйста.
Молодо́й челове́к	Вот она́.
Пи́тер	Ско́лько сто́ит?
Молодо́й челове́к	Сто пятьдеся́т рубле́й.
Пи́тер	Где плати́ть?
Молодо́й челове́к	Иди́те в ка́ссу.
Пи́тер	Спаси́бо.

▶ Диало́г 3

Later in the morning, Peter and Anton Pavlovich pop into a café.

Анто́н Па́влович	Что вы хоти́те, Пи́тер?
Пи́тер	Я хочу́ фрукто́вый сок и́ли чай, пожа́луйста.
Анто́н Па́влович	Де́вушка, иди́те сюда́, пожа́луйста. У вас есть фрукто́вый сок?
Официа́нтка	Извини́те, нет.
Анто́н Па́влович	Что у вас есть?
Официа́нтка	Чай, ко́фе, минера́льная вода́, пепси-ко́ла.
Пи́тер	Да́йте, пожа́луйста, чай с лимо́ном и с са́харом.

| Антóн Пáвлович | И кóфе с молокóм. |
| Официáнтка | Чай с лимóном и с сáхаром, и кóфе с молокóм. Сейчáс. |

▶ Диалóг 4

While they wait for their drinks, Peter and Anton Pavlovich look at their purchases.

Антóн Пáвлович	Что у вас есть?
Пи́тер	Вот кни́га «Áнна Карéнина» и матрёшки.
Антóн Пáвлович	Как хорошó. Это óчень краси́вые матрёшки. Пи́тер, э́то вáша кассéта?
Пи́тер	Да, э́то моя́ кассéта, «Ру́сский джаз».
Антóн Пáвлович	И вот мой компáкт-ди́ск. Óпера «Бори́с Годунóв».
Официáнтка	Вот чай и кóфе.
Пи́тер	Спаси́бо.
Антóн Пáвлович	*Oh look, it's twelve o'clock. We can speak English now!*

▶ Numerals 10–100

10	дéсять	dyesyat'
20	двáдцать	dvatsat'
30	три́дцать	treetsat'
40	сóрок	sorak
50	пятьдеся́т	pidisyat
60	шестьдеся́т	shesdisyat
70	сéмьдесят	syemdyesyat
80	вóсемьдесят	vosyemdyesyat
90	девянóсто	dyevinosta
100	сто	sto
146	сто сóрок шесть	sto sorak shest' etc.

If you are hoping to visit Russia, you will need to learn relatively high numbers to cope with the prices in roubles.

A rouble is **рубль** in Russian, and you may hear it in different forms: **рубль, рубля, рублей**. As long as you recognize the number which goes with it this should be no problem, and if you do get confused, you could carry a notepad and ask salespeople to write down the price for you: **Напишите, пожалуйста** (napeesh<u>ee</u>tye, pazh<u>a</u>lsta), *write please*. Practise the numbers in this unit until you can say them almost without thinking. Every time you see a number in your daily life, say it in Russian, as long as doing so doesn't distract you from driving or working!

Language patterns

1 Plural adjectives

In English, the adjective form is the same whether you are describing one or several items: *big blue balloon*, *big blue balloons*. In Russian, you will remember that there are three forms of singular adjectives to match the singular nouns: masculine, feminine and neuter. (See page 38.) Now that you know how to form plural nouns (e.g. **конфеты** *sweets*), you may want to use adjectives with them. This is easy as it doesn't matter if the plural noun you are referring to is masculine, feminine or neuter. There is only one type of plural adjective ending: **-ые**. This may also be written **-ие** if the spelling rule applies (see **Summary of language patterns**).

краси́вые кни́ги	*beautiful books*
хоро́шие конфе́ты	*good sweets*
больши́е пи́ццы	*big pizzas*

The same ending is used with the plural form **какие...?** *what sort of...?*

Какие сувениры и подарки? *What sort of souvenirs and presents?*

2 My balalaika and your balalaika

In the same way as there are masculine, feminine, neuter and plural forms of adjectives and nouns, there are also different forms of the words *my* and *your*.

Masculine	*Feminine*	*Neuter*	*Plural*
мой паспорт	**моя** балалайка	**моё** пианино	**мои** кассеты
my passport	*my balalaika*	*my piano*	*my cassettes*
ваш паспорт	**ваша** балалайка	**ваше** пианино	**ваши** кассеты
your passport	*your balalaika*	*your piano*	*your cassettes*

As you would expect, these words use the typical endings: **-й** and the consonant **-ш** for masculine forms, **-я** and **-а** for feminine forms, **-ё** and **-e** for neuter forms, and **-и** for plurals.

3 I want to buy a balalaika

Did you notice what happens to the endings of the feminine nouns in **Диалог 1**? Peter says: Я хочу купить книги, матрёшки, шоколад, **водку** и **балалайку**. Водка and балалайка have changed to водку and балалайку. Once again, this is the accusative form. It will always occur when a feminine noun is the person or thing which has something done to it, or in grammatical terms, is the direct object of a verb. By direct object, we mean that a noun answers the question *what?* asked after the verb. Here are some examples of direct objects in English:

She baked **bread**.	She baked **what**?	**Bread**.
He likes **opera, books, wine**.	He likes **what**?	**Opera, books and wine**.
He plays the **balalaika**.	He plays **what**?	**Balalaika**.

And some in Russian:

Я хочу купить **балалайку**.	*You want to buy what?*	*Balalaika*.
Я хочу **пепси-колу**.	*You want what?*	*Pepsi-cola*.

4 Imperatives: do this, do that!

Did you realize that you can already give people eight different orders or requests in Russian? **Здра́вствуйте** *hello* was the first one you learned, and it means literally *Be healthy!*

Others which you know are

извини́те *excuse (me)* покажи́те *show (me)*
повтори́те *repeat* иди́те *go*
напиши́те *write* да́йте *give (me)*
скажи́те *tell (me)*

Add пожа́луйста to be polite, and you should be able to get things done!

Exercises

1 Choose a question word from the list below to complete these dialogues.

   a _____ теа́тр? Вот он.
   b _____ вас зову́т? Меня́ зову́т Ни́на.
   c _____ вы идёте? Я иду́ на по́чту.
   d _____ вы хоти́те? Я хочу́ суп, хлеб и во́дку.
   e _____ э́то? Э́то Са́ша. Он – мой сын.

   Как? Что? Где? Кто? Куда́?

2 You work in a Russian kiosk. You cannot keep everything on display, but you have a list so that you know what is tucked away in boxes. A tourist comes up and asks if you have various items. Carry out an imaginary conversation with the tourist. If you have the items he asks for, tell him all about them. If not, say Извини́те, нет. Here is your list.

хоро́шие бана́ны	лимона́д
биле́ты в теа́тр	матрёшки
ру́сская во́дка	папиро́сы и сигаре́ты
кассе́ты	компакт-ди́ски
америка́нские конфе́ты	план
ко́фе	сувени́ры
	цветы́

The first example has been done for you.

a **Tourist** У вас есть сувениры?
You Да, есть. Вот красивые русские матрёшки.
b **Tourist** У вас есть балалайка?
c **Tourist** У вас есть сигареты? Какие? Русские или американские?
d **Tourist** У вас есть бананы?

Now carry on the conversation. You could ask him if he wants any sweets, or he could ask you how much something costs.

3 Say the following phone numbers, and check them off below.

a 65 – 43 – 74 **b** 14 – 58 – 92 **c** 123 – 89 – 12
d 135 – 91 – 36 **e** 117 – 54 – 22

i сто семнадцать – пятьдесят четыре – двадцать два
ii сто двадцать три – восемьдесят девять – двенадцать
iii сто тридцать пять – девяносто один – тридцать шесть
iv шестьдесят пять – сорок три – семьдесят четыре
v четырнадцать – пятьдесят восемь – девяносто два

4 Which orders or requests would you use in the following circumstances? You want someone to:

a repeat something **e** tell you something
b show you something **f** write something
c give you something **g** excuse you
d go somewhere

i идите, пожалуйста **ii** повторите, пожалуйста
iii скажите, пожалуйста **iv** покажите, пожалуйста
v напишите, пожалуйста **vi** извините, пожалуйста
vii дайте, пожалуйста

5 You are in a possessive mood. Every time Boris claims that an item belongs to him, you contradict him and say it is yours.

Борис Это мой микроскоп.
Вы Нет, это не ваш микроскоп. Это мой микроскоп.

Choose from **мой/моя/моё/мои** and **ваш/ваша/ваше/ваши** to fill in the blanks.

a **Борис** Это моё радио. **Вы** Нет, это не в ____ радио.
Это м ____ радио.
b **Борис** Это моя книга. **Вы** Нет, это не в ____ книга.
Это м ____ книга.

c	**Бори́с**	Это мой гита́ры.	**Вы**

c **Бори́с** Это мой гита́ры. **Вы** Нет, э́то не в ____ гита́ры. Это м ____ гита́ры.

d **Бори́с** Это мой биле́т. **Вы** Нет, э́то не в ____ биле́т. Это м ____ биле́т.

For more practice, you could try the same thing in a more generous mood, adding your own ideas.

Бори́с Это ва́ши сигаре́ты?
Вы Нет, э́то не мой сигаре́ты. Это ва́ши сигаре́ты.

▶ **6** Listen to find out what people want. Tick off the items on the list below as you hear them mentioned. Then listen again and underline each feminine item asked for. These will have changed their endings from **-а** to **-у** and **-я** to **-ю**. If you don't have the recording, make up sentences on this model: **Я хочу́ котле́ту, сала́т и ко́фе с молоко́м.**

вино́	конфе́ты	чай с лимо́ном
во́дка	пи́цца	ко́фе с са́харом
суп	смета́на	омле́т
борщ	фру́кты	пепси-ко́ла

7 Link each adjective to a suitable noun by joining them with a line.

Большо́й	сад
ма́ленькое	конфе́ты
краси́вые	челове́к
ру́сские	вино́
интере́сная	папиро́сы
молодо́й	теа́тр
ботани́ческий	кни́га
хоро́шие	ра́дио
бе́лое	цветы́

8 Use this grid to work on your numbers. Cover up all but one line of numbers, and read out the ones you see. Try it again in a day or two, and see if you are any quicker.

1	14	36	97	12
8	122	3	88	45
64	199	20	17	150
7	13	65	10	63
144	21	19	5	111

Test yourself

There are many situations which you could now handle if you were visiting Russia. Answer these questions to test yourself.

1 Что вы хотите?
2 Куда вы идёте?
3 Что это?
4 Метро закрыто?
5 Это ваш билет? (*Yes*).

07

В гости́нице
at the hotel

In this unit you will learn
- how to give your particulars when booking into a hotel
- how to say the letters of the alphabet and fill in a form
- how to say what nationality you are and what you do
- how to say where you work
- how to specify 'this' or 'that'
- how to count from 100 to 1,000

Before you start

If you are thinking of visiting Russia at any time you will need somewhere to stay. You may be fortunate enough to have friends there, or you may need to book into a **гостиница** (gasteenitsa) *hotel*. The language in this unit will enable you to do this, and it will also be useful whenever you need to give or ask for personal details. You may find it particularly helpful to be able to use the alphabet in case anyone asks **Как это пишется?** (Kak eta peeshetsa?) *How is that written?* In this unit, you will also learn to count up to 1,000 so make sure you know your numbers up to 100 first.

🛈 Hotel accommodation

If you are travelling to Russia on a tourist visa, you will have to arrange your accommodation before you arrive. At present this means getting a private invitation to stay in a home or booking a hotel. Getting a business visa means that you do not need to prebook accommodation. When you arrive at your hotel you will meet the **администратор** *administrator* at the reception desk. Each floor of a big hotel may also have a **дежурная** (dyizhoornaya), a woman on duty who sits at a table on the landing.

▶ Saying the alphabet in Russian

In Russian, as in English, the name of a letter sometimes sounds different from the sound that the letter makes. If you had not thought of this before, say *h*, *w*, or *y* out loud in English and think how confusing the letter names might be to a foreign visitor. You may need to know the names of Russian letters to spell something, for example your name or the name of your home town, so here they are, in the correct order. Familiarize yourself with them before you move on to the dialogues. You will see the letter first, for example C c. Then you see the name of the letter in Russian **эс** and finally the English transliteration of the letter name (es). You can listen to them on your recording.

Alphabet guide

Glance back through the book, picking a few words at random and spelling them out loud.

А а	**а**	a
Б б	**бэ**	(beh *as in bed*)
В в	**вэ**	(veh)
Г г	**гэ**	(geh)
Д д	**дэ**	(deh)

Е е	е	(yeh)
Ё ё	ё	(yoh)
Ж ж	жэ	(zheh)
З з	зэ	(zeh)
И и	и	(ee)
Й й	и	**и кра́ткое** (ee kr<u>a</u>tkoye *short* и)
К к	ка	(ka)
Л л	эль	(el')
М м	эм	(em)
Н н	эн	(en)
О о	о	(o)
П п	пэ	(peh)
Р р	эр	(air)
С с	эс	(es)
Т т	тэ	(teh)
У у	у	(oo)
Ф ф	эф	(ef)
Х х	ха	(kha)
Ц ц	цэ	(tse)
Ч ч	че	(che)
Ш ш	ша	(sha)
Щ щ	ща	(shsha)
ъ	**твёрдый знак**	(tvy<u>o</u>rdy znak *hard sign*)
ы	ы	(iy)
ь	**мя́гкий знак**	(my<u>a</u>khky znak *soft sign*)
Э э	э	(eh)
Ю ю	ю	(yoo)
Я я	я	(ya)

Key words and phrases

Диало́г 1

Одну́ мину́точку	Adn<u>oo</u> min<u>oo</u>tuchkoo	*(Wait) one moment*
Слу́шаю вас	Sl<u>oo</u>shayoo vas	*I'm listening to you*
ко́мната	k<u>o</u>mnata	*room*
но́мер	n<u>o</u>myer	*hotel room/number*
Запо́лните э́тот бланк	Zap<u>o</u>lneetye <u>e</u>tot blank	*Fill in this form*
Мо́жно?	M<u>o</u>zhna?	*Is it possible/ Would you mind?*
так	tak	*so*
но	no	*but*
я пишу́	ya peesh<u>oo</u>	*I write*
Как э́то пи́шется?	Kak <u>e</u>ta p<u>ee</u>shetsa?	*How is that spelt?*

А́нглия	Angleeya	England
Кто вы по профе́ссии?	Kto vy pa prafyessee?	What are you by profession?
учи́тельница/ учи́тель	oocheetyelneetsa/ oocheetyel	teacher (f/m)
я рабо́таю	ya rabotayoo	I work
в	v	in
шко́ла	shkola	school
гражда́нство	grazhdanstva	nationality/citizenship
англича́нка	angleechanka	Englishwoman
бага́ж	bagash	luggage
чемода́н	chimodan	suitcase
су́мка	soomka	bag
аккордео́н	akordeon	accordion
ключ	klyooch	key

Диало́г 2

душ	doosh	shower
ва́нная	vannaya	bathroom
туале́т	tooalyet	toilet
буфе́т	boofyet	snack bar
внизу́	vneezoo	downstairs

Диало́г 3

Где вы живёте?	Gdye vy zheevyotye?	Where do you live?
Где вы рабо́таете?	Gdye vy rabotayetye?	Where do you work?
инжене́р	eenzhinyer	engineer
не́мец	nyemyets	German man
францу́женка	frantsoozhenka	French woman
я живу́	ya zheevoo	I live
продаве́ц/ продавщи́ца	pradavyets/ pradavshsheetsa	shop assistant (m/f)
коне́чно	kanyeshna	of course
ру́сский/ру́сская	rooskee/ rooskaya	Russian man/woman
америка́нец	amyirikanyets	American man
врач	vrach	doctor
испа́нка	eespanka	Spanish woman

Dialogues

▶ Диало́г 1

Fiona arrives at a hotel where she has reserved a room.

Фио́на   Здра́вствуйте.
Администра́тор   Одну́ мину́точку. Да, слу́шаю вас.

Фио́на	Меня́ зову́т Фио́на Ха́рисон. Я хочу́ ко́мнату, пожа́луйста.
Администра́тор	(*looks through bookings*) Фио́на Ха́рисон? Да, вот ва́ша фами́лия. Ва́ша ко́мната но́мер 38 (три́дцать во́семь).
Фио́на	Спаси́бо.
Администра́тор	Запо́лните э́тот бланк.
Фио́на	(*handing the form to the administrator for help*) Мо́жно, пожа́луйста? Я говорю́ по-ру́сски, но пло́хо пишу́.
Администра́тор	Мо́жно. Как ва́ша фами́лия?
Фио́на	Фами́лия Ха́рисон, и и́мя Фио́на.
Администра́тор	Так, Ха́рисон. Как э́то пи́шется, Фио́на?
Фио́на	Ф - и - о - н - а.
Администра́тор	Како́й у вас а́дрес?
Фио́на	А́нглия, Ше́лтон, у́лица Кро́сли, дом 13 (трина́дцать).
Администра́тор	И кто вы по профе́ссии?
Фио́на	Я учи́тельница. Я рабо́таю в шко́ле в Ше́лтоне.
Администра́тор	Како́е у вас гражда́нство?
Фио́на	Я англича́нка.
Администра́тор	Ваш па́спорт, пожа́луйста.
Фио́на	Вот он.
Администра́тор	Спаси́бо. У вас есть бага́ж?
Фио́на	Да, вот мой чемода́н, моя́ су́мка и мой аккордео́н.
Администра́тор	Вот ваш ключ.

▶ Диало́г 2

Fiona is shown to her room.

Администра́тор	Вот ва́ша ко́мната. Вот у вас телеви́зор, телефо́н и балко́н. И в коридо́ре душ, ва́нная и туале́т.
Фио́на	Спаси́бо. Скажи́те, в гости́нице есть рестора́н?
Администра́тор	Да, рестора́н, буфе́т и бар. Но рестора́н сейча́с закры́т.
Фио́на	Как жаль! Как попа́сть в буфе́т?
Администра́тор	Буфе́т напра́во. Э́то недалеко́.
Фио́на	И бар?
Администра́тор	Бар внизу́.

▶ Диало́г 3

As you may have guessed from her luggage, Fiona has come to Moscow to an international conference of accordion players. At their first meeting, Fiona gets the ball rolling by asking everyone to introduce themselves and say where they work.

Фио́на   Кто вы по профе́ссии? Где вы живёте и где вы рабо́таете?

Карл   Меня́ зову́т Карл. Я инжене́р. Я рабо́таю в институ́те в Берли́не. Я не́мец.

Брижи́т   Здра́вствуйте, меня́ зову́т Брижи́т. Я францу́женка. Я учи́тельница и я живу́ в Лио́не. Я там рабо́таю в шко́ле.

Серге́й   Меня́ зову́т Серге́й. Я продаве́ц и я рабо́таю в магази́не здесь в Москве́. Я, коне́чно, ру́сский.

Грег   Здра́вствуйте, я америка́нец и меня́ зову́т Грег. Я актёр и я живу́ в Нью Йо́рке.

Ири́на   Я врач. Меня́ зову́т Ири́на. Я рабо́таю в поликли́нике в Но́вгороде. Я ру́сская.

Хуани́та   Меня́ зову́т Хуани́та. Я продавщи́ца и рабо́таю в магази́не. Я живу́ в Барсело́не. Я испа́нка.

▶ Numerals 100–1,000

100	сто	sto	600	шестьсо́т	shes-sot
200	две́сти	dvyestee	700	семьсо́т	syemsot
300	три́ста	treesta	800	восемьсо́т	vasyemsot
400	четы́реста	chyetiryesta			
500	пятьсо́т	pitsot	900	девятьсо́т	dyevitsot
1,000	ты́сяча	tysyacha			
1,539	ты́сяча пятьсо́т три́дцать де́вять			tysyacha pitsot treetsat dyevyat'	

Practise these numbers until you are confident with them, testing yourself with numbers which you see around you every day.

Mechanics of the language

1 *How to say 'in'*

You will remember that in Unit 5 you met the words **в** and **на**, meaning *to*, as in **Как попа́сть в теа́тр?** *How do I get to the theatre?* There the words **в** and **на** triggered the accusative case in the following word. However, when **в** and **на** mean *in* or *at* a certain place, they trigger a different case, known as the *prepositional case*, in the following word. Again, you use **в** unless you see (**на**) next to the word in your vocabulary list. You saw **в** used a good deal in **Диало́г 3**. Did you notice what happened to the ending of each word following **в**?

Masculine	**Feminine**
(институ́т) в институ́т**е**	(шко́ла) в шко́л**е**
(теа́тр) в теа́тр**е**	(поликли́ника) в поликли́ник**е**
(Но́вгород) в Но́вгород**е**	(Москва́) в Москв**е́**

Masculine words generally add the ending **-е** and feminine words replace the ending **-а** with **-е**.

2 How to say which one you mean (demonstrative pronouns)

Did you notice in **Диало́г 1** that Fiona was told to fill in *this* form, **Запо́лните э́тот бланк**. **Э́тот** is the word for *this* or *that* which is used to point out masculine words. So, **Да́йте, пожа́луйста, э́тот чемода́н** would mean *Please give me **that** suitcase*. If you want to refer to a feminine noun, use **э́та** instead. ***This** girl is my daughter* would be **Э́та де́вушка – моя́ дочь**. For neuter words you need to use **э́то**, as in **Покажи́те, пожа́луйста, э́то ра́дио** *Please show me **that** radio*. To refer to plural nouns use **э́ти**, as in **Э́ти биле́ты – мои́**. ***These** tickets are mine*.

▶ 3 Гражда́нство *Nationality*

In **Диало́г 3** you met people of different nationalities. As you would expect, there are different words in Russian to refer to the male and female of a particular nationality, so a Russian man is **ру́сский** and a Russian woman is **ру́сская**. In the chart below you can see the name of the country, the words for a man and woman of that nationality, and finally the language which they speak. You could make up sentences to practise: **Вы ру́сский? Вы, коне́чно, говори́те по-ру́сски!**

	Country (страна́)	Man (мужчи́на)	Woman (же́нщина)	Language (язы́к)
Russia	Росси́я Rasseeya	ру́сский roosky	ру́сская rooskaya	по-ру́сски pa-roosky

England	**Áнглия**	**англичáнин**	**англичáнка**	**по-англи́йски**
	Angleeya	angleechanin	angleechanka	pa-angleesky
America	**Амéрика**	**америкáнец**	**америкáнка**	**по-англи́йски**
	Amyereeka	ameree-kanyets	amereekanka	pa-angleesky
Japan	**Япóния**	**япóнец**	**япóнка**	**по-япóнски**
	Yaponiya	yaponyets	yaponka	pa-yaponsky
Spain	**Испáния**	**испáнец**	**испáнка**	**по-испáнски**
	Eespaniya	eespanyets	eespanka	pa-eespansky
France	**Фрáнция**	**францýз**	**францýженка**	**по-францýзски**
	Frantsiya	frantsoos	frantsoozhenka	pa-frantsoozsky
Germany	**Гермáния**	**нéмец**	**нéмка**	**по-немéцки**
	Germaniya	nyemyets	nyemka	pa-nemyetsky

Exercises

▶ **1** You are staying in St Petersburg when a friend calls you asking for the phone numbers of hotels in the city. You look in the directory and read out the names and numbers of the following hotels. The line is poor so you have to spell them out clearly. Read them out loud and check them on the recording.

i Астóрия	311–42–06	**iv** Оли́мпия	119–68–00
ii Еврóпа	312–00–72	**v** Санкт-Петербýрг	542–94–11
iii Карéлия	226–35–15	**vi** Коммодóр	119–66–66

2 Tony, a visiting sports coach, has to fill in a registration form **анкéта** at the hotel reception desk. Match the information required with his personal details. His written Russian is not very good, so he spells out his details for the **администрáтор**. Read the spellings out loud.

Анкéта	
a Фами́лия	_____
b И́мя	_____
c Áдрес	_____
d Граждáнство	_____
e Профéссия	_____
f Нóмер пáспорта	_____

i Англичáнин **ii** Кáртер **iii** Трéнер **iv** Áнтони
v Р 243569 О **vi** Áнглия, Стóкпорт, Э́дуард Стрит, дом 35.

3 See if you can guess what nationality these people are.

a шотлáндец/шотлáндка **b** португáлец/португáлка
c ирлáндец/ирлáндка **d** норвéжец/норвéжка

4 Below you have a jumbled up table of information about four people. You are told their **и́мя** *name*, **гражда́нство** *nationality*, **профе́ссия** *job* and **где рабо́тает** *where he or she works*. See if you can sort out the information so that it makes sense, i.e. so that a French person with a French name is working in a French city. Make up a sentence about each person. The first one has been done for you: **a** Мари́ – францу́женка. Она́ врач. Она́ рабо́тает в больни́це в Пари́же.

	И́мя		Гражда́нство		Профе́ссия		Где рабо́тает
a	Мари́	i	ру́сский	1	учи́тель	A	в теа́тре в Арха́нгельске
b	Ханс	ii	францу́женка	2	актёр	B	в шко́ле в Берли́не
c	Бори́с	iii	англича́нка	3	продавщи́ца	C	в больни́це в Пари́же
d	Дже́нни	iv	не́мец	4	врач	D	в магази́не в Бирминге́ме

5 Match up the questions and answers so that they make sense.

a	Где вы рабо́таете?	i	Моя́ фами́лия Бра́дли.
b	Кто вы по профе́ссии?	ii	Иди́те пря́мо и буфе́т нале́во.
c	Как попа́сть в буфе́т?	iii	Я рабо́таю в шко́ле.
d	Вы говори́те по-англи́йски?	iv	Нет, магази́н закры́т.
		v	Я врач.
e	Как ва́ша фами́лия?	vi	Меня́ зову́т Серге́й.
f	Магази́н откры́т?	vii	Нет, я говорю́ по-францу́зски.
g	Как вас зову́т?		

6 Remembering that after **в** and **на** (meaning *in* or *at*) you have to change the ending of the following word, choose the correct form in these sentences.

a Я рабо́таю в больни́ца / больни́це в Арха́нгельске / Арха́нгельск.

b –Где футболи́сты? –Футболи́сты на стадио́н / стадио́не.

c В гости́нице / гости́ница есть буфе́т?

d –Молодо́й челове́к, где здесь бар? –Бар внизу́, в рестора́н / рестора́не.

7 Underline the correct demonstrative form (**э́тот, э́та, э́то, э́ти**) in the following sentences.

(**Э́тот, Э́та, Э́то, Э́ти**) кни́га о́чень интере́сная.

Покажи́те, пожа́луйста, (**э́тот, э́та, э́то, э́ти**) па́спорт.

(**Э́тот, Э́та, Э́то, Э́ти**) сигаре́ты не мой. Они́ ва́ши.

Да́йте, пожа́луйста, (**э́тот, э́та, э́то, э́ти**) ра́дио.

8 Read out loud the following selection of international dialling codes from Russia. Try to work out which countries are represented, and match them up with their English equivalents.

a	Австра́лия	61	**i**	*Germany*
b	Бангладе́ш	880	**ii**	*Canada*
c	Болга́рия	359	**iii**	*Fiji*
d	Гайа́на	592	**iv**	*Israel*
e	Герма́ния	49	**v**	*Ethiopia*
f	Изра́иль	972	**vi**	*Australia*
g	Кана́да	1	**vii**	*Bulgaria*
h	Сингапу́р	676	**viii**	*Guyana*
i	Фи́джи	679	**ix**	*Singapore*
j	Эфио́пия	251	**x**	*Bangladesh*

Test yourself

The dialogue below, between a hotel administrator and a tourist called Richard Rigby, has been written down in the wrong order. Unscramble it, beginning with the phrase in bold print.

Администра́тор	**Ри́чард Ри́гби**
1 Вы америка́нец?	**2** У вас есть ко́мната?
3 Запо́лните э́тот бланк, пожа́луйста.	**4** Здра́вствуйте.
5 Слу́шаю вас.	**6** Нет, я англича́нин.
7 Да. Как вас зову́т?	**8** Меня́ зову́т Ри́чард Ри́гби.

Before moving on to the next unit, say your own name with a Russian accent, and then try spelling out the sound of your name in Russian letters. Some sounds are tricky to reproduce, but here are a few clues from common English names.

Carol	Кэ́рол	*George*	Джордж
Catherine	Ка́трин	*Hugh*	Хью
Jane	Джейн	*John*	Джон
Susan	Сью́зан	*Simon*	Са́ймон
Wendy	Уэ́нди	*William*	Уи́льям

08

кото́рый час?

what time is it?

In this unit you will learn
- how to tell the time
- how to say the days of the week
- how to talk about meals and daily routine
- how to make arrangements

Before you start

If you go to Russia, or meet Russians at home, you need to understand when things are happening and at what time public places open and close. For this, you need to be able to tell the time and know the days of the week. With the structures introduced in this unit you will be able to make arrangements and feel in control.

i Завтрак, обед, ужин *Breakfast, dinner, supper*

Завтрак (zaftrak) *breakfast* may be **каша** (kasha) *porridge*, meat, cheese, fish or eggs and tea or coffee. There is nearly always bread on a Russian meal table as well. At midday you may have a second breakfast if your main meal is to be in the evening.

Обед (abyet) *dinner* is the main meal and may be eaten at any time from midday to late evening. It may include **закуски** (zakoosky) *starters*, a soup and a main dish, followed by cake and tea or coffee.

Ужин (oozhin) *supper* is a light meal, served in the evening.

▶ Telling the time

To ask the time, you say:

Который час? (Katory chas?) literally *Which hour?* or **Сколько сейчас времени?** (Skol'ka syeychas vryemyinee?) literally *How much now time?*

Telling the time on the hour is easy.

Сейчас час.	Syeychas chas	*Now it's one o'clock.*
Сейчас два часа.	Syeychas dva chasa	*Now it's two o'clock.*

3.00	**Три часа**	tree chasa
4.00	**Четыре часа**	chyetirye chasa
5.00	**Пять часов**	pyat' chasov
6.00	**Шесть часов**	shest' chasov
7.00	**Семь часов**	syem' chasov
8.00	**Восемь часов**	vosyem' chasov
9.00	**Девять часов**	dyevyat' chasov
10.00	**Десять часов**	dyesyat' chasov
11.00	**Одиннадцать часов**	adeenatsat' chasov
12.00	**Двенадцать часов**	dvyenatsat' chasov

Полдень	Poldyen'	*Midday*
Полночь	Polnoch'	*Midnight*

Час means *hour*. A watch or clock is **часы́**, literally *hours*. Notice that **час** has different endings depending on which number it follows. After one you use **час**, after two, three and four you use **часа́** and after 5–20 you use **часо́в**. To complete the 24-hour clock, after 21 you use **час**, and after 22, 23 and 24 you use **часа́**.

To ask *At what time?* say **В кото́ром часу́?**

To say *At five o'clock* say **В пять часо́в**.

Telling the time if it is not on the hour can be done in a number of ways, but the easiest is to do it digitally, for example 10.20 is **де́сять часо́в два́дцать мину́т** and 4.45 is **четы́ре часа́ со́рок пять мину́т**.

▶ Key words and phrases

Диало́г 1		
когда́	kagda	when
музе́й открыва́ется	moozyey atkrivayetsa	the museum opens
выходно́й день	vykhadnoy dyen'	day off
вто́рник	ftorneek	Tuesday
музе́й-кварти́ра	moozyey-kvarteera	former flat preserved as museum
среда́	sryida	Wednesday
зоологи́ческий музе́й	za-alageechesky moozyey	zoological museum
по́здно	pozdna	late
пя́тница	pyatneetsa	Friday

Диало́г 2		
конце́рт начина́ется	kantsyert nachinayetsa	the concert begins
четве́рг	chitvyerk	Thursday
ра́но	rana	early
ка́ждый день	kazhdy dyen'	every day

Диало́г 3		
у́тром	ootrum	in the morning
я встаю́	ya fstayoo	I get up
я за́втракаю	ya zaftrakayoo	I have breakfast
я иду́	ya eedoo	I go (on foot in one direction)
рабо́та (на)	rabota	work
я обе́даю	ya abyedayoo	I have dinner
ве́чером	vyechirom	in the evening
я у́жинаю	ya oozhinayoo	I have supper
я смотрю́	ya smatryoo	I watch
я ложу́сь спать	ya lazhoos' spat'	I go to bed

Диало́г 4

Где мы встре́тимся?	Gdye my fstry<u>e</u>timsa?	*Where shall we meet?*
за́л Филармо́нии	zal Feelarm<u>o</u>nee	*Philharmonic hall*
Встре́тимся	Fstry<u>e</u>timsa	*Let's meet*

Dialogues

▶ Диало́г 1

Steven is visiting his friend Cа́ша in St Petersburg for a week. They are trying to plan their time. There are several museums which Steven wants to visit, but first he must find out which **выходно́й день** *(vykhadnoy dyen') day off each museum has. Cа́ша looks through the phone directory to find out details.*

Сти́вен Cа́ша, когда́ открыва́ется ру́сский музе́й?

Cа́ша Ру́сский музе́й открыва́ется в 10 часо́в. Выходно́й день – вто́рник.

Сти́вен И музе́й-кварти́ра Пу́шкина?

Cа́ша Одну́ мину́точку. Да, музе́й-кварти́ра Пу́шкина открыва́ется в 10 часо́в. Выходно́й день – среда́.

Сти́вен И когда́ открыва́ется зоологи́ческий музе́й?

Cа́ша Зоологи́ческий музе́й открыва́ется по́здно, в 11 часо́в. Выходно́й день – пя́тница.

▶ Диало́г 2

When they have planned their days, they think about the evenings. They want to go to a concert and see a film.

Сти́вен Когда́ начина́ется конце́рт?

Cа́ша Конце́рт в четве́рг. Он начина́ется ра́но, в 6 часо́в.

Сти́вен И когда́ начина́ется фильм?

Cа́ша Ка́ждый день фильм начина́ется в 4 часа́ и в 7 часо́в.

▶ Диало́г 3

Steven wants to fit in with Sasha's life, so Sasha tells him about his daily routine.

Cа́ша У́тром я встаю́ в 8 часо́в и за́втракаю в 9 часо́в. Пото́м я иду́ на рабо́ту в библиоте́ку. Библиоте́ка открыва́ется в 10 часо́в. Я там обе́даю, и ве́чером я у́жинаю до́ма в 7 часо́в. Пото́м я смотрю́ телеви́зор и по́здно ложу́сь спать.

▶ Диало́г 4

*Before Sasha leaves for work, Steven asks where they should meet
before going to the concert.*

Сти́вен   Где мы встре́тимся, Са́ша?
Са́ша   Конце́рт начина́ется в 6 часо́в в за́ле Филармо́нии.
          Встре́тимся в 5 часо́в в библиоте́ке. Мо́жно, Сти́вен?
Сти́вен   Мо́жно.

Mechanics of the language

▶ 1 Days of the week

Note that the days of the week and months are written with lower
case letters in Russian.

Monday	понеде́льник	panidyel'neek
Tuesday	вто́рник	ftorneek
Wednesday	среда́	sryida
Thursday	четве́рг	chitvyerk
Friday	пя́тница	pyatneetsa
Saturday	суббо́та	soobota
Sunday	воскресе́нье	vaskrisyen'ye

To ask what day it is, say **Како́й сего́дня день?** (Kakoy sivodnya
dyen'?) Notice that the word **сего́дня** *today* is not pronounced as it
is spelt, the **г** being pronounced as a **в**. To say what day it is, say
Сего́дня суббо́та (Sivodnya soobota) *today is Saturday.*

If you want to say *on* a day of the week, use **в**. If the day of the week
ends in **-a**, change **-a** to **-y**, for example, **в суббо́ту**.

Notice that when you say *on Wednesday* the stress changes from
среда́ to **в сре́ду**.

on Monday	в понеде́льник	fpanidyel'neek
on Tuesday	во вто́рник	vo vtorneek
on Wednesday	в сре́ду	fsryedoo
on Thursday	в четве́рг	fchyetvyerk
on Friday	в пя́тницу	fpyatneetsoo
on Saturday	в суббо́ту	fsoobotoo
on Sunday	в воскресе́нье	v-vaskrisyen'ye

2 First, second, third . . .   ordinal numerals

In the next unit you will be learning the months so that you can say the date in Russian. To prepare for this you need to know the ordinal numerals in Russian, *first, second, third* etc. Once you get past the first few, they are formed quite logically by adding an adjective ending to the numerals you already know. In this unit you will meet the ordinal numerals from *first* to *tenth* in their masculine forms, for use with masculine nouns (**деся́тый эта́ж** dyesy<u>a</u>ty et<u>a</u>sh *tenth floor*).

i When you are in Russia, remember that the ground floor is called **пе́рвый эта́ж** (py<u>e</u>rvy et<u>a</u>sh), so an English first floor will be **второ́й эта́ж** (ftar<u>oy</u> et<u>a</u>sh).

In the next unit you will need to become familiar with *first* to *31st* in order to deal with any date which may arise.

1st	**пе́рвый**	py<u>e</u>rvy
2nd	**второ́й**	ftar<u>oy</u>
3rd	**тре́тий**	try<u>e</u>ty
4th	**четвёртый**	chitvy<u>o</u>rty
5th	**пя́тый**	py<u>a</u>ty
6th	**шесто́й**	shest<u>oy</u>
7th	**седьмо́й**	syidm<u>oy</u>
8th	**восьмо́й**	vas'm<u>oy</u>
9th	**девя́тый**	divy<u>a</u>ty
10th	**деся́тый**	disy<u>a</u>ty

Exercises

▶ 1 Listen to the recording and jot down (using numbers) the times that places open and events begin.

a Бассе́йн открыва́ется в . . .
b О́пера начина́ется в . . .
c Буфе́т открыва́ется в . . .
d Марафо́н начина́ется в . . .
e Галере́я открыва́ется в . . .

f Конце́рт начина́ется в . . .
g Зоопа́рк открыва́ется в . . .
h Моя́ рабо́та начина́ется в . . .
i Фильм начина́ется в . . .

2 Кото́рый час? What would you say for these times?

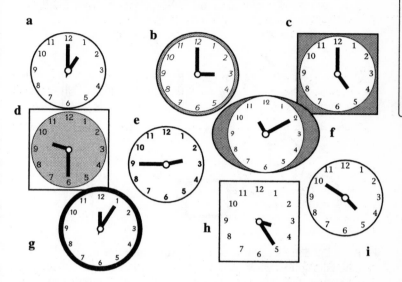

3 Look at the pictures on the next page and fill in the blanks in the captions. If you need to, choose from the verbs below in brackets.

a В _____ часо́в я _____ .
b В _____ часо́в я _____ .
c В _____ часо́в я _____ на рабо́ту.
d В час я _____ на рабо́те.
e В _____ часо́в я у́жинаю до́ма.
f В _____ часо́в я _____ телеви́зор.
g В _____ часо́в я ложу́сь спать.

(встаю́   иду́   обе́даю   за́втракаю   смотрю́)

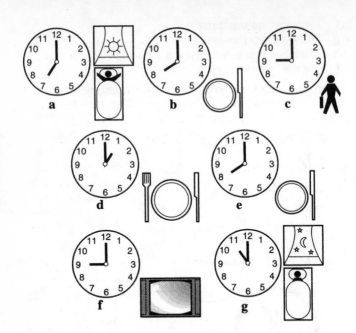

4 Read the details of these St Petersburg museums in your English language guide book, and tell your Russian friend out loud at what time they open, on which days they are closed, and what their telephone numbers are.

		Time of opening	Day off	Telephone number
a	*Museum of Anthropology and Ethnography* Музе́й антрополо́гии и этногра́фии	11.00	Sat	218-14-12
b	*Museum of Musical Instruments* Музе́й музыка́льных инструме́нтов	12.00	Tues	314-53-55
c	*Museum Apartment of A. A. Blok* Музе́й-кварти́ра А. А. Бло́ка	11.00	Wed	113-86-33
d	*Museum of the Arctic and Antarctic* Музе́й А́рктики и Анта́рктики	10.00	Mon	311-25-49

5 Opposite is Anna's diary. Note the usual abbreviations for the days of the week. Each day she is seeing someone different and doing a different activity.

Пн.	Вт.	Ср.	Чт.	Пт.	Сб.	Вс.
Cáша	Táня	Óля	Ю́рий	Máша	Ди́ма	Кири́лл
фильм	обе́д	о́пера	футбо́л	экску́рсия	концéрт	джаз

In the bottom of her bag she has seven scraps of paper on which her friends wrote down where they would meet her. See if you can match each scrap of paper to the right day.

a Встре́тимся на стадио́не
в 3 часá.

b Встре́тимся в кинотеáтре
в 7 часо́в.

c Встре́тимся до́ма в 6
часо́в.

d Встре́тимся в теáтре о́перы
и балéта в 7 часо́в.

e Встре́тимся в зáле
Филармо́нии в 6 часо́в.

f Встре́тимся в цéнтре
джáзовой му́зыки в 2 часá

g Встре́тимся в автóбусе в
час.

6 Here is a list of departments placed next to the lift in a multi-storey shop.

Шестóй этáж:	Факс.
Пя́тый этáж:	Сéйфы. Линóлеум. Сувени́ры.
Четвёртый этáж:	Видеомагнитофóны, видеоплéйеры, телеви́зоры, видеокассéты, тю́неры.
Трéтий этáж:	Музыкáльные инструмéнты. Фóто.
Вторóй этáж:	Парфюмéрия. Космéтика.
Пéрвый этáж:	Гомеопати́ческая аптéка. Óптика – контáктные ли́нзы.

On which floor would you be likely to find **a** contact lenses **b** perfume **c** a saxophone **d** a matryoshka doll **e** a safe **f** a fax **g** a video player **h** linoleum **i** lipstick?

7 Read the complete meal menus below and decide which one you would be likely to have for зáвтрак, обéд and у́жин.

a
закýски
суп
хлеб
котлéта
фрýкты
винó
чай с
лимóном

b
кáша
хлеб
мя́со
кóфе

c
омлéт
хлеб
чай

8 Remember how the words **в** and **на** may be used in two different ways. The first way you met was in Unit 5 **Как попасть в галерею?** *How do I get to the gallery?* Here **в** means *to*, and it changes the ending of following feminine nouns from -**a** to -**y** and from -**я** to -**ю**. Masculine and neuter nouns do not change. These are called *accusative* endings.

The second way of using **в** and **на** you met in Unit 7: **Я работаю в магазине в Москве** *I work in a shop in Moscow.* Here **в** means *in* or *at* and it usually changes the ending of following nouns to -**e**. These are called *prepositional* endings.

Choose the correct endings in the following sentences, depending on whether they use **в** and **на** to mean *to* or *in*.

a Я работаю в театр / театре в Новгород / Новгороде.

b Я иду в библиотеку / библиотеке.

c Вы работаете в университет / университете или в школу / школе?

d –Куда вы идёте? Я иду в институт / институте.

e Извините, пожалуйста. Как попасть в поликлинику / поликлинике.

▶ **9** Listen to the recording. Anna is talking about some of the things she does on each day of the week. Fill in the gaps with the correct day of the week in English, and then say each whole sentence out loud in Russian.

a В _____ я работаю в институте.

b В _____ я обедаю в ресторане.

c В _____ вечером я смотрю телевизор.

d В _____ я встаю рано и слушаю радио.

e В _____ утром я иду в библиотеку. Потом в 2 часа я иду в институт.

f В _____ я ложусь спать очень поздно.

g В _____ я встаю и завтракаю поздно.

10 This is a notice you might see on a shop door.

Магазин работает			
Пн	с 9.00	до	19.00
Вт	с 10.00	до	20.00
Ср	с 10.00	до	20.00
Чт	с 10.00	до	20.00
Пт	с 10.00	до	20.00
Сб	с 11.00	до	16.00
Вс	выходной день		
Перерыв на обед 13.00 – 14.00			

a On which day does the shop open early in the morning?
b When is the lunch break?
c On which day does the shop open late in the morning?
d On which day does the shop not open?
e At what time does the shop close on Saturdays?

КАССА МУЗЕЯ
ВЫХОДНОЙ ДЕНЬ – ПЯТНИЦА

---

11 On which day does the museum not open?

Test yourself

1 Say the days of the week in the correct order and then in reverse order.
2 Say what time it is now.
3 How would you ask *When does the bank open?*
4 Ask *When does the film start?*
5 Tell a friend *Let's meet at 7 o'clock at the restaurant.*

09

вы любите спорт?

do you like sport?

In this unit you will learn
- how to talk about leisure activities
- how to say the date
- how to talk about likes and dislikes
- how to use verbs in different forms
- how to use numerals over 1,000

Before you start

When practising your Russian, do not worry too much about getting the word endings right, as you will still be understood even if you make a mistake. Concentrate on communicating, and with practice you will make fewer errors. Do not let fear of making a mistake stop you from trying to get your message across, as this is how you learn.

▶ Once you make Russian friends you will probably want to express your likes and dislikes and say what you do in your free time. Here are some useful structures:

Я о́чень люблю́ му́зыку	**I really love** music
Я **люблю́** смотре́ть телеви́зор	**I love/like** watching television
Я **не люблю́** чита́ть	**I don't like** reading
Я **совсе́м не люблю́** гуля́ть	**I really don't like** walking
Я **игра́ю в** бадминто́н	**I play** badminton
Я **игра́ю на** гита́ре	**I play** the guitar
Я **хожу́ в** кино́	**I** (habitually) **go to** the cinema

ℹ Пра́здники *Public holidays*

Here are just a few of the **пра́здники** (pr<u>a</u>zdneeky) *public holidays* which are celebrated in Russia.

Но́вый год	1 января́	(N<u>o</u>vy got)	New Year, 1st January
Рождество́	7 января́	(Razhdyestv<u>o</u>)	Orthodox Christmas, 7th January
Же́нский День	8 ма́рта	(Zh<u>e</u>nsky dyen')	Women's Day, 8th March
День Побе́ды	9 ма́я	(Dyen' pab<u>ye</u>dy)	Victory Day, 9th May, end of World War II

The greeting **С пра́здником** (s pr<u>a</u>zdneekum) means literally *(I congratulate you) with the holiday*, and may be applied to any occasion. To wish someone a *Happy New Year* say **с но́вым го́дом** (s n<u>o</u>vym g<u>o</u>dum). On New Year's Eve, Grandfather Frost **Дед Моро́з** (Dyet Mar<u>o</u>s) with his helper the Snowmaiden **Снегу́рочка** (Snyeg<u>oo</u>rachka) gives out presents by the tree **ёлка** (y<u>o</u>lka). *Happy Birthday* is rather a mouthful, **с днём рожде́ния** (s dnyom razhdy<u>e</u>niya), literally *with the day of birth*.

▶ Months

The names of the months, which are all masculine, are easy to recognize.

January	**янва́рь**	yinv<u>a</u>r'	*July*	**июль**	eey<u>oo</u>l'
February	**февра́ль**	fyevr<u>a</u>l'	*August*	**а́вгуст**	<u>a</u>vgoost
March	**март**	mart	*September*	**сентя́брь**	syenty<u>a</u>br'
April	**апре́ль**	apry<u>e</u>l'	*October*	**октя́брь**	akty<u>a</u>br'
May	**май**	maee'	*November*	**ноя́брь**	nay<u>a</u>br'
June	**ию́нь**	eey<u>oo</u>n'	*December*	**дека́брь**	dyek<u>a</u>br'

Key words and phrases

хо́бби	kh<u>o</u>bbee	*hobby*

я о́чень люблю́
  чита́ть
	ya <u>o</u>chen' lyooblyoo
	  cheet<u>a</u>t'
		I really love reading

вы чита́ете	vy cheet<u>a</u>yetye	*you read*
я чита́ю	ya cheet<u>a</u>yoo	*I read*
газе́та	gazy<u>e</u>ta	*newspaper*
то́же	t<u>o</u>zhe	*also*
рома́н	ram<u>a</u>n	*novel*
интере́сно	intiry<u>e</u>sna	*That's interesting*

я совсе́м не люблю́
  чита́ть
	ya savsy<u>e</u>m nye
	  lyoobly<u>oo</u> cheet<u>a</u>t'
		I really don't like reading

я игра́ю в бадминто́н	ya eegr<u>a</u>yoo v badme<u>e</u>nt<u>o</u>n	I play badminton
гуля́ть	gool<u>ya</u>t'	to go for a walk
му́зыка	m<u>oo</u>zyka	music
я игра́ю на саксофо́не	ya eegr<u>a</u>yoo na saksaf<u>o</u>nye	I play the saxophone
ходи́ть на конце́рты	khad<u>ee</u>t' na kantsy<u>e</u>rty	to go (habitually) to concerts
путеше́ствовать	pootyish<u>e</u>stvovat'	to travel
пя́тое октября́	py<u>a</u>toye aktyabry<u>a</u>	5th of October
Ди́ксиленд	D<u>ee</u>kseelend	Dixieland
Вы хоти́те пойти́	Vy khat<u>ee</u>tye paeet<u>ee</u>	Do you want to go?

Dialogue

▶ Диало́г

George is introduced to Lyudmila, and they talk about their leisure interests. Listen to the recording or read the dialogue and answer the following questions: What interests does George have? What sports does Lyudmila play? Now listen or read again. What instrument does George play? Where do they decide to go and when?

Людми́ла	Каки́е у вас хо́бби?
Джордж	Я о́чень люблю́ чита́ть.
Людми́ла	Чита́ть? Каки́е кни́ги вы чита́ете?
Джордж	Ка́ждый день я чита́ю газе́ты, и я то́же люблю́ чита́ть рома́ны.
Людми́ла	Интере́сно. Вы лю́бите ру́сские рома́ны?
Джордж	Да, о́чень люблю́. А вы, у вас есть хо́бби?
Людми́ла	Да, но я совсе́м не люблю́ чита́ть! Я люблю́ спорт. Я игра́ю в бадминто́н и в те́ннис, и я люблю́ гуля́ть.
Джордж	Вы лю́бите му́зыку?
Людми́ла	Да, я о́чень люблю́ джаз.
Джордж	Я то́же. Я игра́ю на саксофо́не. В Ло́ндоне я о́чень люблю́ ходи́ть на конце́рты.
Людми́ла	В Ло́ндоне? Скажи́те, вы не ру́сский?
Джордж	Нет, я англича́нин. Я живу́ в Ло́ндоне.
Людми́ла	Вы хорошо́ говори́те по-ру́сски.
Джордж	Спаси́бо. Я говорю́ по-ру́сски и по-францу́зски, и я о́чень люблю́ путеше́ствовать.
Людми́ла	Интере́сно. Джордж, вы лю́бите джаз и сего́дня пя́тое октября́. Сего́дня ве́чером я иду́ на конце́рт – Ди́ксиленд. Вы хоти́те пойти́ на конце́рт?

Джордж	Да, коне́чно я хочу́. Спаси́бо. Когда́ начина́ется конце́рт?
Людми́ла	В семь часо́в. Встре́тимся здесь в шесть часо́в.
Джордж	Хорошо́. Спаси́бо, Людми́ла.
Людми́ла	Пожа́луйста.

▶ Numerals 1,000–20,000

1,000	ты́сяча	tisyacha
2,000	две ты́сячи	dvye tisyachee
3,000	три ты́сячи	tree tisyachee
4,000	четы́ре ты́сячи	chyetirye tisyachee
5,000	пять ты́сяч	pyat' tisyach
6,000	шесть ты́сяч	shest' tisyach
7,000	семь ты́сяч	syem' tisyach
8,000	во́семь ты́сяч	vosyem' tisyach
9,000	де́вять ты́сяч	dyevyat' tisyach
10,000	де́сять ты́сяч	dyesyat' tisyach
20,000	два́дцать ты́сяч	dvatsat' tisyach

Practise these numbers in whichever way has proved successful for you with lower numbers.

Mechanics of the language

1 Како́е сего́дня число́? *What is the date today?*

In answer to the question **Како́е сего́дня число́?** (Kak<u>o</u>ye siv<u>o</u>dnya cheesl<u>o</u>?) literally *which today number?*, you need the ordinal numbers which you learned in the previous unit. This time they need their neuter ending **-ое** to agree with the neuter **число́**. This is followed by the month with the ending **-а** or **-я** which gives the meaning *of*.

▶ Ordinal numbers 1st–31st with neuter endings for forming dates:

1st	**пе́рвое**	py<u>e</u>rvoye	5th	**пя́тое**	py<u>a</u>toye
2nd	**второ́е**	ftar<u>o</u>ye	6th	**шесто́е**	shest<u>o</u>ye
3rd	**тре́тье**	try<u>e</u>t'ye	7th	**седьмо́е**	syedm<u>o</u>ye
4th	**четвёртое**	chyetvy<u>o</u>rtoye	8th	**восьмо́е**	vas'm<u>o</u>ye

9th	**девя́тое**	dyevy<u>a</u>toye	17th	**семна́дцатое**	syemn<u>a</u>tsatoye
10th	**деся́тое**	dyesy<u>a</u>toye	18th	**восемна́дцатое**	vasyemn<u>a</u>tsatoye
11th	**оди́ннадцатое**	ad<u>ee</u>natsatoye	19th	**девятна́дцатое**	dyevitn<u>a</u>tsatoye
12th	**двена́дцатое**	dvyen<u>a</u>tsatoye	20th	**двадца́тое**	dvats<u>a</u>toye
13th	**трина́дцатое**	treen<u>a</u>tsatoye	21st	**два́дцать пе́рвое**	dvatsat' py<u>e</u>rvoye
14th	**четы́рнадцатое**	chyet<u>i</u>rnatsatoye	22nd	**два́дцать второ́е**	dvatsat' ftar<u>o</u>ye
15th	**пятна́дцатое**	pitn<u>a</u>tsatoye	30th	**тридца́тое**	treets<u>a</u>toye
16th	**шестна́дцатое**	shestn<u>a</u>tsatoye	31st	**три́дцать пе́рвое**	tr<u>ee</u>tsat' py<u>e</u>rvoye

The months with endings **-a** or **-я** for forming dates:

**января́, февраля́, ма́рта, апре́ля, ма́я, ию́ня,
ию́ля, а́вгуста, сентября́, октября́, ноября́, декабря́**

So, **Сего́дня пя́тое а́вгуста** means *today is 5th August.*

12 Jan.	**двена́дцатое января́**	2 Dec.	**второ́е декабря́**
7 May	**седьмо́е ма́я**	6 Feb.	**шесто́е февраля́**
30 Sept.	**тридца́тое сентября́**	19 Mar.	**девятна́дцатое ма́рта**

To say *on* a certain date, the ending of the ordinal numeral should change to **-ого**, pronounced -ovo. **Двена́дцатого а́вгуста** – *on 12th August.*

To say *in* June, you use **в** and change the ending of the month to **-е**.

**в январе́, в феврале́, в ма́рте, в апре́ле, в ма́е, в ию́не,
в ию́ле, в а́вгусте, в сентябре́, в октябре́, в ноябре́,
в декабре́**

---

in spring	**весно́й**
in summer	**ле́том**
in autumn	**о́сенью**
in winter	**зимо́й**

2 Verbs

Verbs are 'doing words' for example, *run, read, talk, sleep*. You have met some Russian verbs in phrases where they are already in their correct form: **Вы говори́те** по-ру́сски? It is hard to say anything without verbs, so to make up sentences yourself you will need to understand how they work. There are two main groups of verbs in Russian, which we will call group 1 and group 2. The infinitive is the form you will find if you look up a verb in the dictionary.

Look at this English verb.

to work (*infinitive*)		
(*singular*)		(*plural*)
I	work	we	work
you	work	*y*ou	work
he/she/it	work**s**	they	work

The same verb in Russian **рабóтать** is a group 1 verb, and it changes its endings more than its English equivalent. You have already met the two forms which are underlined in the box below.

рабóтать (*infinitive*) to work		
(*singular*)		(*plural*)
я	<u>рабóта**ю**</u>	мы	рабóта**ем**
ты	рабóта**ешь**	<u>вы</u>	<u>рабóта**ете**</u>
он/онá/онó	рабóта**ет**	они́	рабóта**ют**

To make the different forms of a group 1 verb, remove the **-ть** from the infinitive and add the endings in bold type. This applies to other group 1 verbs you have met, for example, **знать**, **понимáть**, **зáвтракать**, **обéдать**, **ýжинать**, **читáть**, **игрáть**, **гуля́ть**.

You have also met some group 2 verbs for example, **говори́ть**.

говори́ть (*infinitive*) to speak/talk		
я	<u>говор**ю́**</u>	мы	говор**и́м**
ты	говор**и́шь**	<u>вы</u>	<u>говор**и́те**</u>
он/онá/онó	говор**и́т**	они́	говор**я́т**

To make the different forms of a group 2 verb, remove the last three letters from the infinitive and add the endings in bold type. You have also met **люби́ть** which is a group 2 verb. It is slightly unusual in the **я** form, because it inserts an **л** before the ending: **я люблю́**. In future vocabulary lists you will often see 1 or 2 next to a verb indicating which group it belongs to so that you know what to do with it.

Some verbs are irregular, i.e. they do not follow the patterns given above, like **хотéть** (khaty<u>e</u>t') *to want*.

я	<u>хочý</u>	мы	хоти́м
ты	хóчешь	<u>вы</u>	<u>хоти́те</u>
он/онá/онó	хóчет	они́	хотя́т

Another verb which is unusual is the group 1 verb **жить** (zheet') *to live*.

я	<u>живу́</u>	мы	<u>живём</u>
ты	<u>живёшь</u>	вы	<u>живёте</u>
он/она́/оно́	живёт	они́	живу́т

3 I love to, I want to, I play ...

• To say *I love doing something* say **Я люблю́** + verb infinitive: e.g. **Я люблю́ чита́ть** *I love reading*.

• To say *I love something* say **Я люблю́** + noun. Remember that the noun is a direct object, so it needs accusative endings. If it is feminine -**a** will change to -**у** and -**я** to -**ю**: e.g. **Я люблю́ му́зыку** *I love music*. If it is masculine or neuter it will not change: e.g. **Я люблю́ спорт** *I love sport*.

• To say *I want to do something* say **Я хочу́** + verb infinitive: e.g. **Я хочу́ говори́ть по-ру́сски** *I want to speak Russian*. **Я хочу́ есть бана́н и пить ко́фе** *I want to eat a banana and drink some coffee*. (**Пить** is the verb *to drink* and **есть** is the verb *to eat* – spelled exactly like **есть** in **у меня́ есть**.)

• To say *I play a sport* say **Я игра́ю в** + sport: e.g. **Я игра́ю в бадминто́н/в футбо́л/в гольф** *I play badminton/football/golf*.

• To say *I play an instrument* say **Я игра́ю на** + instrument, using the prepositional ending -**е**: e.g. **Я игра́ю на гита́ре/на балала́йке** *I play the guitar/balalaika*.

• To say *I (habitually) go somewhere* say **Я хожу́ в/на** + place. Remember you are going *to* the place, so you need to use an accusative ending. If the place is feminine -**a** will change to -**у** and -**я** to -**ю**: e.g. **Я хожу́ в больни́цу/на вокза́л** *I go to the hospital/station*.

Exercises

1 On a visit to Russia you have a programme of cultural events to choose from. Read it out loud, including the dates, and answer the questions. For the first event, you will say: **Суббо́та пе́рвое октября́. Пье́са. Оте́лло.** (**Пье́са** is a *play*).

сб. 1 октября́	Пье́са. Оте́лло
вс. 2 октября́	Пье́са. Три сестры́
пн. 3 октября́	Пье́са. Клау́строфобия
вт. 4 октября́	О́пера. Бори́с Годуно́в
ср. 5 октября́	Конце́рт. Ди́ксиленд «Ми́стер Джаз»
чт. 6 октября́	Конце́рт. Бах, Шу́берт и Шу́ман
пт. 7 октября́	Пье́са. Три мушкетёра

a If you liked classical music, which evening would suit you?
b If you liked jazz, which evening would interest you?
c What is the title of the Chekhov play on Sunday?
d On which evening could you see an opera?

2 Volodya is writing an illustrated letter to his little niece saying what he likes to do at different times of year.

Весно́й я люблю́ путеше́ствовать.
Ле́том я люблю́ игра́ть в те́ннис и чита́ть на пля́же.
О́сенью я люблю́ гуля́ть в па́рке.
Зимо́й я люблю́ игра́ть в хокке́й и смотре́ть телеви́зор.

Now respond by saying what you like doing at different times of year. You could also add what you like doing at different times of day: **у́тром** (ootrum) *in the morning*, **днём** (dnyom) *in the afternoon*, **ве́чером** (vyechirom) *in the evening*, **но́чью** (noch'yoo) *at night*.

▶ **3** Listen to the recording, and write down in English which activities the following people like and dislike. You may not catch every word they say, but try to pick out the relevant details.

a Бори́с **b** Ли́за **c** Андре́й **d** Ни́на

4 Како́е сего́дня число́? Read these dates out loud, and fill in the blanks.

a 1 Jan. – но́вый год.
b 7 Jan. – рождество́.
c 8 March – же́нский день.
d 9 May – день побе́ды.
e Сего́дня _____
f Мой день рожде́ния
  (*birthday*) _____.

For the remaining dates, say *on* 13th June **трина́дцатого ию́ня**
and so on.

g 13 June, 24 December, 31 October
h 6 September, 3 October, 14 February

Pick some more dates at random from a calendar and practise
until you feel confident.

5 Below are 12 jumbled sentences. Match the correct halves
together.

a	Я игра́ю на	i	хо́бби?
b	Я игра́ю в	ii	девя́тое апре́ля.
c	Я хожу́ в	iii	лимона́д.
d	Я рабо́таю в	iv	по-ру́сски.
e	Я хочу́ есть	v	па́рке.
f	Я гуля́ю в	vi	хокке́й.
g	Я говорю́	vii	сала́т.
h	Я хочу́ пить	viii	му́зыку.
i	Сего́дня	ix	саксофо́не.
j	Я о́чень люблю́	x	магази́не.
k	Я хочу́	xi	библиоте́ку.
l	Каки́е у вас	xii	смотре́ть телеви́зор.

▶ 6 What are these numbers? Write down the answers in figures.

a шесть ты́сяч
b четы́рнадцать ты́сяч пятьсо́т
c два́дцать ты́сяч три́ста во́семьдесят
d пять ты́сяч три́ста со́рок шесть
e девятна́дцать ты́сяч девятьсо́т два́дцать три
f две ты́сячи четы́реста оди́ннадцать
g ты́сяча две́сти девяно́сто во́семь.
h де́сять ты́сяч пятьсо́т три́дцать оди́н

Now look at your answers and see if you can say the numbers in
Russian without looking at the questions! Good luck!

7 Choose the right endings for these verbs.

a Я рабо́таю/рабо́таете в шко́ле.
b Вы говорю́/говори́те по-ру́сски?
c Я не понима́ете/понима́ю.
d Я люблю́/лю́бите чай с лимо́ном.

e Вы живу́/живёте в Ло́ндоне?

f Ка́ждый день я за́втракаю/за́втракаете до́ма.

g О́сенью я гуля́ю/гуля́ете в па́рке.

8 Никола́й Никола́евич has agreed to answer some questions for a survey you are conducting. Can you ask him the following questions in Russian?

a What is your name?   **e** Where do you work?

b Are you Russian?   **f** Do you have any hobbies?

c Where do you live?   **g** Do you like sport?

d What is your profession?

Could you answer these questions in Russian if you were asked?

9 **Когда́ мы встре́тимся?** When shall we meet?

You are making arrangements to meet Russian friends. Read out **a** and **b** and jot down the dates and times in English. Then change **c** and **d** into Russian and say them out loud.

a В суббо́ту, двадцать пя́того ма́я, в шесть часо́в.

b В четве́рг, три́дцать пе́рвого ию́ля, в де́вять часо́в два́дцать пять мину́т.

c On Monday, 8th February, at 7.30.

d On Friday, 16th March, at 5 o' clock.

10 What do you think these people like to do in their free time?

a Я хожу́ в билья́рдный клуб.

b Я люблю́ смотре́ть спу́тниковое ТВ.

c Я люблю́ игра́ть в сну́кер и в америка́нский пул.

d Я люблю́ компью́терные и́гры.

e Я хожу́ в казино́.

f Я о́чень люблю́ фен-шу́й.

Test yourself

▶ Listen to Андре́й talking about himself. Put ticks in the boxes below to show what he likes and dislikes. If you do not have the recording, work from the text opposite.

		Я о́чень люблю́	Я люблю́	Я не люблю́	Я совсе́м не люблю́
a	Work				
b	Sport				
c	Music				
d	Watching TV				
e	Travel				
f	Cinema				

Здра́вствуйте! Меня́ зову́т Андре́й. Я живу́ в Москве́. Я – студе́нт в университе́те и в суббо́ту и в воскресе́нье я рабо́таю в рестора́не. Я официа́нт. Я не люблю́ рабо́тать в рестора́не. Я о́чень люблю́ спорт, и игра́ю в хокке́й, в футбо́л, в те́ннис и в бадминто́н. Я люблю́ му́зыку, игра́ю на гита́ре и хожу́ на конце́рты. Я совсе́м не люблю́ смотре́ть телеви́зор. Ле́том я о́чень люблю́ путеше́ствовать и зимо́й я люблю́ ходи́ть в кино́.

Now talk about yourself in Russian, your likes and dislikes. You might like to make a recording. Try to imitate the accent of the people you have heard on the recording.

10

входи́те, пожа́луйста!
do come in!

In this unit you will learn
- how to talk about home and family (yours and theirs!)
- how to be a guest in a Russian home
- how to read a public transport route plan

Before you start

In the last few units you have built up a lot of vocabulary and new structures. In this unit you should aim to consolidate everything you have learned before moving on to the second section of the book. You now know enough to experiment and make up sentences of your own, and you are able to hold a conversation in Russian. If you don't understand what is being said to you, don't panic. Try to guess what is being said, or ask for an explanation of a particular word or phrase. If you can't think how to express yourself, don't give up, but paraphrase or simplify what you want to say. You learn best by trying things out and building up your skills, just as you build up muscles in physical exercise. You will probably find that people are very willing to help you.

ℹ Семья́ (Sim'ya) *The family*

In many Russian families, three generations share one home. Living space in cities is at a premium, so you may find that the дива́н in the living room is a sofa by day and a bed by night. **Ба́бушка** *grandmother* may help to bring up the children and run the home while the parents work. Pre-school children may attend **я́сли** (yasly) *nursery* and **де́тский сад** (dyetskee sat) *kindergarten*. If you visit a Russian home, you may be offered slippers **та́почки** (tapochkee) to wear when you arrive, as outdoor shoes are not generally worn inside. Be prepared for warm hospitality from your Russian hosts.

Да́ча (Dacha) *A country house, but much more besides*

A *dacha* can be anything from a structure like a garden shed to a two-storey hunting lodge in the country. Russian city dwellers fortunate enough to have a **да́ча** may use it and its plot of land to grow fruit, vegetables and flowers and to rear chickens and pigs, visiting at weekends to enjoy the fresh air and to bring home-grown produce back to the city. They may house the grandparents and children there in the warmer months, and they gather berries and mushrooms in the woods.

Прести́жные райо́ны (Presteezhneeye rayony)
Prestige areas

In the 1990s a boom began in creating elite properties for the more affluent Russians. Large buildings in older prestigious areas of cities were converted into **эли́тные кварти́ры** *elite apartments*. New blocks of apartments were also built to high standards, often with a **консье́рж** *concierge* and a **домофо́н** *entrance phone* to control access. At the same time, communities of exclusive housing sprang up on the edges of cities, consisting of properties described as **дом** *house* or **ко́ттедж** *cottage*, but sometimes covering in excess of **сто квадра́тных ме́тров** *100 square metres* and set in guarded compounds. Even the more modest properties of such communities may boast **комфо́рт** *comfort*, **ками́н** *a fireplace*, **джаку́зи** *a jacuzzi* and **климатоте́хника** *climate control*.

Маршру́ты (Marshrooty) *Transport routes*

When finding your way around a Russian city you may need to consult a plan of bus, trolleybus and tram routes. Major roads on the route will be named. You already know **у́лица** *street*, **проспе́кт** *avenue*, **пло́щадь** *square* and **мост** *bridge*, but here are two more useful words: **на́бережная** (nabyiryezhnaya) *embankment* and **шоссе́** (shossey) *highway*.

Key words and phrases

Диало́г 1

входи́те	vkhad<u>ee</u>tye	come in
сади́тесь	sad<u>ee</u>tyes'	sit down
семья́	sim'y<u>a</u>	family
Да, есть	Da, yest'	Yes, I have/he has/ they have, etc.
посмотри́те	pasmatr<u>ee</u>tye	look (imperative)
у меня́ (есть)	oo miny<u>a</u> (yest')	I have
альбо́м	al'b<u>o</u>m	album
жена́	zhen<u>a</u>	wife
муж	moosh	husband
де́ти	dy<u>e</u>tee	children
ви́дите	v<u>ee</u>deetye	you see
их зову́т	eekh zav<u>oo</u>t	they are called
маши́на	mash<u>ee</u>na	car
её зову́т	yiy<u>o</u> zav<u>oo</u>t	she is called
да́ча (на)	d<u>a</u>cha	dacha (country house)
мать/оте́ц	mat'/aty<u>e</u>ts	mother/father
на пе́нсии	na py<u>e</u>nsee	on a pension (retired)
их	eekh	them
его́ зову́т	yiv<u>o</u> zav<u>oo</u>t	he is called
энерги́чный	inyerg<u>ee</u>chnee	energetic
дере́вня	dyiry<u>e</u>vnya	countryside/village
дя́дя/тётя	dy<u>a</u>dya/ty<u>o</u>tya	uncle/aunt

Диало́г 2

у́лица Ми́ра	<u>oo</u>leetsa M<u>ee</u>ra	street (of) peace
у нас (есть)	oo nas (yest')	we have
гости́ная	gast<u>ee</u>naya	living room
спа́льня	sp<u>a</u>l'nya	bedroom
ку́хня	k<u>oo</u>khnya	kitchen (also cookery)
но́вый/ста́рый	n<u>o</u>vy/st<u>a</u>ry	new/old
прекра́сный	prikr<u>a</u>sny	fine
столо́вая	stal<u>o</u>vaya	dining room
на́ша соба́ка	n<u>a</u>sha sab<u>a</u>ka	our dog (на́ш works like ва́ш)
река́ Мо́йка (на)	ryik<u>a</u> M<u>o</u>ika	River Moika
кабине́т	kabeeny<u>e</u>t	study
вид	veet	view
так прия́тно	tak preey<u>a</u>tna	so pleasant

Диало́г 3

почему́?*	pachem<u>oo</u>?	Why?
потому́, что	patam<u>oo</u> shta	because

*A child who is always asking Why? is called a почему́чка (pachem<u>oo</u>chka)!

магази́н	magaz<u>ee</u>n	*shop*
по магази́нам	pa magaz<u>ee</u>nam	*round the shops*
наш го́род	nash g<u>o</u>rat	*our city*
истори́ческий	eestar<u>ee</u>cheskee	*historical*
споко́йно	spak<u>o</u>ina	*peaceful*
лес, в лесу́	lyes, vlyes<u>oo</u>	*forest, in the forest*
Приезжа́йте к нам в го́сти	Preeyezh<u>ai</u>tye k nam vg<u>o</u>stee	*Come and visit us (literally Come to us as guest)*

Dialogues

▶ Диало́г 1

Sally goes with Ната́ша to visit Никола́й. Once the introductions are over, she asks him if he has any family. He gets out his photos. How many children does he have, and where do his parents live in the summer?

Никола́й   Входи́те, Са́лли! Меня́ зову́т Никола́й.

Са́лли   О́чень прия́тно, Никола́й.

Никола́й   О́чень прия́тно, Са́лли. Сади́тесь, пожа́луйста. *(sitting down on toy car)* Извини́те! Скажи́те, у вас есть семья́?

Никола́й   Да, есть. Посмотри́те, у меня́ здесь альбо́м. Это моя́ жена́, и вот де́ти, ви́дите? У меня́ сын и дочь. Их зову́т Алёша и Ли́за. Алёша о́чень лю́бит маши́ны и Ли́за лю́бит спорт. Жена́ – учи́тельница. Её зову́т Га́ля. Жена́ и де́ти сейча́с на да́че.

Са́лли   На да́че? Как хорошо́. *(looking at next photo)* А кто э́то? Мать и оте́ц?

Никола́й   Да, э́то ма́ма и па́па. Они́ на пе́нсии, и ле́том они́ живу́т на да́че. Я их о́чень люблю́. И вот мой брат. Его́ зову́т Ви́ктор. Он студе́нт, хорошо́ говори́т по-неме́цки и по-англи́йски и хо́чет путеше́ствовать.

Са́лли   Интере́сно...

Никола́й   И вот моя́ сестра́. Её зову́т И́ра. Она́ о́чень энерги́чная де́вушка, игра́ет в баскетбо́л и лю́бит гуля́ть в дере́вне. И вот дя́дя и тётя. Они́ инжене́ры, рабо́тают на фа́брике в Новосиби́рске.

▶ Диало́г 2

Серёжа, Tim and Бе́лла are comparing photos of their homes. Match their descriptions to the pictures.

Серёжа Я живу́ в кварти́ре на у́лице Ми́ра. У нас в кварти́ре гости́ная, спа́льня, ку́хня, ва́нная и балко́н. Кварти́ра но́вая, и у нас есть лифт и телефо́н. А где вы живёте, Тим?

Тим Я живу́ в до́ме в Ливерпу́ле. Э́то ста́рый, большо́й дом. У нас больша́я гости́ная, прекра́сная столо́вая, ма́ленькая ку́хня, три спа́льни и ва́нная.

Серёжа У вас есть сад?

Тим Да, у нас большо́й сад. На́ша соба́ка, Три́кси, лю́бит там игра́ть.

Бе́лла У меня́ ста́рая кварти́ра в до́ме на реке́ Мо́йке. Она́ краси́вая. У меня́ в кварти́ре гости́ная, кабине́т, ку́хня и ва́нная. У меня́ прекра́сный вид на ре́ку Мо́йку. Там так прия́тно!

▶ Диало́г 3

You are conducting interviews again. This time you are asking why people have chosen to live in the city or in the country. Where do Anna and Sasha prefer to live, and why?

Вы	Почему́ вы лю́бите жить в го́роде?
А́нна	Я люблю́ жить в го́роде потому́, что мо́жно ходи́ть на концéрты, в теáтр, в кино́, по магази́нам. Наш го́род истори́ческий, краси́вый. Мы живём в цéнтре и у нас есть стáнция метро́ недалеко́.
Вы	Сáша, почему́ вы лю́бите жить в дере́вне?
Сáша	Я люблю́ жить в дере́вне потому́, что там споко́йно и мо́жно гуля́ть в лесу́. Приезжáйте к нам в го́сти. В дере́вне о́чень прия́тно.

Mechanics of the language

1 У вас есть...? *Do you have...?*

You have already met this question, which means literally *by you is there?* The answer is **Да, есть** (Da, yest') *Yes, there is.* Or in full it may be **Да, у меня́ есть...** (Da, oo mi̱n̲y̲a̱ yest'...) *Yes, by me there is ...* If you want to make a statement rather than ask a question, simply omit the question mark: **У вас есть брат** *You have a brother.* **У вас есть** does not function like a verb, but is simply a phrase which is used in place of the verb *to have.* To ask or say that different people have something, use these forms:

я	**У меня́**	oo mi̱n̲y̲a̱	*I have*	мы	**У нас**	oo nas	*we have*
ты	**У тебя́**	oo ti̱by̲a̱	*you have*	вы	**У вас**	oo vas	*you have*
он/оно́	**У него́**	oo n̲yi̱vo̱	*he/it has*	они́	**У них**	oo neekh	*they have*
она́	**У неё**	oo n̲yiyo̱	*she has*				
кто	**У кого́?**	oo kavo̱	*who has?*				

You may choose whether or not to include the word **есть** in your statements. **Есть** adds emphasis: **У меня́ есть газе́та** *I do have a newspaper.*

У меня́, у тебя́ etc. may also mean *at my home, at your home,* or even *in my country.* This is a very useful phrase for making comparisons between cultures: **У вас рождество́ седьмо́го января́, но у нас рождество́ два́дцать пя́того декабря́.** *In your country Christmas is on 7 January, but in our country Christmas is on 25 December.*

2 More about verbs

You already know that **я хожу** is used to say: *I go somewhere habitually*, and **я иду** is usually used to say *I am going somewhere now*. Here are the verbs **ходить** and **идти** in full. They both refer to going on foot, not by transport.

ходить *to go habitually*		**идти** *to go on one occasion*	
я хожу	мы ходим	я иду	мы идём
ты ходишь	вы ходите	ты идёшь	вы идёте
он ходит	они ходят	он идёт	они идут

Куда вы ходите каждый день в 7 часов?	*Where do you go every day at 7 o'clock?*
Куда вы идёте?	*Where are you going now?*

3 Points of the compass

You may wish to say in which part of the country your town or city is. The points of the compass are: **север** (sy_e_vyir) *north*, **юг** (yook) *south*, **запад** (z_a_pat) *west*, **восток** (vast_o_k) *east*. To say **in the north** etc., use **на** with the prepositional endings, adding **-e** to the end of the following word.

на севере
на западе
на востоке
на юге
в центре

} Австралии, Америки, Англии, Ирландии, России, Уэльса, Шотландии
of *Australia, America, England, Ireland, Russia, Wales, Scotland*

север

запад   восток

юг

4 Whose is it?

You have already met **мой** and **ваш**, *my* and *your*. Here are the words meaning *your* (if you address someone as **ты**), and *our*. They are **твой** (tvoy) *your* and **наш** (nash) *our*. Remember that **мой** and **ваш** have different forms to agree with the gender of the nouns to which they refer (see Unit 6). The same is true of **твой** and **наш**.

Masculine	*Feminine*	*Neuter*	*Plural*
твой пáспорт	**твоя** балалáйка	**твоё** пианúно	**твои** кассéты
your passport	*your balalaika*	*your piano*	*your cassettes*
наш пáспорт	**нáша** балалáйка	**нáше** пианúно	**нáши** кассéты
our passport	*our balalaika*	*our piano*	*our cassettes*

The words **егó** (yiv<u>o</u>) *his*, **её** (yiy<u>o</u>) *her* and **их** (eekh) *their* are easier to use as they do not change at all. So, **егó** can used with any noun to mean *his*: **егó пáспорт, егó балалáйка, егó пианúно, егó кассéты. Её** *her* is just as simple, as is **их** *their*.

5 Him, her, them: direct object pronouns

As well as meaning *his*, *her* and *their*, the words **егó, её** and **их** have another meaning: *him*, *her* and *them* in phrases where people are the direct object of the verb. To fill in a few gaps, here is the full range of *me, you, him, her, us, you, them*. You have met many of these forms before, for example in the phrase **Как вас зовýт?** literally *'How you do they call?'*

ты лю́бишь **меня**	*you love me*	вы лю́бите **нас**	*you love us*
я люблю́ **тебя**	*I love you*	они́ лю́бят **вас**	*they love you*
она́ лю́бит **егó**	*she loves him*	мы лю́бим **их**	*we love them*
он лю́бит **её**	*he loves her*		

Exercises

1   Look at these route plans for St Petersburg public transport. What should you catch to go to the following places?

a Finland station **b** Arsenal embankment **c** Revolution Highway
d Moscow Avenue **e** Gor'kovskaya metro station
f Tuchkov Bridge **g** Kazan Square **h** Industrial Avenue

Семна́дцатый троллейбус: Каза́нская пло́щадь – Горо́ховая у́лица – Вите́бский вокза́л – За́городный проспе́кт – Моско́вский проспе́кт

Шестьдеся́т тре́тий трамва́й: Финля́ндский вокза́л – Сампсони́евский мост – ста́нция метро́ «Го́рьковская» – Тучко́в мост

Два́дцать восьмо́й авто́бус: Финля́ндский вокза́л – Арсена́льная на́бережная – шоссе́ револю́ции – Индустриа́льный проспе́кт

▶ 2 Listen to these descriptions of people. Each description mentions where they live, where they work, their family, their hobbies, and something they want to do. Listen and try to note down something in English in each category for each person.

	А́ня	Пи́тер	Леони́д	Зо́я
живёт				
рабо́тает				
семья́				
хо́бби				
хо́чет				

▶ 3 Fill in the blanks in this description of Nadyezhda's home and life, using the words in brackets below. Listen to the recording to check your answers.

Надёжда _____ в кварти́ре в Арха́нгельске, на се́вере Росси́и. У неё но́вая кварти́ра, не о́чень краси́вая, но Надёжда лю́бит там жить потому́, что _____ недалеко́. В кварти́ре, у неё больша́я гости́ная и ма́ленькая спа́льня, _____ и ва́нная. Её муж рабо́тает в Москве́. В кварти́ре живу́т Надёжда, её ма́ма и ____ дочь. Их зову́т Гали́на и Ма́ша. У них кот. Его́ зову́т Го́рби. Ма́ша его́ о́чень _____. Ка́ждый ____Надёжда хо́дит на фа́брику, где она́ рабо́тает. Ма́ша хо́дит в шко́лу, и ба́бушка _____ ____ по магази́нам.

(лю́бит живёт её день магази́ны хо́дит ку́хня)

4 Look at this map of Russia and say where these cities are:

a	Магада́н на _____ Росси́и.	**i**	се́вере
b	Москва́ на _____ Росси́и.	**ii**	ю́ге
c	Ирку́тск на _____ Росси́и.	**iii**	восто́ке
d	Нори́льск на _____ Росси́и.	**iv**	за́паде

▶ **5** Listen to the recording to find out what these people have. Put a tick in the correct columns when you have understood. When you have finished, you could construct an imaginary interview with each person, asking **У вас есть маши́на?** etc. and improvising answers based on your chart and on what you can remember from the recording.

	Маши́на	Брат	Кот	Кварти́ра	Да́ча
Бори́с					
На́стя					
Ли́за					

6 Choose the correct form of the verb to complete each of these sentences.

a – Скажи́те, пожа́луйста. Где здесь банк?
– Извини́те, я не зна́ете/зна́ю/зна́ем.
b – Куда́ вы иду́/идёшь/идёте?
– Я иду́/идёшь/идёте в музе́й.
c Я хоти́м/хо́чешь/хочу́ купи́ть сувени́ры.
d Он хорошо́ говорю́/говори́т/говоря́т по-ру́сски.
e Где ты рабо́таем/рабо́тают/рабо́таешь?

f Ýтром я за́втракаю/за́втракает/за́втракаете в 7 часо́в.

g – У вас есть хо́бби? – Да, я о́чень лю́бит/люблю́/ лю́бят чита́ть.

h Мы игра́ю/игра́ет/игра́ем в хокке́й.

i Они́ у́жинает/у́жинают/у́жинаем по́здно ве́чером.

7 Read this property advert and list its features.

Эли́тный ко́ттедж. Прести́жный райо́н. Электри́чество, вода́, газ, климатоте́хника. Джаку́зи и са́уна. Ками́н. Спу́тниковое ТВ. 250кв.м. Большо́й гара́ж.

Now turn to page 209 to see how confident you feel with all the material so far by doing a revision test.

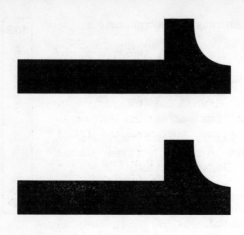

Напишите, пожалуйста!

write it down, please!

In this unit you will learn
- how to read Russian script
- how to write in Russian

Before you start

Before moving on to the second part of the book you have the chance to meet the handwritten form of the language. At some time you may need to read Russian in script rather than the printed form. You may also want to write some Russian yourself, and if you learn some basic writing skills at this stage, it will help you to monitor your progress as you work through the rest of the book. The exercises in the second half of the book will still require you to read, speak and listen to Russian, but some of them will also give you the opportunity to write a little. However, if you choose not to learn to write in script, you can always print your answers or find alternative ways of answering.

Here are the letters of the Russian alphabet in their handwritten forms. Get used to their appearance, and then try copying them down in pencil until you feel confident with them. Carry on to a blank sheet of paper if necessary.

А	а	𝒜 а
Б	б	Ƃ δ
В	в	ℬ в
Г	г	𝒯 г
Д	д	𝒟 g
Е	е	Ɛ е
Ё	ё	Ë ё
Ж	ж	Ж ж
З	з	3 ӟ
И	и	𝒰 и
Й	й	Й й
К	к	𝒦 к

Л	л	*Л*	*л*
М	м	*М*	*м*
Н	н	*Н*	*н*
О	о	*О*	*о*
П	п	*П*	*п*
Р	р	*Р*	*р*
С	с	*С*	*с*
Т	т	*Т*	*т*
У	у	*У*	*у*
Ф	ф	*Ф*	*ф*
Х	х	*Х*	*х*
Ц	ц	*Ц*	*ц*
Ч	ч	*Ч*	*ч*
Ш	ш	*Ш*	*ш*
Щ	щ	*Щ*	*щ*
	ъ		*ъ*
	ы		*ы*
	ь		*ь*
Э	э	*Э*	*э*

Ю	ю	*ЗО ю*
Я	я	*Я я*

When you are happy with the individual letters, move on to looking at some words in hand-written form. Notice that the letters

л   *л*

м   *м*

and я   *я*

must always begin with a little hook, so you cannot join them onto a preceding **o**.   *о*

The letter **т**   *т̄*

is often written with a line above it and

the letter **ш**   *ш*

with a line beneath it so that they can easily be distinguished from surrounding letters. First read the words out loud to make sure you recognize them and then try writing them yourself. The stress marks do not appear on the hand-written words. Carry on to a blank sheet for more practice.

А	а	А́том	*Атом*	*Atom*
Б	б	Борщ	*Борщ*	*Beetroot soup*
В	в	Входи́те	*Входите*	*Come in*
Г	г	Горбачёв	*Горбачёв*	*Gorbachev*
Д	д	Диа́гноз	*Диагноз*	*Diagnosis*
Е	е	Е́льцин	*Ельцин*	*Yeltsin*
Ё	ё	Ёлка	*Ёлка*	*Fir tree*
Ж	ж	Жена́	*Жена*	*Wife*

З	з	Здра́вствуйте	*Здравствуйте*	Hello
И	и	Институ́т	*Институт*	Institute
Й	й	Музе́й	*Музей*	Museum
к	к	Ключ	*Ключ*	Key
Л	л	Ле́том	*Летом*	In summer
М	м	Маши́на	*Машина*	Car
Н	н	Напра́во	*Направо*	On the right
О	о	Официа́нт	*Официант*	Waiter
П	п	Поэ́т	*Поэт*	Poet
Р	р	Росси́я	*Россия*	Russia
С	с	Сын	*Сын*	Son
Т	т	Тра́нспорт	*Транспорт*	Transport
У	у	У́жин	*Ужин*	Supper
Ф	ф	Фа́брика	*Фабрика*	Factory
Х	х	Хорошо́	*Хорошо*	Good
Ц	ц	Царь	*Царь*	Tsar
Ч	ч	Чай	*Чай*	Tea
Ш	ш	Шесть	*Шесть*	Six
Щ	щ	Щи	*Щи*	Cabbage soup

	ъ	Объе́кт	*Объект*	Object
	ы	Ры́нок	*Рынок*	Market
	ь	Ию́нь	*Июнь*	June
Э	э	Эта́ж	*Этаж*	Floor
Ю	ю	Юг	*Юг*	South
Я	я	Япо́ния	*Япония*	Japan

You have now written all the letters of the Russian alphabet in both their lower case and capital forms where possible. For further practice you could try converting words and phrases from elsewhere in the book into handwriting.

Exercises

In the following exercises you will be asked to read and write Russian script. If you decide that writing will not be useful to you, then find another way of responding to the exercises. You may be able to say the answers aloud, or print the words asked for, or group them using numbers or symbols.

1 To test your new skills, see if you can read all the handwritten words in this box. Now sort them into three categories: sport, food and members of the family. If you are going to practise your writing skills, write out the three lists.

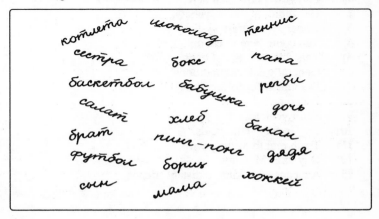

2 Write down or indicate the odd man out in each of these groups.

Город
парк
библиотека
музей
гитара
гастроном

Музыка
балалайка
оркестр
саксофон
инженер
опера

Профессия
врач
больница
учитель
футболист
дипломат

For further practice you could copy out the rest of the words in the boxes.

3 Can you complete the words in the grid using the clues in English given below?

1) Plays are performed here.
2) He studies at the university.
3) Underground train system.
4) You come here to eat out.
5) This dish is made of eggs.
6) General weather conditions.
7) Document for foreign travel.
8) Do come in!
9) Farm vehicle.
10) City in the Netherlands.
11) Tenth month of the year.
12) Day after Monday.
13) A means of talking to distant friends.

1	m̄								
2		m̄							
3			m̄						
4				m̄					
5					m̄				
6						m̄			
7							m̄		
8						m̄			
9					m̄				
10				m̄					
11			m̄						
12		m̄							
13	m̄								

4 Write out the following words, not forgetting the little hooks at the start of *л*, *м*, and *я*.

кассета _____

водка _____

администратор _____

ресторан _____

телевизор _____

институт _____

рекорд _____

атом _____

Now take the first letter of each word to make another word. What is it? Can you write it?

5 Identify at least five words from this menu and write them out. A translation is provided in the **Answers** at the back of the book.

МЕНЮ

ХОЛОДНЫЕ ЗАКУСКИ
Салат
Грибы
Икра
Колбаса
Сыр

ПЕРВЫЕ БЛЮДА
Борщ
Щи

ВТОРЫЕ БЛЮДА
Рыба
Котлеты
Курица
Омлет
Пицца
Сосиски

СЛАДКИЕ БЛЮДА
Фрукты
Мороженое
Конфеты

НАПИТКИ
Минеральная вода
Фруктовый сок
Пиво
Вино
Водка

6 Read these words and write down or say the missing word in each sequence.

a Север, юг, запад и _____.

b Брат и сестра, тётя и дядя, бабушка и _____.

c Май, июнь, июль, _____, сентябрь, октябрь

d Десять, двадцать, _____, сорок, пятьдесят

e Англия, англичанин. Франция, француз. _____, русский.

Continue to practise your writing little and often, and refer back to this unit frequently to make sure that you are not learning any bad habits!

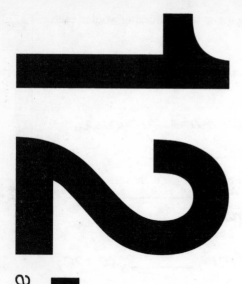

12

В аэропорту
at the airport

In this unit you will learn
- what to do and say on the plane
- what to do and say at the airport

Before you start, revise

- greetings, page 25
- times, dates and numbers, pages 76, 90, 224
- *my* and *your*, page 60 and *whose is it?* page 106
- how to use the verb **хотеть**, page 92

Now that you have reached the second half of the book, you should need less help with reading Russian, so the transliteration of words will no longer be shown. There will still be lots of listening and speaking, and in many exercises you can choose whether to write in Russian or not. To test your reading skills, there will be exercises and anecdotes both in print and script. The Russian anecdote has a long tradition, and by reading anecdotes from the Soviet era and the modern day you can learn a lot about the history, culture and humour of the Russian people. Some of the anecdotes appear on the recording.

ℹ️ Паспорт, виза и декларация *Passport, visa and declaration*

When you arrive in Russia you will have to show your **паспорт, виза** and **декларация**. The declaration is a form declaring any foreign currency and valuables you are taking into Russia. This is stamped on entry, and you may be asked to show it again on exit, declaring what you are taking out and showing receipts for goods purchased and money exchanged.

В самолёте *In the aeroplane*

If you travel on a Russian plane, you will feel that you are on Russian territory from the moment you board, and you may want to try out your Russian immediately. Here are some signs that you may see:

Не курить *No smoking*
Застегните ремни *Fasten your seat belts*

Learn the key words, some of which you already know, and then listen to or read the dialogue.

самолёт	*aeroplane*	**пиво**	*beer*
стюардесса	*stewardess*	**журналы**	*magazines*
место	*seat/place*	**градус**	*degree* (temperature)
обедать	*to have dinner*		

▶ Диало́г 1 Где моё ме́сто? *Where's my seat?*

Вы	Где моё ме́сто?
Стюарде́сса	Покажи́те, пожа́луйста, биле́т.
Вы	Вот он.
Стюарде́сса	Спаси́бо. Шестна́дцатое «а». Напра́во, пожа́луйста.

(*Once you are in the air, the stewardess asks you a question.*)

Стюарде́сса	Вы хоти́те обе́дать?
Вы	Обе́дать? Да, коне́чно, о́чень хочу́.
Стюарде́сса	И что вы хоти́те пить? У нас минера́льная вода́, вино́, пи́во, ко́фе и чай.
Вы	Да́йте, пожа́луйста, бе́лое вино́.
Стюарде́сса	Хоти́те журна́лы, газе́ты?
Вы	Да, пожа́луйста. У вас есть англи́йские газе́ты?
Стюарде́сса	Да, англи́йские и америка́нские.

(*Just before landing, the pilot gives you some information.*)

Пило́т	В Москве́ сейча́с восемна́дцать часо́в три́дцать пять мину́т, температу́ра – пятна́дцать гра́дусов.

Exercise 1

Say in English and Russian:

a your seat number **б** what you chose to drink **в** the time using the 24-hour clock, and the temperature in Moscow.

Exercise 2

Read through the dialogue aloud, altering the information as follows:

a Your seat number is now 9 «б» on the left. **б** The stewardess offers you lemonade, fruit juice, and coffee with milk. **в** You choose fruit juice. **г** You ask for a Russian magazine.

Exercise 3

Listen to the recording and note down, using a numeral and a Russian letter, the seat numbers as the stewardess reads them out:

a

б

в

г

and the time and temperature in these cities:

д В Краснода́ре
е В Арха́нгельске
ж В Петербу́рге

ℹ Аэропо́рт *The airport*

Once you arrive at the airport in Russia, you may see these signs. The first group you will already recognize.

| аэропо́рт | *буфе́т* | сувени́ры |

| *НЕ КУРИ́ТЬ* | ПАРФЮМЕ́РИЯ |

| *спра́вочное бюро́* | ка́сса | ТУАЛЕ́Т |

Exercise 4

The following groups of words you have not seen before. Work out what they mean.

а вы́ход   вы́хода нет   вы́ход на поса́дку
б тамо́женный контро́ль   вы́дача багажа́   транзи́т
    па́спортный контро́ль   № ре́йса
в регистра́ция   кра́сный коридо́р   зал ожида́ния   вход

exit/boarding gate (exit to embarkation)/no exit/luggage reclaim/passport control/flight number/customs control/transit/red channel/check-in/entrance/waiting room

ℹ️ Па́спортный контро́ль *Passport control*

Upon arrival at the airport, you will first go through passport control, and then on to customs – **тамо́женный контро́ль**.

Отку́да вы?	*Where are you from?*	**то́лько**	*only*
нарко́тик	*narcotics*	**до́ллар**	*dollar*
фу́нт сте́рлингов	*pound sterling*	**доро́жный чек**	*traveller's cheque*

▶️ Диало́г 2 Отку́да вы? *Where are you from?*

Де́вушка	Да́йте, пожа́луйста, па́спорт.
Джеймс	Вот он.
Де́вушка	Спаси́бо. А где ва́ша ви́за?
Джеймс	Извини́те. Вот она́.
Де́вушка	Вы тури́ст и́ли бизнесме́н?
Джеймс	Я тури́ст.
Де́вушка	Вы англича́нин?
Джеймс	Да, англича́нин.
Де́вушка	Отку́да вы?
Джеймс	Я живу́ в Пре́стоне, на се́вере А́нглии.
Де́вушка	Хорошо́. Вот ваш па́спорт.
Джеймс	Спаси́бо.

James moves on to customs.

Молодо́й челове́к	Это ваш бага́ж?
Джеймс	Да, это мой чемода́н и моя́ су́мка. И вот моя́ деклара́ция.
Молодо́й челове́к	Спаси́бо. У вас в багаже́ есть нарко́тик?
Джеймс	Нет.
Молодо́й челове́к	У вас есть фу́нты сте́рлингов?
Джеймс	Нет, то́лько до́ллары и доро́жные че́ки.
Молодо́й челове́к	Хорошо́. Вот ва́ша деклара́ция. До свида́ния.

▶️ Listen to the dialogue several times, then work on it by covering up James's lines and answering the questions yourself, altering information as you choose.

Exercise 5

In the **деклара́ция** you are asked to declare any foreign currency, weapons, drugs and valuables. Underline the items in this handwritten list which you think you should declare.

до́ллары
план
компью́тер

кни́га
фу́нты сте́рлингов

пистоле́т
ви́за
минера́льная вода́

доро́жные че́ки
ка́мера
газе́та

Exercise 6

▶ Last week you rang your friend, **Валенти́н**, to tell him when you would be arriving in Moscow. Read through what he says first, and familiarize yourself with the new words. Then complete your side of the conversation.

здравствуй	*hello*	**поня́тно**	*understood*
ты бу́дешь	*you will be*	**так**	*so*
А́нна бу́дет	*Anna will be*		

а You *Hello. Valentin?*
Валенти́н Алло́! Стив, э́то ты?
б You *Yes. How are you?*
Валенти́н Хорошо́, спаси́бо. Стив, когда́ ты бу́дешь в Москве́?
в You *On Friday.*
Валенти́н Шесто́го ию́ля?
г You *Yes, on the 6th of July.*
Валенти́н В кото́ром часу́?
д You *At 18:40.*
Валенти́н И А́нна то́же бу́дет на самолёте.
е You *Yes, of course.*
Валенти́н И како́й но́мер ре́йса?
ж You *The flight number is SU242.*

| **Валенти́н** | SU две́сти со́рок два. Поня́тно. Так, мы встре́тимся в аэропорту́ шесто́го ию́ля в восемна́дцать часо́в со́рок мину́т. До свида́ния, Стив. |
| **3 You** | *Goodbye, Valentin.* |

Well done! Did you notice the unusual ending on **аэропо́рт** when Valentin says *at the airport?* You would expect to see **-е**, but instead you see **-у**. This happens with a few masculine nouns, including **сад** *garden*, and **лес** *forest*: **в саду́** *in the garden*, **в лесу́** *in the forest*.

The verb **быть** *to be* in the future tense (i.e. not what is happening now, but what *will* happen in the future), which you also met in this dialogue, is very useful when making arrangements, so here it is:

я бу́ду	I will be	**мы бу́дем**	we will be
ты бу́дешь	you will be	**вы бу́дете**	you will be
он/она́ бу́дет	he/she will be	**они́ бу́дут**	they will be

Exercise 7

You are flying to St Petersburg, and you need to ring your Russian friend with the details. Prepare what you will say on the phone.

Flight no. BA 878
Arrival in St Petersburg: 19.40
Date of travel: Thursday 26 Jan.

At last you have completed the formalities, and you see Валенти́н waiting for you.

наконе́ц	*at last*
Как долете́ли?	*How was (your flight)?*
прекра́сно	*fine*
Как вы пожива́ете?	*How are you (getting on)?*
пожива́ть [1]	*to get on*
немно́жко	*a little*
уста́л/уста́ла/уста́ли	*tired (m/f/pl)*
как всегда́	*as always*
ждать [1] (я жду, ты ждёшь, они́ ждут)	*to wait*
ско́ро	*soon*

▶ Диало́г 3 Здра́вствуй, Валенти́н!
Hello, Valentin!

Валенти́н Здра́вствуй, Стив! Здра́вствуй, А́нна! Наконе́ц!
А́нна Здра́вствуй, Валенти́н! Как прия́тно тебя́ ви́деть!
Валенти́н Как долете́ли?
Стив Прекра́сно, спаси́бо.
Валенти́н Как вы пожива́ете? Хоти́те есть, пить?
А́нна Спаси́бо нет, Валенти́н. Я немно́жко уста́ла.
Стив Я то́же немно́жко уста́л. Но я, как всегда́, о́чень хочу́ есть и пить.
Валенти́н Хорошо́, мы ско́ро бу́дем до́ма. Ири́на там ждёт.

Exercise 8

Listen to the dialogue or read it and find the Russian for:

а How lovely to see you!
б How are you?
в I am a little tired.
г as always
д We will soon be at home.

Exercise 9

▶ Read out loud the arrival dates and times of these travellers. Listen to the recording to check your pronunciation.

а Са́лли бу́дет в Со́чи 16/а́вг., в 22,30.
б Станисла́в бу́дет в Му́рманске 5/ноя., в 10,15.
в Лю́ба бу́дет в Москве́ 29/ма́я, в 13,50.
г А́лла бу́дет в Ирку́тске 10/фев., в 15,20.

ℹ Обме́н валю́ты *Currency exchange*

Now that you are through passport control and customs, you may need to change some money into roubles. To do this you need to find a sign saying **обме́н валю́ты** *exchange of currency*. Check the exchange rate – **курс** – and don't forget to get your **деклара́ция** stamped and keep your receipt.

Exercise 10

Look at these numerals 1–10 written by hand, and copy them until you can write them authentically without looking at the original.

Exercise 11

▶ At the information office **спра́вочное бюро́** of the airport you overhear people asking where the check-in **регистра́ция** is for various flights **ре́йсы:** Скажи́те, пожа́луйста, где регистра́ция, рейс во́семьсот се́мьдесят де́вять (879) в Ло́ндон?

For practice, you decide to note down the flight numbers. Listen to the recording and fill in the numbers as a Russian would write them.

а Рейс _____ в Де́ли.
б Рейс _____ в Амстерда́м.
в Рейс _____ в Цю́рих.
г Рейс _____ в Пари́ж.
д Рейс _____ в Нью-Йо́рк.

Exercise 12

Rearrange the words in these questions so that they make sense. You could choose to say the sentences out loud, number the words, or write them.

а пить вы что хоти́те?
б ва́ша как фами́лия?
в ме́сто моё где?
г вас фу́нты есть сте́рлингов у?
д ва́ша чемода́н э́то и су́мка ваш?

Exercise 13

Match up the questions and answers.

а) Где моё место?
б) Где ваша виза?
в) Вы бизнесмен?
г) Это ваш багаж?
д) У вас есть доллары?
е) Что вы хотите пить?
ж) У вас есть русские газеты?

1) Нет, я турист.
2) Нет, это не мой багаж.
3) Нет, у меня есть фунты.
4) Чай, пожалуйста.
5) Пятое «г», налево.
6) Да, русские и английские.
7) Вот она.

▶ **Анекдо́т** *Anecdote*

This anecdote from pre-glasnost days is about a Russian emigré in America recalling life in the Soviet Union. He explains why he chose to emigrate. There is one key phrase you need before you begin: **Нельзя́ пожа́ловаться** *Mustn't grumble.*

Интервьюе́р	Проду́кты есть в Москве́?
Ру́сский эмигра́нт	Нельзя́ пожа́ловаться.
Интервьюе́р	И как тра́нспорт в Москве́?
Ру́сский эмигра́нт	Нельзя́ пожа́ловаться.
Интервьюе́р	Как там больни́цы?
Ру́сский эмигра́нт	Нельзя́ пожа́ловаться.
Интервьюе́р	И как там шко́лы?
Ру́сский эмигра́нт	Нельзя́ пожа́ловаться.
Интервьюе́р	Почему́ вы сейча́с живёте в Аме́рике?
Ру́сский эмигра́нт	Потому́, что здесь мо́жно пожа́ловаться.

1 Which four aspects of Soviet life was the emigré questioned about?
2 What was his reason for emigrating?

Congratulations on successfully negotiating the airport! Now it's time to look at other situations in which you might find yourself if visiting Russia or entertaining Russian guests at home.

13

как попасть на Московский вокзал?

how do I get to Maskovsky station?

In this unit you will learn
- how to use public transport
- how to ask for further directions

Before you start, revise

- directions, Unit 5
- numbers and telling the time, page 76
- how to say *to* Moscow and *in* Moscow, pages 47, 70

Russian distinguishes between going somewhere on foot and by some means of transport, so two verbs which will be useful to you are идти *to go on foot* and éхать *to go by transport*.

идти	*to go on foot*		éхать	*to go by transport*	
я иду		мы идём	я éду		мы éдем
ты идёшь		вы идёте	ты éдешь		вы éдете
он/она идёт		они идут	он/она éдет		они éдут

ℹ Городской трáнспорт *Public transport*

To find the stop for a bus, trolleybus or tram, look out for these signs.

А for a bus **автóбус**, **П** for a trolleybus **троллéйбус**, **Т** for a tram **трамвáй**. The signs for buses and trolleybuses are usually attached to a wall, but tram signs are suspended from cables over the road.

To travel on any of these vehicles you need a ticket **талóн**. These may be bought from kiosks or from the bus driver, singly or in strips of ten called a little book **кнúжечка**. Plain clothes inspectors fine people travelling without a ticket. Some people prefer to buy a season ticket **едúный билéт**. When you get on, you should get your ticket punched at one of the little contraptions mounted in the vehicle. If it is too crowded to reach one, ask someone to do it for you: **Пробéйте талóн, пожáлуйста**. If someone is trying to get off when the vehicle is crowded they will say: **Вы сейчáс выхóдите?** *Are you getting off now?* If you are not, you should try to let them past.

автóбус	*bus*
троллéйбус	*trolleybus*
трамвáй	*tram*
останóвка (на)	*stop*
останóвка автóбуса	*bus stop*
останóвка троллéйбуса	*trolleybus stop*
останóвка трамвáя	*tram stop*
талóн	*ticket (bus, trolleybus and tram)*
кнúжечка	*little book (strip of ten tickets)*
едúный (билéт)	*season ticket*
пешкóм	*on foot*
минýта	*minute*

Как попа́сть в...?	How do I get to ...?
Сади́тесь на пя́тый авто́бус	Get on to bus no. five
Пробе́йте тало́н, пожа́луйста	Punch my ticket, please
Когда́ мне выходи́ть?	When do I need to get off?
Че́рез три остано́вки	after three stops

▶ **Диало́г 1 Как попа́сть в цирк?** *How do I get to the circus?*

Robert has arranged to meet Slava at the circus, but he doesn't know how to get there.

Ро́берт Де́вушка, извини́те, пожа́луйста, как попа́сть в цирк?

Де́вушка В цирк? Сади́тесь на четы́рнадцатый трамва́й.

Ро́берт Где остано́вка?

Де́вушка Там, напра́во. Ви́дите?

Ро́берт Да. А мо́жно пешко́м?

Де́вушка Мо́жно.

Ро́берт Ско́лько мину́т пешко́м, и ско́лько на трамва́е?

Де́вушка Пешко́м два́дцать – три́дцать мину́т. А на трамва́е де́сять.

On the tram

Ро́берт Извини́те, я е́ду в цирк. Когда́ мне выходи́ть?

Ба́бушка Че́рез три остано́вки.

Ро́берт Пробе́йте тало́н, пожа́луйста.

Exercise 1

▶ Listen to the dialogue above, and say **а** which tram Robert has to catch **б** where the tram stop is **в** how long it would take on foot **г** how long it would take by tram **д** how many stops he has to travel.

Now work through the dialogue playing the parts of де́вушка and ба́бушка, and altering these details: **е** Robert needs bus no. eight **ж** the bus stop is straight ahead **з** it will take 30–40 minutes on foot and 15 on the bus **и** he needs to get off after four stops.

Exercise 2

You see this sign on a bus. What must you not do?

В АВТОБУСЕ НЕЛЬЗЯ КУРИТЬ!

ℹ️ Метро́ *The metro*

To spot a metro station **ста́нция метро́** look out for a big red letter **М**. To enter the metro, you buy a ticket **биле́т** from the window at the station, insert it into the automatic barrier, pass through the turnstile and you are free to travel as far as you want for a certain number of journeys until you exit the metro system. The metro generally runs from at least six a.m. to midnight. At each station an announcement is made. The order varies, but it will usually include the name of the station you are at, **Ста́нция «Лубя́нка»**, the name of the next station, **Сле́дующая ста́нция – «Кита́й Го́род»**, and a warning to be careful because the doors are shutting, **Осторо́жно. Две́ри закрыва́ются**.

ста́нция метро́	metro station
биле́т	ticket
автома́т	slot
турнике́т	turnstile
переса́дка	change
без переса́дки	without a change
с переса́дкой	with a change
де́лать переса́дку	to make a change
дое́дете до ста́нции ...	go as far as station ...

Look out for these signs:

ВХОД	entrance
ВЫХОД	exit
НЕТ ВХО́ДА	no entrance
НЕТ ВЫ́ХОДА	no exit
К ПОЕЗДА́М	to the trains
ПЕРЕХО́Д НА СТА́НЦИЮ «ТЕАТРА́ЛЬНАЯ ПЛО́ЩАДЬ»	Transfer to station 'Theatre Square'

▶️ Диало́г 2 На метро́ *On the metro*

Martin has heard that the view over Moscow from the University is worth seeing. He has left his plan of the metro at the hotel so he stops Valya and asks her the way.

Ма́ртин Скажи́те пожа́луйста, как попа́сть в университе́т?
Ва́ля На метро́?
Ма́ртин Да, на метро́.
Ва́ля Хорошо́. Там нале́во ста́нция метро́. «Парк Культу́ры».

Ма́ртин	Поня́тно.
Ва́ля	На метро́ дое́дете до ста́нции «Университе́т».
Ма́ртин	Это далеко́?
Ва́ля	Нет, четы́ре остано́вки.
Ма́ртин	Спаси́бо.

Exercise 3

a In the dialogue above, which station does Martin go from?

б Which station must he go to?

в How many stops does he have to go?

Exercise 4

You are staying with Lydia in Moscow, but she has to work today. She writes you out a list of places you could visit and how to get there.

	станция метро
Кремль	Александровский сад
Ботанический сад	Ботанический сад
Рынок	Пушкинская
Дом книги	Арбатская
ГУМ	Площадь Революции

Which metro station do you need for **a** the Kremlin **б** the market **в** the book shop **г** the botanical gardens **д** the department store *GUM*?

Another friend wants to meet you later. Arrange which metro station to meet at and write it down so you don't forget. (You choose which one!)

Now make up questions and answers based on the information above, for example – Скажи́те, пожа́луйста, как попа́сть в Кремль? – Дое́дете до ста́нции «Алекса́ндровский сад».

i Вокза́л *The train station*

Russian trains offer differing degrees of comfort: **мя́гкий** *soft* (*seated*), **жёсткий** *hard* (*seated*) and **спа́льный** *sleeper*. Each train has a **проводни́к** or **проводни́ца** *conductor*, who checks tickets and supplies bedding and tea on long journeys. The names of main-line stations refer to the places to and from which trains travel, so **Ки́евский вокза́л** in Moscow is where you would catch a train to Kiev, and **Моско́вский вокза́л** in St Petersburg is where you would catch a train to Moscow. If Russian friends are going to see you off on a long journey, you may find that before leaving home, everyone sits down for a moment in silence. This is a tradition meant to bring the traveller safely back home.

вокза́л (на)	station
по́езд (*pl* поезда́)	train(s)
ско́рый по́езд	express train
электри́чка	suburban electric train
ваго́н	carriage
купе́	compartment
ме́сто	seat
ваго́н-рестора́н	dining car
расписа́ние	timetable
отправле́ние	departure
платфо́рма	platform
обра́тный биле́т	return ticket
биле́т в оди́н коне́ц	single ticket
мя́гкий ваго́н	soft (seated) carriage
жёсткий ваго́н	hard (seated) carriage
спа́льный ваго́н	sleeper carriage
По́езд отхо́дит в 7 часо́в	The train leaves at 7 o'clock
проводни́к, проводни́ца	conductor
касси́р	ticket office cashier
пассажи́р	passenger
для куря́щих	for smokers
для некуря́щих	for non-smokers

Look out for these notices:

ВЫ́ХОД В ГО́РОД	exit to the town
ЗАЛ ОЖИДА́НИЯ	waiting room
БУФЕ́Т	snack bar
КА́ССА	ticket office

▶ Диало́г 3 Когда́ отхо́дит по́езд? *When does the train leave?*

Trevor wants to travel to Moscow by train to see Konstantina. First, he goes to the **ка́сса** *to get a ticket.*

Тре́вор Да́йте, пожа́луйста, оди́н обра́тный биле́т в Москву́ на шесто́е а́вгуста.

Касси́р Одну́ мину́точку... Хорошо́. По́езд семь, ваго́н трина́дцать.

Тре́вор Когда́ отхо́дит по́езд?

Касси́р У́тром, в де́сять часо́в три́дцать мину́т.

Шесто́го а́вгуста. На платфо́рме:

Тре́вор Это трина́дцатый ваго́н?

Проводни́ца Да. Ваш биле́т, пожа́луйста.

Тре́вор Вот он.

Проводни́ца Второ́е ме́сто. Иди́те в пе́рвое купе́, пожа́луйста.

Тре́вор Скажи́те, в по́езде есть ваго́н-рестора́н?

Проводни́ца Есть.

Тре́вор Когда́ он открыва́ется?

Проводни́ца В оди́ннадцать часо́в.

Exercise 5

Re-read the dialogue above and find out **а** on which date Trevor wants to travel **б** the number of his train and carriage **в** the departure time **г** the seat number **д** the opening time of the dining car.

– Мя́гкий ваго́н ищу́.

Exercise 6

ищу́	I am looking for

Read this timetable and give out information about it, for example, **По́езд но́мер пятьсо́т оди́ннадцать в Петербу́рг отхо́дит в де́вять часо́в три́дцать шесть.**

РАСПИСÁНИЕ		
ПÓЕЗД		*ОТПРАВЛÉНИЕ*
№ 511	ПЕТЕРБУ́РГ	9.36
№ 96	НÓВГОРОД	12.55
№ 716	ИВÁНОВО	20.47
№ 82	ТУ́ЛА	23.05

Now look back to Trevor's dialogue at the ticket office and substitute the St Petersburg train for Trevor's train, altering the dialogue accordingly. Perhaps you could change other details as well, or write down part of the conversation in English or Russian.

ℹ️ Такси́ *Taxi*

Official taxis are black Volgas with a chequered pattern and the letter **T** on the door, and the fare is supposed to be metered. There are also private unmetered taxis, but some Russians prefer to hitch a lift with a passing vehicle and negotiate a fare.

такси́	*taxi*
маршру́тное такси́	*fixed-route minibus taxi*
маши́на	*car*
автомоби́ль (*m*)	*car*
стоя́нка такси́ (на)	*taxi rank*
Такси́! Свобо́дно?	*Taxi! Are you free?*
Куда́ пое́дем?	*Where are we going?*
Не волну́йтесь	*Don't worry!*

▶️ Диало́г 4 Такси́! *Taxi!*

Lorna is in a hurry to catch a train at **Моско́вский вокза́л** *so she flags down a taxi.*

Ло́рна Такси́! Свобо́дно?
Такси́ст Сади́тесь. Куда́ пое́дем?
Ло́рна На Моско́вский вокза́л, пожа́луйста.
Такси́ст Когда́ отхо́дит ваш по́езд?
Ло́рна В де́вять часо́в со́рок мину́т.
Такси́ст Не волну́йтесь. Мы ско́ро бу́дем на вокза́ле.

Exercise 7

а At what time does her train leave?

б Will she be in time to catch it?

в Now put yourself in Lorna's position. You are going to Kiev, so you need to go to **Киевский вокзал** and your train leaves at ten o'clock. What will you say to the taxi driver?

Now that you know all the forms of transport, here is a summary of how to say *I am going to the university **on the bus** etc.* **Я еду в университет на автобусе.**

Exercise 8

Would you understand these instructions and signs?

а **Садитесь на пятый троллейбус** means

автобус		автобусе
троллейбус		троллейбусе
трамвай		трамвае
такси	**на** }	такси
метро		метро
машина		машине
автомобиль		автомобиле
поезд		поезде

    i   Get on trolleybus no. 15

    ii Get on trolleybus no. 5

    iii Get on trolleybus no. 50

б **ВЫХОД В ГОРОД** means

    i To the trains   **ii** No exit   **iii** Exit to the town

в **Дайте, пожалуйста, обратный билет** means

    i   Please give me a return ticket.

    ii Please give me a single ticket.

    iii Please give me a metro ticket.

Exercise 9

How would you say:

а How do I get to the Kremlin?

б Where is the bus stop?

в Are you getting off now?

г I am going to the Botanical Gardens on the metro.

д What time does the train leave?

▶ Анекдóт 1 *Anecdote 1*

This anecdote is about a man and a little boy on a bus. The words below will help you to understand it, but you need only learn **éсли** *if* for active use. Notice that the man is addressed as **дя́дя** *uncle*, meaning that he is probably too old to be called **молодóй человéк**.

вхóдит	*(he) gets on*
пробивáет (талóн)	*punches (a ticket)*
мáльчик	*boy*
éсли я теря́ю	*if I lose*
éсли вы теря́ете	*if you lose*
дурáк	*fool*

Человéк вхóдит в автóбус и пробивáет три талóна.

Мáльчик	Дя́дя, почемý у вас три талóна?
Человéк	Éсли я теря́ю пéрвый талóн, у меня́ вторóй есть.
Мáльчик	А éсли вы теря́ете вторóй талóн?
Человéк	У меня́ трéтий есть.
Мáльчик	А éсли вы теря́ете трéтий талóн?
Человéк	Я не дурáк! У меня́ еди́ный билéт.

1 Why does the man punch the third **талóн** *ticket*?
2 Why does he not need any **талóны** *tickets* at all?

Анекдóт 2 *Anecdote 2*

This anecdote is set in a train and is about someone who can't find his way back to his carriage from the dining car. Again, you do not need to learn the vocabulary for active use, although **Что вы!**, or **Что ты!**, *What?!* is excellent for expressing amazement!

я не пóмню	*I can't remember*
что вы!	*What on earth?!*
за окнóм	*through the window*
был	*there was*

В пóезде éдет дурáк. Он обéдает в вагóн-ресторáне.

Дурáк	Извини́те, дéвушка, я не пóмню, где мой вагóн.
Проводни́ца	Что вы! Вы не знáете, где ваш вагóн?
Дурáк	Нет, не знáю. Но за окнóм лес был.

1 Who does he ask to solve his problem?
2 What does he remember seeing through his carriage window?

14

где можно
купить
самовар?

where can I buy a samovar?

In this unit you will learn
- more about shoppping
- what to buy and where

Before you start, revise

- shopping vocabulary from Unit 6, pages 55–6
- numbers, page 224; times, page 76; directions, page 47; days of the week, page 79.

ℹ️ Где плати́ть? *Where do I pay?*

As mentioned before, the system of shopping in some of the more old-fashioned shops involves quite a bit of queueing. The word for a queue is **о́чередь**. First, you queue to find out the availability and price of what you want, then queue a second time at the **ка́сса** to pay for the goods and collect the **чек**. At the cash desk you will need to say for which number department **отде́л** you need the receipt. Finally you queue for a third time to hand over the receipt and collect the goods. This system can make shopping a long process. However, for the language learner the queues and transactions are an opportunity not to be missed! This sort of shopping is far more interesting than using the many Western-style shops and supermarkets where you simply take your goods to the till.

Сувени́ры *Souvenirs*

A samovar **самова́р** is an urn, usually powered by charcoal or electricity, in which water is heated. Very strong tea is made in a tiny tea pot which stands on top of the samovar to keep warm. A little strong tea is poured into a glass and topped up with water from the samovar. Tea may be taken with sugar **са́хар**, lemon **лимо́н** or fruit preserves **варе́нье**.

Other popular souvenirs which you have encountered in earlier units include the balalaika **балала́йка**, which is a triangular stringed musical instrument used for playing Russian folk music, and the *matryoshka* doll **матрёшка**. These dolls are made of wood, brightly painted, and when they are opened they reveal a whole series of smaller dolls hidden inside each other.

Bear in mind that any prices quoted in this book may be out of date.

In this unit there are inevitably a lot of key words, but some of them you already know, and some you will not need to learn for active use. When you have learned as many of them as possible, test yourself by covering up first the English side and then the Russian, saying out loud the words which are hidden.

Key words and phrases

What you say

Мо́жно посмотре́ть?	*May I have a look?*
Покажи́те, да́йте ...	*Show me, give me ...*
Ско́лько сто́ит? Ско́лько сто́ят?	*How much is it? How much are they?*
Напиши́те, пожа́луйста, ско́лько сто́ит	*Please write down how much it is*
Повтори́те, пожа́луйста, ме́дленнее	*Repeat that more slowly please*
У вас есть/есть ли у вас кни́ги о спо́рте?	*Do you have any books about sport?*
Пожа́луйста, да!	*Yes please.*
Спаси́бо, нет!	*No thank you.*
Ско́лько с меня́?	*How much do I owe?*
До́рого/недо́рого	*That's expensive/not expensive*
Всё? Да, всё.	*Is that all? Yes, that's all.*
Где плати́ть? В ка́ссу?	*Where do I pay? At the cash desk?*
Где ка́сса?	*Where is the cash desk?*
Напро́тив.	*Opposite.*
Сто два́дцать рубле́й на второ́й отде́л	*120 roubles for department 2*
Магази́н откры́т/закры́т	*The shop is open/closed*
Я хочу́ купи́ть ...	*I want to buy ...*
Куда́ мне пойти́?	*Where should I go?*
Где продаю́тся газе́ты?	*Where are newspapers sold?*

What the shop assistant says

Слу́шаю вас	*I'm listening (May I help?)*
Вам помо́чь?	*May I help you?*
Что вы хоти́те?	*What do you want?*
Ско́лько вы хоти́те?	*How much do you want?*
Сыр сто́ит 200 рубле́й килогра́мм	*Cheese costs 200 roubles a kilo*

Exercise 1

What does this shop sell?

Где мо́жно купи́ть проду́кты? *Where can you buy food?*

Универса́м *Supermarket*

суперма́ркет	*supermarket*
гастроно́м	*grocer's*
Здесь продаю́тся ...	*Here you can buy ...*
проду́кты	*provisions*
мя́со	*meat*
ры́ба	*fish*
колбаса́	*sausage* (salami)
соси́ска	*sausage* (frankfurter)
ко́фе, чай, са́хар	*coffee, tea, sugar*
конфе́ты	*sweets*
торт	*cake*
вино́, пи́во, во́дка	*wine, beer, vodka*

Моло́чные проду́кты *Dairy produce*

молоко́	*milk*
смета́на	*sour cream*
сыр	*cheese*
ма́сло	*butter*

Бу́лочная *Bakery*

Чёрный/бе́лый хлеб	*black/white bread*
бато́н	*long loaf*
бу́лка	*sweet bread roll*
су́шка	*dry ring-shaped biscuit*

Рынок *Market*

све́жие фру́кты/о́вощи/цветы́	*fresh fruits/vegetables/flowers*
я́блоко (*pl.* я́блоки)	*apple(s)*
гру́ша	*pear*
апельси́н	*orange*
карто́шка	*potato*
помидо́р	*tomato*
огуре́ц (*pl.* огурцы́)	*cucumber(s)*

Ско́лько вы хоти́те? *How much do you want?*

You will find that after any expression of quantity (kilo, litre, packet, etc.) the next word will change its ending: **кило́ бана́нов** *a kilo of bananas*. This is called the *genitive case*. It is not essential for you at this stage to know how this works. Not knowing the endings will not prevent you from understanding or being understood.

кило́	*kilo*		грамм	*gram*
литр	*litre*		метр	*metre*
ба́нка	*jar, tin*		буты́лка	*bottle*
		па́чка	*packet*	
сто грамм/пятьсо́т грамм			100 grams/500 grams	

▶ Диало́г 1 В гастроно́ме *In the grocer's*

Nick is looking for some cheese. Read the dialogue and answer the questions on the next page.

Продавщи́ца	Слу́шаю вас.
Ник	У вас есть сыр?
Продавщи́ца	Есть ли у нас сыр? Да, коне́чно. Вот он.
Ник	Како́й это сыр? Мо́жно посмотре́ть, пожа́луйста?
Продавщи́ца	Мо́жно. Это эсто́нский сыр. Сто́ит две́сти рубле́й кило́.
Ник	Повтори́те, пожа́луйста, ме́дленнее.
Продавщи́ца	Две́сти рубле́й.
Ник	Это до́рого?
Продавщи́ца	Нет, недо́рого. Ско́лько вы хоти́те?
Ник	Пятьсо́т грамм. Ско́лько с меня́?
Продавщи́ца	Сто рубле́й. Всё?
Ник	Да, всё. Где плати́ть?

Продавщица	В кассу.
Ник	А где касса?
Продавщица	Напротив. Видите?
Ник	Да. Спасибо. Какой здесь отдел?
Продавщица	Четвёртый.

Exercise 2

a Where do you think the cheese is from, and how much does it cost? Find the Russian for **б** Could I have a look? **в** How much do you want? **г** Is that all? **д** Opposite.

Now put yourself in Nick's place and work through the dialogue covering up his lines and saying his part.

Exercise 3

The following is a list of products from a supermarket's advertising brochure. Read this list, identify the products, and answer the questions.

Майонез
Сыр Эдамский, Голландия
Киви, Греция
Лимоны, Испания
Мандарины, Испания
Кетчуп, Болгария
Чай индийский
Кофе, Бразилия
Шоколад, Германия
Водка, «Столичная», «Смирнофф», «Абсолют»

---

a Which two fruits from Spain can you buy?
б What sort of cheese is there?
в What has been imported from Bulgaria?
г What sort of tea can you buy?
д Which brands of vodka are listed?

▶ Exercise 4

You are in a **гастроном**. Listen to people asking for things. Underline the items which you hear requested on the list overleaf. For further practice, you could copy the list.

чай   сахар
огурец   колбаса
сосиски   конфеты
банка кофе   торт
кило помидоров   мясо
рыба   бутылка пива

Exercise 5

Find five drinks and six types of food below.

кофе
ФРУКТОВАЯ ВОДА
ВОДКА
СОУСЫ и КЕТЧУПЫ
конфеты
шоколад
КАРАМЕЛЬ
шампанское
ЛАНЧЕН МИТ
чай фруктовый

Exercise 6

Ask in the **гастроно́м** if they have:

a salami sausage **б** tea **в** cake **г** fish **д** milk **е** oranges
ж cucumbers

Ходи́ть по магази́нам *Going round the shops*

Универма́г *Department store*

пода́рок (pl пода́рки)	present(s)
оде́жда	clothes
джи́нсы	jeans
ша́пка	fur hat

Сувени́ры *Souvenirs*

матрёшка	stacking matryoshka *doll*
электри́ческий самова́р	electric samovar
плато́к (pl платки́)	shawl(s)
деревя́нная игру́шка	wooden toy

Киóск *Kiosk*

газéта, журнáл, план	*newspaper, magazine, plan*
откры́тка	*postcard*
морóженое	*ice cream*

Аптéка *Chemist's*

| аспири́н | *aspirin* |
| лекáрство | *medicine* |

▶ Диалóг 2 Рýсские сувени́ры *Russian souvenirs*

Chris is asking Oleg to help organize her day. Read the dialogue several times and then answer the questions below it.

Крис Я сегóдня хочý ходи́ть по магази́нам.

Олéг Что ты хóчешь купи́ть?

Крис Подáрки и сувени́ры. Я хочý купи́ть кни́ги, деревя́нные игрýшки, откры́тки и самовáр. Я óчень люблю́ рýсский чай с лимóном.

Олéг Поня́тно. Кни́ги и откры́тки продаю́тся в магази́не «Дом Кни́ги». Это недалекó.

Крис А где продаю́тся самовáры и игрýшки?

Олéг В магази́не «Рýсский сувени́р». Котóрый сейчáс час?

Крис Дéвять часóв.

Олéг Хорошó. «Дом Кни́ги» открывáется в дéвять часóв.

Крис Как попáсть в «Дом Кни́ги»?

Олéг Три останóвки на автóбусе. Останóвка там, напрóтив.

Later, in «Ру́сский сувени́р»

Де́вушка	Вам помо́чь?
Крис	Пожа́луйста, да! Покажи́те, пожа́луйста, э́тот самова́р. Нет, вот э́тот. Оле́г, како́й э́то краси́вый самова́р! Де́вушка, э́то электри́ческий самова́р?
Де́вушка	Да, электри́ческий. Отку́да вы?
Крис	Я англича́нка, живу́ в Ло́ндоне.
Де́вушка	Не волну́йтесь. Моя́ тётя живёт в Ло́ндоне, и она́ говори́т, что на́ши самова́ры хорошо́ там рабо́тают.
Крис	Поня́тно. Покажи́те, пожа́луйста, э́ти деревя́нные игру́шки. Да, кра́сные и зелёные. И вот э́ти жёлтые.
Де́вушка	Вот э́ти?
Крис	Да. Спаси́бо. Напиши́те, пожа́луйста, ско́лько они́ сто́ят.

Exercise 7

Read the shopping list in the left-hand column and match up the items with an appropriate shop from the right-hand column. You could then rewrite the list correctly.

аспири́н	кио́ск
ма́сло	сувени́ры
са́хар	ры́нок
вино́	моло́чные проду́кты
моро́женое	универса́м
цветы́	апте́ка
хлеб	универма́г
самова́р	було́чная
ша́пка	гастроно́м

Exercise 8

а What does Chris want to do today?
б What four things does she want to buy?
в Is it far to the book shop?
г Where is the bus stop?
д What is the Russian for *she says that*?
е How does Chris know that the samovar will work in England?
ж What colours are the toys she wants to look at?

Now you could make up your own dialogue, buying things which you would particularly like.

▶ Exercise 9

Listen to the three conversations. Note down in Russian or English what Sasha wants to buy, the shop he needs and the directions he is given.

	Са́ша хо́чет купи́ть ...	Магази́н	Куда́?
а			
б			
в			

Exercise 10

Here is an alphabetical list of the types of shops you could find in a major Russian city, and of items to buy. You have met many of the words, and the rest you can probably work out.

Автомоби́ли
Антиквариа́т
А́удио-Видеоте́хника
Бу́лочная
Гастроно́м
Диети́ческие проду́кты
Диза́йн-сту́дия
Кни́ги
Колбаса́
Косме́тика
Моло́чные проду́кты
Музыка́льные инструме́нты

Мя́со
О́вощи-фру́кты
О́птика
Пода́рки
Ры́ба
Спорти́вные това́ры
Сувени́ры
Таба́к
Цветы́
Часы́

Read the list and underline where you think you could buy **а** spectacles **б** a watch **в** a bread roll **г** antiques **д** food for a special diet **е** a herring **ж** a trombone **з** a video player **и** a car.

АУДИО
ВИДЕО
ФОТО
Мойка, 56 ◀||||

Exercise 11

How would you say:

a I want to buy some bread, cheese, tomatoes and tea.
б Where can I buy a newspaper?
в That's all.
г Repeat that, please.
д Do you have any white wine?
е How much is it?

Анекдо́т *Anecdote*

This anecdote from the times of food shortages in the Soviet era is set in an empty butcher's shop opposite an empty fish shop. How would you say the punchline in English?

Ба́бушка	У вас есть мя́со?
Продаве́ц	Нет.
Ба́бушка	У вас есть колбаса́?
Продаве́ц	Нет.
Ба́бушка	У вас есть соси́ски?
Продаве́ц	Нет.
Ба́бушка	У вас есть ры́ба?
Продаве́ц	Нет. Ры́бы нет в магази́не напро́тив.

▶ And finally, here is a tongue twister for you to learn by heart to practise the letters **с** and **ш**. It means *Sasha walked along the road and sucked a biscuit* (lit. *walked Sasha along road and sucked biscuit*).

Шла Са́ша по шоссе́ и соса́ла су́шку.

15

В чём дело?

what's the matter?

In this unit you will learn
- how to book a hotel room
- how to complain
- how to sort out problems

Before you start, revise

- vocabulary and structures from Unit 7
- у вас есть . .? Unit 10, page 104

When learning new vocabulary, decide which words it will be most useful to learn and which you only need to recognize. Test yourself by covering up the English words first and then the Russian words, and see how many you can remember.

ℹ В гости́нице *At the hotel*

Like hotels the world over, you will find that Russian hotels vary, but many will provide these facilities: a restaurant **рестора́н**, bar **бар**, café **кафе́**, shops **магази́ны**, post office **по́чта**, service desk **бюро́ обслу́живания**, bureau de change **обме́н валю́ты**, lost property office **бюро́ нахо́док**, cloakroom **гардеро́б**, lifts **ли́фты** and hairdresser's **парикма́херская**.

ОТ СЕБЯ/К СЕБЕ *PUSH/PULL*

От себя́ and **к себе́** mean literally *away from yourself* and *towards yourself*. This is what you will see on doors in public buildings to tell you when to push and when to pull.

Заказа́ть но́мер *Booking a room*

У вас есть свобо́дный но́мер/ свобо́дная ко́мната?	*Do you have a free room?*
но́мер на одного́ с ва́нной	*a room for one with a bath*
но́мер на двои́х с ду́шем	*a room for two with a shower*
но́мер на день	*a room for a day*
но́мер на 2,3,4 дня	*a room for 2, 3, 4 days*
но́мер на 5,6 дней	*a room for 5, 6 days*
но́мер на неде́лю	*a room for a week*
день, неде́ля, ме́сяц, год	*day, week, month, year*
Ско́лько сто́ит но́мер в день?	*How much is a room per day?*
Мо́жно заказа́ть но́мер?	*Could I book a room?*
но́мер на одного́ на четы́рнадцатое ма́я	*a room for one for 14 May*
к сожале́нию	*unfortunately*
к сча́стью	*fortunately*
за́втрак начина́ется/конча́ется в . . .	*breakfast starts/finishes at . . .*
Когда́ на́до заплати́ть?	*When do I have to pay?*
вчера́, сего́дня, за́втра	*yesterday, today, tomorrow*
счёт	*the bill*
пра́вильно/непра́вильно	*that's right/that's not right*

▶ Диало́г 1 У вас есть свобо́дный но́мер?

Do you have a free room?

Steve has just arrived at a hotel without having made a reservation.
Listen to or read the dialogue. When you have got the gist of the
conversation, look at the questions below and answer them.

Стив	У вас есть свобо́дный но́мер на сего́дня?
Администра́тор	Да, есть. Како́й но́мер вы хоти́те?
Стив	Но́мер на одного́ с ва́нной, пожа́луйста.
Администра́тор	К сожале́нию, у нас то́лько большо́й но́мер на двои́х с ду́шем.
Стив	Скажи́те, пожа́луйста, ско́лько сто́ит но́мер на двои́х?
Администра́тор	Сто два́дцать до́лларов в день.
Стив	Э́то до́рого. Когда́ на́до заплати́ть?
Администра́тор	За́втра.
Стив	В кото́ром часу́ начина́ется за́втрак?
Администра́тор	В семь часо́в. И конча́ется в де́вять часо́в.
Стив	Мо́жно обе́дать в гости́нице?
Администра́тор	Коне́чно, мо́жно. В гости́нице о́чень хоро́ший рестора́н. Вот ваш ключ. Ваш но́мер – 104.
Стив	Спаси́бо. А как попа́сть в но́мер 104? У меня́ чемода́н и больша́я су́мка.
Администра́тор	Лифт пря́мо и напра́во.

Exercise 1

a What sort of room does Steve want? **б** What is he offered? **в** How
much does it cost per day? **г** When does he have to pay? **д** What is the
earliest he may have breakfast? And the latest? **e** Can he have dinner
in the hotel? **ж** What luggage does he have? **з** Where is the lift?

Exercise 2

Steve decides to go out and explore the town, but first he must give
his key to the woman on duty on his landing.

Дежу́рная	Молодо́й челове́к, где ваш ключ?
Стив	Вот он. Скажи́те, в кото́ром часу́ но́чью закрыва́ется вход?
Дежу́рная	В по́лночь.
Стив	Спаси́бо. А где здесь бар?
Дежу́рная	Внизу́. Нале́во.

a At what time does the entrance to the hotel close? **б** Where is the
bar?

▶ Exercise 3

Listen to these customers. What sort of rooms do they want, and for how long?

a

б

в

▶ Exercise 4

Complete your part of this dialogue.

a	**You**	*Do you have a free room?*
	Администра́тор	Да. Како́й но́мер вы хоти́те?
b	**You**	*A double room with a bath, please.*
	Администра́тор	Одну́ мину́точку. Да, у нас есть но́мер на двои́х с ва́нной. Сто́ит сто до́лларов в день.
c	**You**	*Good. What time is dinner?*
	Администра́тор	Обе́д начина́ется в шесть часо́в.
d	**You**	*Is there a lift here? I have a big suitcase.*
	Администра́тор	Да, лифт пря́мо, ви́дите?
e	**You**	*Yes, I see.*
	Администра́тор	Вот ваш ключ. Ваш но́мер – 34.
f	**You**	*Thank you. Room number 34. Is that right?*
	Администра́тор	Да. пра́вильно. Но́мер 34.
g	**You**	*Thank you very much. Goodbye.*

В но́мере *In the hotel room*

окно́	window	ва́нная	bathroom
дверь (f)	door	туале́т	toilet
стол	table	душ	shower
стул	chair	ва́нна	bath
кре́сло	armchair	кран	tap
шкаф	cupbord	одея́ло	blanket
крова́ть (f)	bed	поду́шка	pillow
ла́мпа	lamp	полоте́нце	towel
телефо́н	telephone	мы́ло	soap
телеви́зор	television	шампу́нь (m)	shampoo
часы́	clock	зе́ркало	mirror

To help you learn this vocabulary you could make labels for your furniture at home.

Exercise 5

The vocabulary list above is a checklist of things which should be in each hotel room. Look at the pictures and make a list in Russian (written or spoken) of those things which Simon has in his room. Or you could underline the items in the vocabulary list. Make another list of what is missing in his room.

В номере холодно *It's cold in my room*			
жáрко	*it's hot*	**тихо**	*it's quiet*
теплó	*it's warm*	**грязно**	*it's dirty*
хóлодно	*it's cold*	**мне хóлодно**	*I'm cold*
шýмно	*it's noisy*	**мне плóхо**	*I feel bad*

Exercise 6

Choose appropriate words from the list above to describe what it is like in these places.

а	На пля́же	_____	и _____.
б	В Антáрктике	_____	и _____.
в	На концéрте	_____	и _____.
г	В больни́це	_____	и _____.
д	В бассéйне	_____	и _____.

Чем я могу́ вам помо́чь? *How may I help you?*

Мо́жно ещё одея́ло, пожа́луйста	Could I have another blanket, please?
Я хочу́ заказа́ть биле́т в теа́тр на за́втра	I want to book a theatre ticket for tomorrow
Я хочу́ заказа́ть такси́ на за́втра на 10 часо́в	I want to book a taxi for tomorrow at ten
Куда́ вы пое́дете?	Where are you going?
Я хочу́ позвони́ть домо́й в Австра́лию	I want to call home to Australia
код в Австра́лию	the code for Australia
Мо́жно принести́ за́втрак в но́мер?	Could you bring breakfast to my room?

▶ Диало́г 2 Алло́! *Hello!*

*Your friend Katya is a hotel administrator. You go to work with her one day, and overhear the following conversations at her desk and while she is on the phone. To say hello on the phone you say **Алло́!***

Клайв	Извини́те, я хочу́ позвони́ть домо́й в Австра́лию. Мо́жно?
Ка́тя	Мо́жно. Код в Австра́лию 61.
Анна	Алло́, э́то рестора́н?
Ка́тя	Нет, э́то администра́тор.
Анна	Мо́жно принести́ за́втрак в но́мер, пожа́луйста? Мне пло́хо.
Ка́тя	Мо́жно. Что вы хоти́те?
Анна	Чай с лимо́ном и фру́кты, пожа́луйста.
Тре́вор	Алло́, администра́тор?
Ка́тя	Да, слу́шаю.
Тре́вор	Я хочу́ заказа́ть такси́ на за́втра на 10 часо́в.
Ка́тя	Куда́ вы пое́дете?
Тре́вор	На вокза́л.
Ка́тя	У вас есть бага́ж?
Тре́вор	Да, чемода́н.

Exercise 7

а Where does Clive want to phone, and what code does he need?
б What does Anna want the restaurant to send to her room, and why?
в Where does Trevor want to go, and when?

To practise your writing, you could pretend to be the administrator and jot down notes in English or Russian to remind you what your customers wanted.

Проблéмы! *Problems!*

Всё хорошó?	*Is everything all right?*
В чём дéло?	*What's the matter?*
кáжется, мы потеря́ли ключ	*It seems we have lost the key*
горя́чая/холóдная водá не идёт	*The hot/cold water is not running*
окнó выхóдит на плóщадь	*The window looks out onto the square*
окнó не открывáется/закрывáется	*The window won't open/shut*
телефóн не рабóтает	*The telephone doesn't work*
Как это мóжет быть?	*How can that be?*
У меня́ пропáл бумáжник/ фотоаппарáт/кошелёк (m)	*I have lost my wallet/camera/ purse*
У меня́ пропáла су́мка (f)	*I have lost my bag*
У меня́ пропáло пальтó (n)	*I have lost my coat*
У меня́ пропáли дéньги/ докумéнты (pl)	*I have lost my money/documents*
я, ты, он не/довóлен (m)	*I am, you are, he is un/happy*
я, ты, онá не/довóльна (f)	*I am, you are, she is un/happy*
мы, вы, онú не/довóльны (pl)	*We, you, they are un/happy*
Спасúбо большóе	*Thank you very much*

▶ Диалóг 3 Извинúте *Excuse me*

Read these dialogues, imagining you are the administrator.

а

Эдна Извинúте, в нóмере жáрко.

Кáтя Окнó откры́то?

Эдна Нет, закры́то. Окнó выхóдит на плóщадь, и там óчень шу́мно.

б

Марк Извинúте, мне хóлодно. Мóжно ещё одея́ло, пожáлуйста?

Кáтя Мóжно. Какóй ваш нóмер?

Марк Нóмер 73. Там хóлодно, кран не закрывáется и телевúзор плóхо рабóтает.

в

Ванесса	Извините, кажется, мы потеряли ключ.
Катя	Какой ваш номер?
Ванесса	Шестнадцать.
Катя	Вот ваш ключ.
Ванесса	Здесь? У вас? Как это может быть? Спасибо большое.

г

Билл	Дайте, пожалуйста, счёт.
Катя	Вот счёт. Номер на двоих на неделю. Правильно?
Билл	Да, правильно.
Катя	Всё хорошо?
Билл	Да, здесь очень приятно. В номере тепло и тихо. Спасибо большое. Мы очень довольны.

д

Катя	В чём дело? Вы недовольны?
Гари	Мы очень недовольны. Горячая вода не идёт, телефон не работает и в номере грязно.

Exercise 8

Make brief notes in English of the conversations above.

Exercise 9

On the next page you will find a list of repair work for a hotel. What needs putting right in these rooms? Read the list out loud including the numbers, before summarizing the problems in English.

номер 9, телевизор не работает
номер 14, телефон плохо работает
номер 23, кран не закрывается
номер 31, холодно, окно не закрывается
номер 35, жарко, окно не открывается
номер 40, шумно
номер 52, грязно
номер 55, радио не работает

Exercise 10

You have been put in a room which is cold, dirty and noisy. The television doesn't work, the tap won't turn off and the window looks out onto the station. Bad luck! What will you say to the hotel administrator?

▶ Exercise 11

Listen to the recording, and describe what these four people have lost.

а   в

б   г

Exercise 12

Below is a page from a hotel brochure. What facilities are there in this hotel, on which floor are they and when are they open? Where telephone numbers are provided, read them out in Russian. Don't forget that the first floor in Russian is the ground floor in English!

Пе́рвый эта́ж	
Гардеро́б	(переры́в на обе́д* 14.00–15.00)
Бюро́ нахо́док	10.00–16.00
Рестора́н	8.00–23.00 тел. 229-02-31
Второ́й эта́ж	
Дире́ктор	тел. 229-569-28
Администра́тор	тел. 229-899-57
Бюро́ обслу́живания	8.00–22.00 тел. 229-08-46
Газе́тный кио́ск	8.00–16.00
Буфе́т	8.00–22.00
Тре́тий эта́ж	
По́чта	8.00–20.00 тел. 229-33-13
Парикма́херская	8.00–20.00 тел. 229-29-09
Бар	14.00–24.00
*lunch break	

And finally, remembering that the word **гости́ница** comes from **гость** *a guest*, here is a proverb – the equivalent of *there's no place like home* (lit. *Being a guest is good, but being at home is better*).

> **В гостя́х хорошо́, а до́ма лу́чше**

16

приятного
аппетита!
bon appétit! enjoy your meal!

In this unit you will learn
- how to read a menu and order a meal
- how to buy a snack, ice creams or drinks
- what to say if you are eating at a friend's home

Before you start, revise

- likes and dislikes, page 87
- prices, pages 58–9
- Unit 6, dialogue 3, page 57

ℹ️ Хочу́ есть и пить *I'm hungry and thirsty*

As a visitor to Russia, you will find a variety of options if you want to eat out, varying from high-class restaurants to bars and kiosks selling food and drinks on the street. Many museums, train stations and department stores may have a stand-up snackbar **буфе́т**. If you are opting for a full meal you will start with appetizers **заку́ски**, followed by a soup, or first course **пе́рвое блю́до**, which may be beetroot soup **борщ** or cabbage soup **щи**. Then will come a main, or second, course **второ́е блю́до**, usually based on meat or fish with side dishes **гарни́р**, and finally dessert **сла́дкое**. Much Russian cuisine contains meat, but if you are a vegetarian then salads and dishes with mushrooms **грибы́** can usually be found, and are very good. If it is a special occasion, the meal may be accompanied by vodka **во́дка**, wine **вино́** and champagne **шампа́нское**.

The verbs 'to eat' *есть* and 'to drink' *пить*

есть (irregular)	*to eat*			**пить** (1)	*to drink*		
я ем	I eat	мы еди́м	we eat	я пью	I drink	мы пьём	we drink
ты ешь	you eat	вы еди́те	you eat	ты пьёшь	you drink	вы пьёте	you drink
он ест	he eats	они́ едя́т	they eat	он пьёт	he drinks	они́ пьют	they drink

В рестора́не *At the restaurant*

Ключевы́е слова́

Я о́чень хочу́ есть/пить!	I'm really hungry/thirsty
Мы хоти́м стол на пять/шесть челове́к	We want a table for five/six people
Официа́нт/ка, иди́те сюда́, пожа́луйста	Waiter/waitress, come here please
Да́йте, пожа́луйста, меню́	Please give me/us the menu
Слу́шаю вас	Can I help you? (I'm listening)
Что вы хоти́те заказа́ть?	What do you want to order?
Что вы хоти́те есть/пить	What do you want to eat/drink?
Что вам?	What would you like?
Что вы рекоменду́ете?	What would you recommend?
На заку́ску, на пе́рвое, на второ́е, на сла́дкое	For a starter, for 1st/2nd course, for dessert
Я хочу́ заказа́ть шашлы́к	I want to order kebab (shashlik)

Да́йте мне, пожа́луйста, хлеб с колбасо́й	Please give me bread with salami sausage
Вот вам бутербро́д	Here's your sandwich
чай с лимо́ном, с са́харом, с молоко́м	tea with lemon, sugar, milk
чай без лимо́на, без са́хара, без молока́	tea without lemon, sugar, milk
Прия́тного аппети́та! (Priyatnuva appiteeta!)	Bon appétit!
Да́йте, пожа́луйста, счёт	Please give me the bill
Ско́лько с меня́?	How much do I owe?
С вас ...	You owe ...

Bear in mind that any prices quoted in this book may be out of date.

▶ Диало́г 1 В кафе́ In the café

Henry visits a small café for a snack.

Хе́нри Официа́нтка! Да́йте, пожа́луйста, меню́.

Официа́нтка Здра́вствуйте. Вот меню́. Слу́шаю вас. Что вы хоти́те?

Хе́нри Чай, пожа́луйста.

Официа́нтка С лимо́ном?

Хе́нри Да, с лимо́ном и с сахаро́м.

Официа́нтка Э́то всё?

Хе́нри Нет. У вас есть бутербро́ды?

Официа́нтка Есть.

Хе́нри Да́йте, пожа́луйста, хлеб с колбасо́й.

Официа́нтка Вот вам чай с лимо́ном и с са́харом, и хлеб с колбасо́й.

Хе́нри Ско́лько с меня́?

Официа́нтка С вас девяно́сто рубле́й.

Exercise 1

Listen to the dialogue above. **a** How does Henry like his tea? **б** What does he want to eat?

▶ Exercise 2

Now complete your part of a dialogue in the café.

a **You** *You would like to see the menu.*

   Официа́нт Вот вам меню́. Что вы хоти́те?

б **You** *You ask for coffee and ice cream.*

   Официа́нт Ко́фе без молока́?

в	**You**	*No, you want your coffee with milk and sugar.*
	Официа́нт	Вы хоти́те шокола́дное моро́женое или вани́льное?
г	**You**	*You don't understand. Ask the waiter to repeat it.*
	Официа́нт	Что хоти́те? Шокола́дное моро́женое и́ли вани́льное?
д	**You**	*You understand now. Ask for vanilla ice cream.*
	Официа́нт	Вот вам ко́фе и вани́льное моро́женое. Прия́тного аппети́та!
е	**You**	*Thank the waiter. Ask him how much it all costs.*
	Официа́нт	С вас сто со́рок рубле́й.

Below is a dinner menu from the Hotel Ukraine. Study the headings, and see how many dishes you can work out. Find those which you don't know from the vocabulary list overleaf and learn them, testing yourself by covering up first the English words and then the Russian. You could then see how many dishes you can remember from each category.

Гости́ница «Украи́на»

Меню́

Заку́ски

Сала́т моско́вский
Грибы́ в смета́не
Икра́ чёрная
Икра́ кра́сная
Сыр голла́ндский

Пе́рвые Блю́да

Щи
Борщ украи́нский
Суп с гриба́ми

Вторы́е блю́да

Шашлы́к
Беф-стро́ганов
Ку́рица

Гарни́р

Рис
Грибы́

Сла́дкие блю́да

Компо́т
Шокола́дное моро́женое
Фру́кты
Торт Наполео́н

Напи́тки

Кра́сное вино́
Бе́лое вино́
Ко́фе
Чай инди́йский
Чай с лимо́ном
Тома́тный сок
Газиро́ванная вода́
Минера́льная вода́
Во́дка
Конья́к

грибы́	mushrooms	ку́рица	chicken
смета́на	sour cream	рис	rice
икра́	caviar	компо́т	stewed fruit
сыр	cheese	торт	cake
щи	cabbage soup	напи́тки	drinks
борщ	beetroot soup	сок	juice
шашлы́к	kebab	газиро́ванная вода́	sparkling water

Using the menu on page 163 as a guide, write out a meal which you would like to order, or underline the dishes which you would select. Now make up a conversation with a waiter, ordering what you have chosen. The waiter begins: **Слу́шаю вас. Что вы хоти́те заказа́ть?**

Exercise 3

In a hotel you see a notice telling you at what time and on which floor you may get your meals. A Russian standing next to you is trying to read the notice as well, but he has just broken his spectacles. Explain the details to him.

На пе́рвом этаже́ рабо́тает рестора́н.

За́втрак	– с 8.00 до 10.00
Обе́д	– с 13.00 до 15.00
У́жин	– с 18.00 до 20.00

На второ́м этаже́ рабо́тает гриль-ба́р. Здесь мо́жно заказа́ть ко́фе и бутербро́ды.

За столо́м *At the table*

стол	table	хлеб	bread
стул	chair	ма́сло	butter
блю́до	dish	нож	knife
таре́лка	plate	ви́лка	fork
ча́шка	cup	ло́жка	spoon
стака́н	glass	соль *(f)*	salt
рю́мка	wine glass	пе́рец	pepper
салфе́тка	serviette		

▶ Диало́г 2 В рестора́не *In the restaurant*

Victoria is ordering a meal in a restaurant. Read the dialogue before answering the questions below.

Виктория	Молодой человек! Я хочу заказать, пожалуйста.
Официант	Слушаю вас.
Виктория	На закуски у вас есть салат московский?
Официант	Извините, нет.
Виктория	Жаль. Что вы рекомендуете?
Официант	Я рекомендую грибы в сметане.
Виктория	Хорошо, на закуски – грибы в сметане. На первое, у вас есть борщ?
Официант	Нет, сегодня у нас есть только щи.
Виктория	Так, на первое – щи, на второе – шашлык с рисом, и на сладкое – фрукты.
Официант	Понятно, на закуски – грибы в сметане, на первое – щи, на второе – шашлык с рисом, и на сладкое – фрукты. А что вы хотите пить?
Виктория	У вас есть вино?
Официант	Да, какое вино вы хотите?
Виктория	Дайте белое вино, и чай, пожалуйста.
Официант	Чай с сахаром?
Виктория	Нет, чай с лимоном без сахара.
Официант	Это всё?
Виктория	Да, это всё, спасибо. Нет! Вот идёт мой брат! Дайте, пожалуйста, ещё рюмку и тарелку. Здравствуй, Николай. Что ты хочешь есть и пить?

Exercise 4

a What two things are not available today?

б What does Victoria order, and how does she like her tea?

в She sees someone come into the restaurant. Who is it, and what does Victoria ask for on his behalf?

Exercise 5

Did you notice how Victoria asked for *another* ещё glass and plate? – **Дайте, пожалуйста, ещё рюмку и тарелку.** Don't forget to change -а to -у and -я to -ю if you are asking for a feminine object. How would you ask for an extra cup, spoon, knife and chair?

▶ Exercise 6

Now imagine you are a bilingual waiter in the Кафе «Тбилиси» taking down a Russian customer's order. Listen to the recording and jot down in English or Russian what the customer wants.

Exercise 7

Look at this picture. Make sure that you know how to say everything on the table in Russian. Then cover the picture and try to remember everything. You could try writing a list in Russian.

Exercise 8

How would you ask for: Moscow salad, mushroom soup, beef stroganoff, rice, chocolate ice cream, white wine and coffee with milk? Now ask for the bill.

▶ Exercise 9

See if you can unscramble the dialogue below. It is set in a **буфе́т**. The first sentence is in bold type. Listen to the recording to check your answer.

а Да́йте, пожа́луйста, хлеб, сыр и ко́фе.
б Что у вас есть сего́дня?
в С вас пятдеся́т рубле́й.
г Да, да́йте чай без са́хара.
д Извини́те, у нас нет ко́фе. Вы хоти́те чай?
е Спаси́бо. Ско́лько с меня́?
ж **Слу́шаю вас.**
з У нас сего́дня хлеб, сыр, колбаса́, шокола́д и фру́кты.
и Вот вам хлеб, сыр и чай.

Exercise 10

Imagine that you are running a restaurant in Russia. Fill out the menu below, putting at least two items in each column, and don't forget the date at the top.

МЕНЮ

_____ 200____ го́да

Заку́ски	Пе́рвое блю́до	Второ́е блю́до	Сла́дкое	Напи́тки

Exercise 11

Ка́ша is any sort of porridge dish cooked with grains and liquid. There is a Russian saying: **Щи да ка́ша – пи́ща на́ша** *Cabbage soup and porridge are our food.* What ingredients do you need to make a milky rice pudding? See if you can read them out loud from the recipe below, including the numerals.

Каша рисовая молочная
рис   100 грамм
масло   25 грамм
сахар   20 грамм
соль   5 грамм
молоко   260 миллилитров
вода   200 миллилитров

У друзей *With friends at their home*

You can now cope with anything which is likely to occur in a restaurant, but what about visiting friends at their home? Here are some phrases which may help.

Входите, раздевайтесь!	*Come in, take your coat off!*
розы	*roses*
нормально	*fine, OK*
Угощайтесь!	*Help yourself!*
вкусно	*It's tasty*
За ваше здоровье!	*Cheers! Your health!*
Берите ещё ...	*Take some more ...*
Спасибо большое за всё	*Thanks very much for everything*
Уже поздно	*It's late already*
Пора идти	*It's time to go*
Спокойной ночи	*Good night*
До завтра	*Until tomorrow*

Диалог 3 В квартире *In the flat*

▶ Exercise 12

You have been invited to Yulia and Volodya's for supper. Read the dialogue, and say: **а** what you take as a gift, **б** how Volodya is feeling, **в** what is for starters, **г** whether you like it, **д** what you have to drink and **е** why you have to leave.

Юлия   Добрый вечер. Входите, раздевайтесь!

Вы   Добрый вечер. Вот вам маленький подарок – шампанское и цветы.

Юлия   Спасибо большое. Я так люблю розы. Вот идёт Володя.

Вы   Здравствуйте, Володя. Как дела?

Володя   Нормально, спасибо. Всё хорошо. Садитесь, пожалуйста.

Вы   Спасибо. Ой, какие прекрасные закуски. Я очень люблю грибы в сметане и икру.

Юлия   Вот вам тарелка. Угощайтесь!

Вы   Мм! Всё очень вкусно, Юлия.

Володя   И вот вам водка. За ваше здоровье!

Вы   За ваше здоровье!

Юлия   Берите ещё закуски.

Вы   Спасибо большое.

Later that evening, in the entrance hall.

Вы   Уже́ по́здно. Пора́ идти́.
Воло́дя Споко́йной но́чи. До за́втра.
Вы   Спаси́бо за всё. Споко́йной но́чи.

Exercise 13

How would you say:

а I really love champagne.
б Cheers.
в What lovely wine glasses!
г How are you?

▶ Анекдо́т *Anecdote*

To finish off the unit, here is an anecdote set in a bar. Why does the waiter tell the customer it is now safe to drink beer?

Официа́нт Что вам? Вы хоти́те пи́во?
Бори́с   Нет, я на велосипе́де. Да́йте, пожа́луйста, сок.

Че́рез мину́ту ...

Официа́нт Вы мо́жете сейча́с пить пи́во. Ваш велосипе́д кто́-то укра́л.

велосипе́д	*bicycle*
кто́-то укра́л	*someone has stolen*

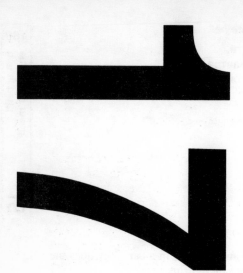

7

На по́чте
at the post office

In this unit you will learn
- how to send a letter,
  postcard, parcel, telegram
- how to make a phone call

Before you start, revise

- numerals, page 224
- telling the time, page 76
- filling in forms, Unit 15

ℹ️ Телефóнная и áдресная кнúга
Telephone directory

Until the 1990s, there was no system of public telephone directories in Russia. If you wanted to find a number, you had to ask at an enquiry office **спрáвочное бюрó**, giving at least the name, patronymic, surname and address of the person you wished to contact. This is why many Russians still carry round a little hand-written book with every phone number they are ever likely to need. However, there are now complete directories available, giving private numbers as well as administrative and commercial numbers. They also offer tourist information, and many have foreign language sections.

On the first page of most directories you will find the emergency phone numbers you might need:

01 **пожáр** fire
02 **милúция** police
03 **скóрая медицúнская пóмощь** ambulance
04 **газ** gas

Learning the Russian alphabet in the correct order will save a lot of time when using a directory. Remember too that Russian directories will boast that they provide everything you need to know not from A to Z, but from **А** to **Я** «**от А до Я**»,

Я хочý позвонúть домóй *I want to call home*

Many Russians use the phone a lot, making long, late calls from the comfort of an armchair. If you want to use the phone, you have several choices. The easiest and cheapest way to make a call is by private telephone, but if this is not possible, you will need to use a pay phone **телефóн-автомáт** or **таксофóн** for local calls, using a pre-payment card or credit card. If the number you want to call is abroad, you may be able to call direct from your hotel or book a call through hotel reception. A less expensive option is to book a call at the telephone section of a main post office **пóчта**, or at the special telephone and telegraph offices **телефóн – телегрáф**. Don't forget the time difference with the country you are calling. If you choose the post office, you book a call at the counter for a certain number of minutes at a certain time and wait for the staff to call out your booth number over the public address system. Then you dash to the right booth (practise your numerals beforehand) and start your call, which is counted from the moment of the announcement. The whole thing can be a little flustering! Some major post offices offer a bookable Internet service available in little computer booths, and they also sell pre-payment cards for home Internet connection on behalf of Internet providers **Интернéт провáйдеры**.

По телефóну *On the phone*

Я хочý позвони́ть в А́нглию/ в Австрáлию	*I want to call England/ Australia*
Мóжно заказáть разговóр на зáвтра на 3 минýты?	*Can I book a 3-minute call for tomorrow?*
Какóй нóмер телефóна?	*What's the phone number?*
Какóй код?	*What's the code?*
Скóлько минýт вы хоти́те заказáть?	*How many minutes do you want to book?*
2, 3, 4 минýты, 5, 6, 7, 8, 9, 10, минýт	*2, 3, 4 minutes, 5–10 minutes*
Когдá вы хоти́те говори́ть?	*When do you want to talk?*
разговóр	*conversation*
чек	*bill, chit*

▶ Диалóг 1 Мóжно заказáть разговóр? *May I book a call?*

Wendy has a call to make, so she goes to the post office to make a booking.

Уэ́нди	Извини́те, пожáлуйста. Я хочý позвони́ть в А́нглию.
Дéвушка	Да. Какóй нóмер телефóна?
Уэ́нди	987–25–55.
Дéвушка	И какóй код?
Уэ́нди	0115.
Дéвушка	Скóлько минýт вы хоти́те заказáть?
Уэ́нди	Четы́ре минýты, пожáлуйста.
Дéвушка	Когдá вы хоти́те говори́ть?
Уэ́нди	Мóжно заказáть разговóр на сегóдня на восемнáдцать часóв?
Дéвушка	Нет, ужé пóздно на сегóдня.
Уэ́нди	Мóжно на зáвтра, ýтром?
Дéвушка	Однý минýточку ... Да, мóжно заказáть разговóр на зáвтра на дéвять часóв. Вот вам чек. Всё поня́тно?
Уэ́нди	Да, поня́тно.

Exercise 1

Choose the correct phrase to complete each sentence.

а Уэнди хочет позвонить

    i в Москву.
    ii в больницу.
    iii в Англию.

б Уэнди хочет заказать разговор

    i на восемнадцать минут.
    ii на сегодня на восемнадцать часов.
    iii поздно вечером.

в Уэнди не может заказать разговор на сегодня потому, что

    i почта закрыта.
    ii девушка не понимает.
    iii уже поздно.

Exercise 2

You have to fill in a form at the post office to request a call to another city. You guess that the title of the form **Заявка на междугородный разговор** probably means *Request for intercity conversation.* **Между** means *between*, so **междугородный** means *intercity* and **международный** means *international* (between nations). Now you have to decide where to put the rest of the details which you assume are being asked for.

Заявка на междугородный разговор

а	С городом	**i**	*How many minutes*
б	Телефон или адрес	**ii**	*Which city*
в	Дата и время вызова	**iii**	*Telephone number and address*
г	Количество минут	**iv**	*Signature*
д	Подпись	**v**	*Date and time of call*

▶ Exercise 3

Listen to the recording and jot down details of where and when people are calling.

To which city   Phone number   At what time   For how many minutes

а
б
в

Exercise 4

An independent telecommunications company is advertising its products and services. What is it offering to its customers? Cover up the right-hand column while you try to work it out.

а	24 часá международная телефóнная связь	**i**	*E-mail*
б	Международные бизнес-лúнии	**ii**	*fax, telex*
в	Кáрточные таксофóны	**iii**	*mobile phones*
г	Электрóнная пóчта	**iv**	*tele-conferences*
д	Телеконферéнции	**v**	*24-hour international phone link*
е	Мобúльные телефóны	**vi**	*telephone modems*
ж	Телефóнные мóдемы	**vii**	*five-year guarantee*
з	Факс, тéлекс	**viii**	*web design*
и	Гарáнтия – 5 лет	**ix**	*international business lines*
к	Веб дизáйн	**x**	*public card phones*

ℹ️ На пóчте *At the post office*

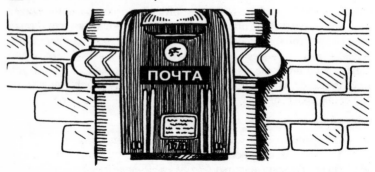

If you want to send something by post **по пóчте** you will need to visit the post office again, unless you already have the stamps and can use a letter box **почтóвый ящик**. The post office is usually open from Monday to Saturday from 9.00 till 21.00 and on Sunday from 10.00 till 20.00. If you only need a stamp **мáрка** then it may be quicker to buy it from your hotel. At the post office, as well as buying stamps, you may buy an envelope **конвéрт**, and send parcels **посылки** and telegrams. Some post offices now also deal with faxes, as do telephone and telegraph offices and hotels. To send a parcel, take the contents only to the post office, where they will be inspected, weighed and wrapped for you. There is usually a long list on the wall of items which may not be sent by post, such as liquids and perishable goods.

письмо	letter
открытка	postcard
посылка	parcel
международная телеграмма	international telegram
конверт	envelope
марка	stamp
авиаписьмо	airmail letter
почтовый ящик	letter box
Что надо делать?	What do I need to do?
Надо заполнить бланк	You need to fill in a form
Где можно купить марки, конверты, открытки?	Where can I buy stamps, envelopes, postcards?
Сколько стоит послать письмо в Великобританию?	How much is it to send a letter to the UK?
Сколько стоит марка на письмо в Германию?	How much is a stamp for a letter to Germany?
Три марки по 500 (пятьсот) рублей	three stamps at 500 roubles each
Я хочу послать посылку в Англию	I want to send a parcel to England
Напишите адрес вот здесь	Write the address right here
Куда, кому, адрес отправителя, вес	Where to, to whom, address of sender, weight
Я хочу послать телеграмму в Англию	I want send a telegram to England
Напишите здесь текст	Write the text here
15 рублей за слово	15 roubles per word

▶ Диалог 2 Я хочу послать письмо в Великобританию *I want to send a letter to Great Britain*

Dan has a lot of things to do at the post office. He goes to a small branch so that everything can be done at one counter, instead of queueing at different windows in the main post office.

Дэн　Извините, девушка, где можно купить марки?

Девушка　Здесь у меня можно всё купить: марки, конверты, открытки. Какие марки вы хотите?

Дэн　Я хочу послать это письмо в Великобританию. Сколько стоит марка на письмо?

Девушка　Шестнадцать рублей. Вот четыре марки по четыре рубля.

Дэн　Спасибо. И я хочу послать телеграмму домой. Сколько стоит?

Девушка　Пятнадцать рублей за слово.

Дэн　Что надо делать?

Девушка　Надо заполнить бланк. Напишите здесь текст.

Дэн　Спасибо. И можно тоже послать эти книги и игрушки в Англию?

Дéвушка	Конéчно мóжно. Нáдо запóлнить бланк. Напишúте áдрес вот здесь.
Дэн	Áдрес в Великобритáнии?
Дéвушка	Да, прáвильно. И напишúте ваш áдрес в Москвé здесь.
Дэн	Понятно. Спасúбо.
Дéвушка	Это всё?
Дэн	Да, всё. Спасúбо вам большóе. До свидáния.

Exercise 5

a What does the girl sell at her counter? **б** What stamps does Dan buy, and what for? **в** What does he have to do to send a telegram? **г** What does he want to send home in a parcel?

Exercise 6

Without looking at the dialogue above, can you remember how to say the following phrases in Russian?

a Three stamps at ten roubles. **б** What do I need to do? **в** Of course you can. **г** That's right. **д** Thanks very much.

And can you fill in these blanks? Write or say your answers.

e Где _____ купúть мáрки?

ж Какúе мáрки вы _____?

з Нáдо _____ бланк.

и _____ всё? Да, всё.

к До _____.

Exercise 7

Choose a suitable question word to fill in the blanks. Question words which you already know are кто? что? где? когдá? кудá? как? почемý? скóлько?

a _____ попáсть на пóчту?

б _____ здесь почтóвый ящик?

в _____ мне пойтú?

г _____ вы по профéссии?

д _____ сейчáс врéмени?

e _____ вас зовýт?

ж _____ у вас есть?

з _____ открывáется пóчта?

Exercise 8

You have just arrived in Moscow and are staying in Room 331 at the hotel Россия on улица Варварка. You can't find Andrei Ivanov's phone number, so you decide to send him a telegram to tell him where you are. His address is Flat 9, Block 26 on Проспект Мира. (Don't forget that Russian addresses begin with the name of the city and work down to the number of the flat and the person's name.) Fill in this form at the post office.

Телеграмма
Куда, кому _____
_____
Текст _____
_____
_____
_____
Фамилия и адрес отправителя _____
_____
_____

Exercise 9

Match up the words which go together.

сын   папа   стол   девушка
соль   дочь   перец
вокзал   яблоки   стул
        поезд
мама   груши   пьеса
театр   молодой человек

Exercise 10

Your friend has received an unexpected letter from Russia, but is unable to read the name and address on the envelope in order to reply. Look at the envelope and find out who has sent it.

Куда *England*
Bristol
Green Lane, 39,

Кому *Macintosh, H.*

Индекс предприятия связи	и адрес отправителя
194358	*Россия*

Санкт - Петербург
Проспект Энгельса
121 - 2 - 69
Кузнецова, Т. И.

Пишите индекс предприятия связи места назначения

▶ Анекдо́т *Anecdote*

Finally, here is an anecdote set in a doctor's office in a busy hospital. The phone rings. It's an enquiry about a patient.

– До́ктор, скажи́те, как пожива́ет Ива́н Ива́нович Ивано́в?
– Хорошо́.
– А когда́ он пойдёт домо́й?
– Е́сли всё пойдёт хорошо́, он пойдёт домо́й за́втра.
– О́чень интере́сно. Спаси́бо.
– Пожа́луйста. А кто говори́т?
– Ива́н Ива́нович Ивано́в.

18

какая сегодня погода?

what's the weather like today?

In this unit you will learn
- how to talk about the weather
- how to talk about your holidays
- how to use a tourist brochure
- how to book an excursion

Before you start, revise

- free time in Unit 9, page 93
- finding your way around town in Unit 5, page 47

ℹ Зи́мний спорт *Winter sports*

From west to east, Russia stretches around 10,000 kilometres, taking in 11 time zones, and its climatic zones from north to south include arctic tundra, forest, steppe and southern deserts, so no generalizations may be made about the climate or weather! This means that whatever you learn to say about the weather will be useful somewhere at some time! However, it would be true to say that in those parts of Russia where the climate permits, many Russians love to participate in winter sports. From a young age they learn to ski **ката́ться на лы́жах**, to skate **ката́ться на конька́х** and to sledge **ката́ться на саня́х**.

О́тпуск *Holidays*

In the past it was difficult for Russians to visit non-Communist countries, but now travel agents can offer a holiday or time-share **тайм-шер** anywhere in the world for those who can afford them. Popular destinations include America **Аме́рика**, the Bahamas **Бага́мы**, Cyprus **Кипр**, Egypt **Еги́пет**, Greece **Гре́ция**, Jamaica **Яма́йка**, Korea **Коре́я**, Malta **Ма́льта**, Tenerife **Тенери́ф**, Thailand **Таила́нд**, Tunisia **Туни́с** and Turkey **Ту́рция**.

Below is a typical advert for a holiday. Read it and check anything you don't understand in the **Answers** section at the back of the book.

Мальта

Рейсы «Аэрофло́та»

Оте́ль *** : 2 -ме́стные номера́, бар, кафе́, дискоте́ки, те́ннис, бассе́йн, шоп-тур, казино́, экску́рсии и да́йвинг. Персона́л говори́т по-ру́сски.

Погóда *The weather*

Какáя сегóдня погóда?	What's the weather like today (si<u>vo</u>dnya)?
Сегóдня хóлодно	Today it's cold
прохлáдно	It's cool
теплó	It's warm
слúшком жáрко	It's too hot
дýшно	It's close
вéтрено	It's windy
тумáнно	It's foggy
пáсмурно	It's overcast
идёт дождь	It's raining
идёт снег	It's snowing
сóлнце свéтит	The sun is shining
морóз	It's frosty
температýра вóздуха	air temperature
температýра водь́	water temperature
плюс 5 грáдусов теплá	+ 5 degrees of warmth (5 above)
мúнус одúн грáдус морóза	– 1 degree of frost (1 below)
вéтер ю́го-зáпадный	The wind is south-westerly
Какóй прогнóз погóды на зáвтра?	What is the weather forecast for tomorrow?
Зáвтра бýдет хóлодно, теплó	Tomorrow it will be cold, warm
Зáвтра бýдет дождь, снег	Tomorrow there will be rain, snow
веснóй, лéтом, óсенью, зимóй	in spring, in summer, in autumn, in winter
веснá, лéто, óсень, зимá	spring, summer, autumn, winter
зúмний спорт	winter sport
Какóй твой любúмый сезóн?	Which is your favourite season?
Мой любúмый сезóн – веснá	My favourite season is spring
Что дéлать?	What is to be done?

▶ Диалóг 1 Сегóдня хóлодно *It's cold today*

Rosemary is spending her first winter in Russia and is determined to make the most of the snow. But her friend Maxim is not so keen.

Рóузмэри	Максúм, ты хóчешь сегóдня катáться на лы́жах в лесý?
Максúм	Нет, не óчень хочý. Сегóдня хóлодно.
Рóузмэри	Конéчно хóлодно! Зимá! Но сегóдня так прекрáсно. Морóз и сóлнце свéтит.
Максúм	Да, но по рáдио говоря́т, что температýра вóздуха сегóдня мúнус дéсять грáдусов. Слúшком хóлодно. Я хочý смотрéть телевúзор и читáть дóма, где теплó.

Róузмэри	Смотре́ть телеви́зор? Макси́м, что ты! Как э́то мо́жет быть? Ты совсе́м не лю́бишь зи́му?
Макси́м	Нет, я люблю́ ле́то, когда́ жа́рко. Мо́жно гуля́ть на пля́же и есть моро́женое.
Róузмэри	Поня́тно. Я то́же о́чень люблю́ ле́то. Но я так хочу́ сего́дня ката́ться на лы́жах. Жаль. Что де́лать?
Макси́м	Мо́жно позвони́ть А́ндрю. Он о́чень лю́бит зи́мний спорт.
Róузмэри	Пра́вильно. На́до позвони́ть А́ндрю. Како́й у него́ но́мер телефо́на?
Макси́м	Семьсо́т три́дцать де́вять, пятна́дцать, со́рок два.

Exercise 1

а What does Rosemary want to do? **б** What is the weather like? **в** What does Maxim want to do? **г** What is his favourite season and why? **д** What does Rosemary decide to do? **е** What is Andrew's phone number?

Exercise 2

Match up the captions with the pictures.

а	идёт дождь
б	тума́нно
в	идёт снег
г	ве́трено
д	со́лнце све́тит

▶ Exercise 3

Listen to the weather forecast and tick the features of the weather which you hear mentioned.

a	Rain	**e**	Temperature −7°
б	Snow	**ж**	Frost
в	Warm	**з**	Sun
г	Cold	**и**	Temperature −17°
д	Northerly wind		

Exercise 4

Look at this weather map for today and play the part of the weather forecaster on television. You could try writing down your script, and check it with the suggested script in the back of the book. Don't forget the points of the compass: *in the north* **на се́вере**, *in the south* **на ю́ге**, *in the west* **на за́паде**, *in the east* **на восто́ке**.

Что ты де́лаешь в свобо́дное вре́мя? *What do you do in your free time?*

де́лать [1]	*to do*
свобо́дное вре́мя	*free time*
лови́ть [2] ры́бу (я ловлю́, ты ло́вишь)	*to go fishing*

собира́ть [1] ма́рки, грибы́	to collect stamps, mushrooms
гото́вить [2] (я гото́влю, ты гото́вишь)	to cook
ката́ться на лы́жах, на конька́х, на саня́х	to ski, skate, sledge
ката́ться на велосипе́де, на ло́шади, на ло́дке	to cycle, ride a horse, go boating
отдыха́ть [1] за грани́цей, на берегу́ мо́ря	to holiday abroad, at the seaside
купа́ться в мо́ре	to swim in the sea
загора́ть [1] на пля́же	to sunbathe on the beach
гуля́ть [1] в лесу́	to walk in the woods
ходи́ть [2] в теа́тр, кино́, (я хожу́, ты хо́дишь)	to go to the theatre, cinema
ходи́ть [2] по магази́нам	to go shopping
игра́ть [1] в футбо́л, в ша́хматы	to play football, chess
игра́ть [1] на гита́ре	to play the guitar
рисова́ть [1] (я рису́ю, ты рису́ешь)	to draw
танцева́ть [1] (я танцу́ю, ты танцу́ешь)	to dance
акти́вный челове́к	active person
обы́чно	usually
ча́сто	often
с удово́льствием	with pleasure
идёт бале́т, о́пера, фильм, пье́са	There is a ballet, opera, film, play on
ты хо́чешь пойти́ в/на ..?	Do you want to go to ..?

▶ Диало́г 2 Каки́е у тебя́ хо́бби? What are your hobbies?

Хе́лен Каки́е у тебя́ хо́бби?

Юра Я о́чень акти́вный челове́к. Зимо́й я люблю́ игра́ть в хокке́й и ката́ться на лы́жах, а ле́том я ча́сто гуля́ю в дере́вне и игра́ю в те́ннис. Я то́же люблю́ купа́ться в мо́ре. О́сенью я собира́ю грибы́ в лесу́. А у тебя́ есть хо́бби?

Хе́лен Да, но я не о́чень акти́вный челове́к. Я люблю́ слу́шать ра́дио, игра́ть в ша́хматы, чита́ть кни́ги, смотре́ть фи́льмы и ходи́ть на конце́рты.

Юра В Ланка́стре есть теа́тр?

Хе́лен Коне́чно есть. Но я не о́чень ча́сто хожу́ в теа́тр в Ланка́стре, потому́, что до́рого сто́ит.

Юра Да, поня́тно. Здесь в Краснода́ре у нас хоро́шие теа́тры. Ты хо́чешь пойти́ в теа́тр за́втра ве́чером?

Хе́лен Да, с удово́льствием!

Exercise 5

From the dialogue above, find out where Helen and Yura are from and what their interests are.

Exercise 6

You are working at a sports complex in a resort on the shores of the Black Sea **Чёрное мо́ре**. You answer an enquiry about what is available for the active holidaymaker. You consult your list of symbols for help and begin: **Здесь мо́жно ...**

▶ Exercise 7

Below are three mini-dialogues. Read or listen to them and match them up with their titles: **(i)** At the kiosk **(ii)** An invitation to the theatre **(iii)** At the theatre.

а

Де́вушка	Ва́ши биле́ты, пожа́луйста.
Ва́ня	Одну́ мину́точку. Вот они́.
Де́вушка	Хоти́те програ́мму?
Ва́ня	Да. Да́йте, пожа́луйста, три програ́ммы.

б

Ла́ра	Скажи́те, пожа́луйста, когда́ идёт бале́т «Жизе́ль»?
Киоскёр	Восьмо́го, девя́того и деся́того апре́ля.

в

Га́ля	У меня́ есть биле́ты в Большо́й теа́тр. Вы свобо́дны?
Чарльс	Коне́чно. Как хорошо́! Биле́ты на сего́дня?

Га́ля	Да, на сего́дня на ве́чер.
Чарльс	Где мы встре́тимся?
Га́ля	У меня́ в кварти́ре в шесть часо́в.

Exercise 8

You are a very unco-operative person. Whatever Liza suggests, whatever the season, you use the weather as an excuse. Find a suitable phrase to get you out of these activities.

а Хо́чешь пойти́ на пляж?
б Хо́чешь ката́ться на велосипе́де?
в Хо́чешь пойти́ на конце́рт?
г Хо́чешь пойти́ в лес собира́ть грибы́?
д Хо́чешь ката́ться на конька́х?
е Хо́чешь купа́ться в мо́ре?
ж Хо́чешь пойти́ на стадио́н на футбо́л?

i Нет, сего́дня идёт дождь.
ii Нет, сего́дня сли́шком хо́лодно.
iii Нет, сего́дня сли́шком жа́рко.
iv Нет, сего́дня тума́нно.
v Нет, сего́дня ве́трено.
vi Нет, сего́дня ду́шно.
vii Нет, сего́дня со́лнце све́тит.

▶ Exercise 9

You want to book an excursion to Novgorod.

а When do you want to go?
б How many are there in your group?
в When does the tour guide **экскурсово́д** tell you to be ready to set off?

Вы	Мо́жно заказа́ть экску́рсию на за́втра в Но́вгород?
Экскурсово́д	Мо́жно. Ско́лько вас челове́к?
Вы	Во́семь.
Экскурсово́д	Хорошо́. В авто́бусе есть свобо́дные места́. Встре́тимся здесь за́втра у́тром в во́семь часо́в.

Exercise 10

Now you are in Novgorod, you have lost the tour guide and you are the only one who speaks any Russian. Help your friends out with this list of facilities in the Russian guidebook. You may not understand every word but you should be able to work out most things. The only word you have to look up is **па́мятник** *a monument*.

1	Спра́вочное бюро́
2	Тури́стский ко́мплекс
3	Гости́ница
4	Ке́мпинг
5	Па́мятник архитекту́ры
6	Музе́й
7	Археологи́ческий па́мятник
8	Теа́тр, конце́ртный зал
9	Стадио́н
10	Рестора́н, кафе́, бар
11	Универса́льный магази́н
12	Ры́нок
13	Стоя́нка такси́
14	Автозапра́вочная ста́нция
15	Железнодоро́жный вокза́л
16	Пляж
17	Сад, парк

Exercise 11

Read this postcard from Sveta to Lena.

a Where is she staying?
б What is the weather like?
в What does she do every day?

Здравствуй, Лена.
Мы отдыхаем в Сочи и живём
в гостинице на берегу моря.
Солнце светит и жарко.
Каждый день я ем
мороженое и играю в
волейбол на пляже.

           Света.

Why not write a postcard describing your ideal holiday?

Exercise 12

Browse through this TV programme listing and use all your powers of deduction to say at what time you would watch television if you were interested in **a** sport **б** politics **в** children's programmes **г** games of chance **д** news.

ТЕЛЕВИДЕНИЕ

6.00 Телеутро	16.55 Чемпионат России по футболу. Полуфинал. ЦСКА - «КамАЗ»
8.30 Олимпийское утро	18.00 Астрология
9.20 Новости Эй-би-си	18.20 Лотто «Миллион»
9.55 Парламентская неделя	19.20 Гандбол. Чемпионат мира.
10.10 Утренний концерт	20.00 Новости
10.25 Утренняя почта	20.40 Спокойной ночи, малыши!
10.45 «Санта-Барбара»	21.00 Спортивный карусель
11.10 Русское лото	21.40 Москва - Кремль
11.30 «Живём и любим»	22.00 Кинотеатр «Си-би-эс»
12.05 Милицейская хроника	22.50 Что? Где? Когда?
12.30 Футбол «Динамо» - «Спартак»	23.50 Футбол «Ювентус» - «Парма»
14.00 Новости и погода	
14.20 Винни-Пух	
14.30 Наш сад	
16.30 Кенгуру	

Exercise 13

a   Как попáсть на зúмний стадиóн?
б   Как попáсть в цирк?

Идúте **i** напрáво **ii** налéво **iii** прáмо.

Exercise 14

Answer these questions about your favourite things.

Како́й твой люби́мый сезо́н? Мой люби́мый сезо́н _____
Како́й твой люби́мый спорт? Мой_____
Кака́я твоя́ люби́мая кни́га?   Моя́ люби́мая кни́га_____
Кака́я твоя́ люби́мая маши́на?_____
Каки́е твои́ люби́мые фи́льмы? Мои́ люби́мые фи́льмы____
Каки́е твои́ люби́мые
   компози́торы/спортсме́ны?   _____

Now you could continue making up questions and answers.

Анекдо́т *Anecdote*

На у́лице, по́здно ве́чером.
– Куда́ ты идёшь так по́здно?
– Пора́ идти́ домо́й.
– Почему́ так ра́но?

▶ And finally, a Russian proverb about making the most of your time. **Лени́вцы** means *lazy people*.

> **За́втра, за́втра, не сего́дня – так лени́вцы говоря́т**

19

у меня болит голова
I've got a headache

In this unit you will learn
- what to do if you feel ill
- how to say what is hurting
- how to say someone's age

Before you start, revise

• how to say *I have* **у меня**, etc., page 104

ℹ️ Ба́ня *The bath house*

The Russian health service provides free emergency medical care for everyone, and there are also many private clinics using state-of-the-art equipment. Many Russians prefer to use natural cures involving herbs and often vodka. Suggested remedies for a cold may include taking a cold shower, chewing garlic, using nose drops made from the juice of an onion, and going to bed warmly dressed with extra blankets and a restorative tumbler of pepper vodka and frequent glasses of tea. All of these treatments are sure to leaving you feeling 'as fresh as a little gherkin' **све́жий как огу́рчик** the next morning! Another favourite cure is a visit to the bath house **ба́ня**. Many bath houses operate on a single sex system, and offer a cold pool, a steam room, bunches of birch twigs to help the circulation, tea and a massage. A visit may take the best part of a day and is extraordinarily relaxing and convivial. Even if you are no better by the end of it, you will hardly care!

Что с ва́ми? *What's the matter with you?*

мне пло́хо	I'm ill
Я чу́вствую себя́ хорошо́/нева́жно/ пло́хо	I feel good/not so good/ bad
я пло́хо сплю	I'm sleeping badly
у меня́ температу́ра	I've got a temperature
меня́ тошни́т	I feel sick/nauseous
мне то жа́рко, то хо́лодно	I'm feeling hot and cold
у меня́ грипп	I've got flu
Что у вас боли́т?	What's hurting?
у меня́ боли́т голова́/у́хо/ зуб/живо́т	my head/ear/tooth/ stomach aches
у меня́ боли́т го́рло/глаз/нос	my throat/eye/nose hurts
у меня́ боли́т рука́/нога́/ спина́/се́рдце	my arm/leg/back/ heart hurts
у меня́ боля́т зу́бы/у́ши/глаза́	my teeth/ears/eyes hurt

▶️ Exercise 1

Listen to Vadim, Tanya and Anton describing their symptoms. Decide which of them, has just run a marathon, has flu or has food poisoning.

Exercise 2

Look at the picture below and number the words below correctly.

[ ] голова́   [ ] глаз   [ ] у́хо   [ ] нос   [ ] зу́бы
[ ] го́рло   [ ] рука́   [ ] нога́   [ ] спина́   [ ] живо́т
[ ] се́рдце

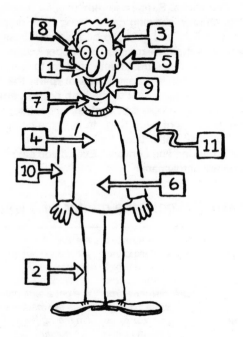

В кабине́те *In the consulting room*

кабине́т	*consulting room*
поликли́ника	*health centre*
больни́ца	*hospital*
апте́ка	*pharmacy*
ско́рая по́мощь	*ambulance*
врач, до́ктор	*doctor*
медсестра́	*nurse*
консульта́ция	*consultation*
симпто́м	*symptom*
диа́гноз	*diagnosis*

рецéпт	prescription
идти́ к врачу́	to go to the doctor's
принима́ть (1) лека́рство	to take medicine
табле́тка	tablet
раз, 3 ра́за в день	once, 3 times a day
откро́йте рот	Open your mouth
я слома́л/а ру́ку	I've (m/f) broken my arm
ле́вый, пра́вый	left, right
серьёзно, несерьёзно	It's serious, not serious
ду́мать [1]	to think
вы́звать ско́рую по́мощь	to send for an ambulance
Не беспоко́йтесь!	Don't worry

▶ Диало́г 1 Скажи́те а-а-а-! *Say 'aah'!*

Listen to this conversation in a doctor's surgery and answer the questions below.

Врач Входи́те. Сади́тесь. Как вас зову́т?

Бра́йан Меня́ зову́т Бра́йан Уи́лкинсон.

Врач Что у вас боли́т? Каки́е у вас симпто́мы?

Бра́йан У меня́ боли́т голова́. Мне то жа́рко, то хо́лодно, и у меня́ температу́ра.

Врач У вас боли́т го́рло?

Бра́йан Да, немно́жко.

Врач Пожа́луйста, откро́йте рот и скажи́те а-а-а.

Бра́йан А-а-а-а-а.

Врач Вы ку́рите?

Бра́йан Нет.

Врач Я ду́маю, что у вас начина́ется грипп. Э́то не о́чень серьёзно. На́до отдыха́ть до́ма и принима́ть лека́рство три ра́за в день. Поня́тно?

Бра́йан Да, поня́тно.

Врач Вот реце́пт.

Бра́йан Спаси́бо. До свида́ния.

Exercise 3

a What is the patient's name?

б What are his symptoms?

в Does he smoke?

г What does the doctor advise?

▶ **Диало́г 2 Это серьёзно!** *That's serious!*

Leaving the surgery, poor Brian falls down the stairs. He is in some pain, but he still manages to speak Russian!

Врач	Что с ва́ми?
Бра́йан	Ой, мне пло́хо. У меня́ боли́т нога́.
Врач	Кака́я нога́? Ле́вая и́ли пра́вая?
Бра́йан	Пра́вая.
Врач	Покажи́те, пожа́луйста. Мо́жно посмотре́ть?
Бра́йан	Да, мо́жно. Ой, я ду́маю, что я слома́л но́гу.
Врач	Да, пра́вильно. Это серьёзно! На́до вы́звать ско́рую по́мощь.
Бра́йан	Да́йте, пожа́луйста, аспири́н.
Врач	Нет, нельзя́. Не беспоко́йтесь. Ско́рая по́мощь ско́ро бу́дет здесь.

Exercise 4

а What has Brian done? **б** What does the doctor send for? **в** What will he not let Brian do?

▶ **Диало́г 3 Ско́рая по́мощь** *First aid*

Meanwhile, back at the hotel, Caroline has found the administrator collapsed on the floor. She phones for an ambulance.

Кэ́ролайн	Алло́, «Ско́рая по́мощь»?
Телефони́ст	Да, слу́шаю вас. В чём де́ло?
Кэ́ролайн	Я не зна́ю, но администра́тор чу́вствует себя́ пло́хо.
Телефони́ст	Како́й у вас а́дрес?
Кэ́ролайн	А́дрес? Извини́те, я не по́мню.
Телефони́ст	Вы в гости́нице?
Кэ́ролайн	Да, в гости́нице «Изма́йлово».
Телефони́ст	Хорошо́. Я зна́ю а́дрес. Так, администра́тор чу́вствует себя́ пло́хо. А что у него́ боли́т?
Кэ́ролайн	Не зна́ю, но я ду́маю, что у него́ боли́т се́рдце.
Телефони́ст	Не беспоко́йтесь. Мы ско́ро бу́дем у вас. Че́рез три мину́ты.

Exercise 5

Caroline is in a bit of a panic, but she is able to tell the switchboard operator everything he needs to know. **а** Where is she staying? **б** What is the matter with the administrator? **в** When will the ambulance be there?

Exercise 6

Read what people say is wrong with them, and underline the most advisable course of action.

а	У меня́ боли́т голова́.	Я принима́ю табле́тку/я чита́ю газе́ту/я иду́ к врачу́.
б	У меня́ грипп.	Я иду́ на рабо́ту/я иду́ в бассе́йн/я иду́ к врачу́.
в	Я слома́ла но́гу.	Я игра́ю в футбо́л/я е́ду в больни́цу/я пью чай.
г	Меня́ тошни́т.	Я ем котле́ты с ри́сом/я принима́ю лека́рство/я игра́ю в волейбо́л.

Exercise 7

Many private hospitals advertise their specialist services in the telephone directories. Which heading would you look under if you wanted:

a   a diagnostic service
б   specialized laboratories
в   Tibetan medicine
г   express analysis
д   advice on preventive medicine
е   physiotherapy
ж   advice on your infectious disease?

  i   Тибе́тская медици́на
  ii   центр превенти́вной медици́ны
  iii   инфекцио́нная больни́ца
  iv   специализиро́ванные лаборато́рии
  v   экспре́сс-ана́лизы
  vi   физиотерапевти́ческая больни́ца
  vii   диагно́стика

Exercise 8

Your medical expertise is called for again! Study the chart below, and fill in the blanks with ticks or crosses to show whether you think certain activities are advisable for your patients. Then tell them what they may and may not do. For example, you might say to Leonid: **Нельзя́ игра́ть в те́ннис, но мо́жно чита́ть газе́ту.** *You must not play tennis, but you may read the paper.*

	(a) игра́ть в те́ннис	(б) чита́ть газе́ту	(в) пить вино́	(г) купа́ться в мо́ре
Леони́д (слома́л но́гу) Ири́на (боля́т глаза́) Арка́дий (тошни́т) Мариа́нна (боли́т се́рдце)				

Ско́лько вам лет? *How old are you?*

во́зраст	*age*
Ско́лько вам/ему́/ей лет?	*How old are you/is he/is she?*
мне два́дцать оди́н год	*I am 21 years old*
ему́ три́дцать три го́да	*he is 33 years old*
ей со́рок шесть лет	*she is 46 years old*

In Russian, you choose a different word for *year* depending on the number.

1 – оди́н **год**
2, 3, 4 – два, три, четы́ре **го́да**
5, 6, 7 etc., up to 20 – пять, шесть, семь, два́дцать **лет**

For numbers over 20, look at the last digit, and if it is 1 use **год**, if it is 2–4, use **го́да**, and if it is 5, 6, 7, 8, 9, or a multiple of 10, use **лет**.

Exercise 9

Choose the correct word for year to complete these phrases. Don't forget to read the numbers out loud!

а Мне 53 _____.
б Ему́ 18 _____.
в Ей 2 _____.
г Ему́ 85 _____.
д Ей 61 _____.

▶ Exercise 10

Listen to the recording and make a note of these patients' names, ages and symptoms.

	И́мя	О́тчество	Во́зраст	Симпто́мы
а				
б				
в				

Exercise 11

Look at this family photograph, invent names and relationships for the people on it and say how old they are. For example, you might say **Э́то мой де́душка. Его́ зову́т Станисла́в и ему́ девяно́сто де́вять лет.** Or **Э́то моя́ дочь. Её зову́т Лю́да и ей три го́да.**

Exercise 12

Find these words in Russian in the wordsearch grid. Words may be written in any direction, vertically, horizontally or diagonally.

flu	leg	doctor (врач)	eye
arm	prescription	back	ears
head	throat	heart	tooth
mouth		stomach	

г	щ	ф	я	н	г	т	г
е	ю	й	о	л	р	о	г
ц	е	с	а	п	л	в	в
е	ц	з	п	о	э	и	р
п	д	и	в	з	ш	ж	а
т	р	а	к	у	р	г	ч
г	е	ж	ы	б	о	о	б
ч	с	п	и	н	а	х	т

▶ Анекдо́т *Anecdote*

Why is this elderly patient unimpressed by the doctor's advice?

> **вы проживёте до ...**   *You will live to ...*

Врач   Éсли вы не ку́рите и не пьёте, вы проживёте до
           девяно́ста лет.
Ба́бушка Э, до́ктор, уже́ по́здно!
Врач   Почему́?
Ба́бушка Мне уже́ девяно́сто три го́да!

And finally, read this Russian proverb and see if you can work out
what the first line means.

> Кто не ку́рит и не пьёт,
> Тот здоро́веньким умрёт.

The whole saying could be translated as *Whoever neither smokes nor
drinks will die healthy.*

20

какой он?

what's he like?

In this unit you will learn
- how to say what people are wearing
- how to say what people look like
- how to describe someone's character
- how to express your opinions and preferences

Before you start, revise

- how to say *my*, *your*, *his*, *her* etc., page 106
- singular adjective endings, page 38

ℹ Оде́жда и о́бувь *Clothes and footwear*

In the Soviet era, fashionable clothes and footwear were often in short supply in the shops. There was a joke at the time that Adam and Eve must have been Soviet citizens because in the garden of Eden they were naked, barefoot, with one apple between them, and they believed they were living in paradise! Nowadays, a wide range of Russian and imported clothes are available in the shops, including many international designer labels. The image of the country **ба́бушка** dressed in padded coat, shawl **плато́к** and felt boots **ва́ленки** has never applied to the younger generation, who have always been as fashion conscious as young people anywhere.

Expressing your opinion

Showing your pleasure, surprise, agreement or regret is something you will want to do as you talk to Russian friends. Don't forget the verbs **люби́ть** *to love*, and **хоте́ть** *to want*. And here is another useful verb, **мочь** *to be able*.

люби́ть [2]		хоте́ть [*irregular*]		мочь [1]	
я люблю́	мы лю́бим	я хочу́	мы хоти́м	я могу́	мы мо́жем
ты лю́бишь	вы лю́бите	ты хо́чешь	вы хоти́те	ты мо́жешь	вы мо́жете
он лю́бит	они́ лю́бят	он хо́чет	они́ хотя́т	он мо́жет	они́ мо́гут

Он в костю́ме *He's wearing a suit*

Как он оде́т? Как она́ оде́та?	*How is he/she dressed?*
брю́ки/он в брю́ках	*trousers/He's wearing trousers*
джи́нсы/она́ в джи́нсах	*jeans/She's wearing jeans*
ю́бка/она́ в ю́бке	*skirt/She's wearing a skirt*
руба́шка/он в руба́шке	*shirt/He's wearing a shirt*
блу́за/она́ в блу́зе	*blouse/She's wearing a blouse*
сви́тер/он в сви́тере	*sweater/He's wearing a sweater*
костю́м/он в костю́ме	*suit/He's wearing a suit*
га́лстук/он в га́лстуке	*tie/He's wearing a tie*
пла́тье/она́ в пла́тье	*dress/She's wearing a dress*
пальто́/он в пальто́	*coat/He's wearing a coat*
ша́пка/он в ша́пке	*hat (fur)/He's wearing a hat*
ту́фли/она́ в туфля́х	*shoes/She's wearing shoes*

ботинки/она в ботинках	ankle boots/She's wearing ankle boots
очки/он носит очки	glasses/He wears glasses
он будет в шапке	He will be wearing a hat

Exercise 1

Listen to or read the dialogues below.

a Where do you think Nikita and Alan are? **б** Describe Nikita's sister. **в** Where and when are Monica and Victor meeting? **г** How will Monica recognize him?

▶ Диалог 1 Как она одета? *How is she dressed?*

Никита Алан, вот моя сестра Маша на платформе. Она нас ждёт.

Алан А я её не знаю. Как она одета?

Никита Она носит очки, и она в пальто, в ботинках и шапке.

Алан Да, вижу. Она красивая. Сколько ей лет?

Никита Двадцать три года.

▶ Диалог 2 Я буду в костюме *I'll be wearing a suit*

Моника Где мы встретимся?

Виктор В ресторане «Восток», в семь часов.

Моника Хорошо. Я буду в платье, а вы?

Виктор Я буду в костюме и в галстуке. Мне сорок лет и я курю сигары.

Как она выглядит? *What does she look like?*

мужчина/женщина	man/woman
брюнет (ка)/блондин (ка)	brunette/blonde (m/f)
высокий/невысокий	tall/short
полный/стройный	chubby/slim
толстый/худой	fat/thin
красивый/некрасивый	good looking/not good looking
молодой/пожилой	young, elderly
светлые, рыжие, тёмные волосы	light, red, dark hair

длинные, короткие волосы	long, short hair
голубые, карие, серые, зелёные глаза	blue, brown, grey, green eyes
с бородой	bearded
лысый	bald

Exercise 2

Tick the correct statements.

Ваня

Галя

а	Ваня невысокий.	**а**	Галя невысокая.
б	Он худой.	**б**	Она стройная.
в	Он пожилой.	**в**	Она молодая.
г	Он красивый.	**г**	Она некрасивая.
д	Он лысый.	**д**	Она блондинка.
е	Он в костюме.	**е**	Она в юбке и блузе.
ж	Он в джинсах.	**ж**	Она в пальто.
з	У него длинные волосы.	**з**	У неё короткие волосы.
и	У него светлые волосы.	**и**	У неё тёмные волосы.
к	Он носит очки.	**к**	Она носит очки.

▶ Exercise 3

You see someone behaving suspiciously, so you ring the police and give them a description. Fill in your half of the conversation. To give the suspect's approximate age, change the order of the words: **ему лет двадцать** *he's about 20* instead of **ему двадцать лет** *he's 20*.

Милиционе́р	Как он вы́глядит?
Вы	*It's a young man.*
Милиционе́р	Ско́лько ему́ лет?
Вы	*He's about 19.*
Милиционе́р	Како́й он? Высо́кий?
Вы	*Yes, he's tall and thin.*
Милиционе́р	Каки́е у него́ во́лосы?
Вы	*He has short, dark hair.*
Милиционе́р	Как он оде́т?
Вы	*He's wearing jeans and a shirt.*
Милиционе́р	Спаси́бо.

Како́й у него́ хара́ктер? *What is his personality like?*

симпати́чный	*nice*
интере́сный	*interesting*
энерги́чный	*energetic*
весёлый	*cheerful*
до́брый	*good*
ми́лый	*sweet*
тала́нтливый	*talented*
у́мный	*clever*
глу́пый	*stupid*
лени́вый	*lazy*
ску́чный	*boring*
неприя́тный	*unpleasant*
проти́вный	*revolting*
Он не челове́к, а мо́края ку́рица	*He is not a man, but a wet hen (i.e. a wimp)*

Exercise 4

Kostya and Kolya are like chalk and cheese. Read this description of Kostya and then fill in the missing words in the description of Kolya.

Ко́стя о́чень интере́сный, энерги́чный челове́к. Он высо́кий, худо́й, и о́чень лю́бит игра́ть в бадминто́н. Он симпати́чный и у́мный студе́нт и тала́нтливый актёр. У него́ коро́ткие, све́тлые во́лосы и он но́сит очки́. Он всегда́ весёлый, и по суббо́там он хо́дит в кино́.

Ко́ля о́чень (*boring, lazy*) челове́к. Он (*short*) и (*fat*) и (*doesn't like*) спорт. Он (*unpleasant*) и (*stupid*) студе́нт. У него́ (*long, dark*) во́лосы (*and green eyes*). По суббо́там он хо́дит в кино́.

Exercise 5

Read these excerpts from the 'lonely hearts' column in a newspaper. Which advertisement would you reply to if you were looking for **a** a cheerful, good-looking man who enjoys the theatre **б** an older woman with a family **в** a young blonde Ukrainian woman, good natured **г** a music-loving man?

i **ВАЛЕ́РИЙ** Молодо́й челове́к, 30 лет, рост 184 см., вес 98 кг., ру́сский, не пью, не курю́. Люблю́ му́зыку, спорт.

ii **СЛА́ВИК** 35 лет, 174 см., 65 кг., стро́йный брюне́т, краси́вый, спорти́вный. Живу́ в го́роде Но́вгороде. До́брый, весёлый хара́ктер. Люблю́ теа́тр, кни́ги.

iii **ТАМА́РА** Симпати́чная де́вушка, 25 лет, рост 165 см., вес 65 кг., блонди́нка, украи́нка, люблю́ цветы́ и со́лнце. По хара́ктеру до́брая.

iv **ЛЮДМИ́ЛА** Же́нщина, лет 53, ру́сская, рост 153 см., во́лосы све́тлые, глаза́ зелёные, энерги́чная. Сын и дочь.

Exercise 6

Match up the descriptions on the next page with the pictures below.

Лев Толсто́й   Ю́рий Гага́рин   А́нна Па́влова

a Молода́я же́нщина, краси́вая, стро́йная, энерги́чная. Лю́бит бале́т.

б Пожило́й челове́к с бородо́й, энерги́чный, у́мный. Лю́бит кни́ги.

в Молодо́й челове́к, краси́вый. весёлый. Коро́ткие, тёмные во́лосы. Лю́бит путеше́ствовать.

По-мо́ему . . . *In my opinion . . .*

Here are some expressions to use in conversation to express your opinions and feelings.

к сожале́нию/к сча́стью	*unfortunately/fortunately*
как ужа́сно/интере́сно/ску́чно	*how awful/interesting/boring*
наве́рно	*probably*
мо́жет быть	*possibly, maybe*
ка́жется	*it seems*
по-мо́ему	*in my opinion*
совсе́м	*quite (completely)*
дово́льно	*quite (fairly)*
немно́жко/мно́го	*a bit/a lot*
пра́вильно/непра́вильно	*That's right/not right*
лу́чше/ху́же	*better/worse*
я о́чень люблю́	*I really love*
я бо́льше люблю́	*I prefer (love more)*
бо́льше всего́ я люблю́	*more than anything I love*
(bol'she vsyivo)	
я совсе́м не люблю́	*I really don't like*
вот почему́	*That's why*
бо́же мой!	*my God!*
как жаль!	*what a pity!*
кошма́р!	*what a nightmare!*
чуде́сно!	*wonderful!*
смешно́!	*that's funny!*
то́чно так!	*exactly!*
ла́дно	*OK*

Диало́г 3 Как жаль! *What a pity!*

▶ Exercise 7

Read these brief dialogues and decide in which one Anatoly expresses
а disappointment **б** horror **в** agreement.

i *Anatoly is visiting Deena at her flat.*

Анато́лий	Ди́на, мо́жно смотре́ть футбо́л по телеви́зору?
Ди́на	Извини́, к сожале́нию, телеви́зор сего́дня не рабо́тает.
Анато́лий	Как жаль! Бо́льше всего́ я люблю́ смотре́ть футбо́л. А по́чему телеви́зор не рабо́тает?
Ди́на	Я не зна́ю. Наве́рно потому́, что он ста́рый.
Анато́лий	По-мо́ему, на́до купи́ть но́вый телеви́зор.
Ди́на	Мо́жет быть. Но ску́чно смотре́ть телеви́зор днём.

ii *Anatoly and Leonid are making plans for the evening.*

Анато́лий Что ты хо́чешь де́лать сего́дня ве́чером?

Леони́д Не зна́ю, но в университе́те идёт хоро́ший конце́рт.

Анато́лий Но ты зна́ешъ, что я совсе́м не люблю́ му́зыку. Лу́чше идти́ в кино́, да?

Леони́д Нет, дово́льно ску́чно. Я бо́льше люблю́ теа́тр. Пойдём на пье́су «Три сестры́». Ла́дно?

Анато́лий Ла́дно.

iii *Vika rings Anatoly with a problem about tickets for their trip.*

Анато́лий Алло́! Ви́ка?

Ви́ка Да, э́то я. Анато́лий, извини́, но я не могу́ сего́дня купи́ть на́ши биле́ты на по́езд.

Анато́лий Как не мо́жешь, Ви́ка?

Ви́ка Я в больни́це, слома́ла ру́ку.

Анато́лий Бо́же мой! Рука́ боли́т?

Ви́ка Коне́чно, ужа́сно боли́т.

Анато́лий Кошма́р! Что де́лать? Кто мо́жет купи́ть биле́ты, е́сли ты в больни́це?

Exercise 8

Match up each problem with a solution.

а	Зал закры́т! Что де́лать?	**i**	Не волну́йтесь. Он слома́л ру́ку. Вот почему́ он в больни́це.
б	В маши́не совсе́м гря́зно!		
в	Я чу́вствую себя́ ху́же!		
г	Я не зна́ю, как попа́сть в гости́ницу!	**ii**	Вот идёт экскурсово́д. Он, наве́рно, зна́ет.
в	Я чу́вствую себя́ ху́же!	**iii**	Вот вода́ и мы́ло.
д	Како́й кошма́р! Мы потеря́ли биле́ты!	**iv**	Мо́жет быть, ва́ши биле́ты в су́мке?
е	Как ужа́сно! Почему́ Ива́н в больни́це?	**v**	Вот табле́тки. Ско́ро бу́дет лу́чше.
		vi	Вот ключ.

▶ Exercise 9

Read or listen to this letter written by a Russian in Minsk, Belarus. He is seeking a penfriend. Make brief notes in English, or write a reply in Russian.

Здравствуйте!

Меня зовут Саша Иванов, мне 18 лет, у меня сестра и брат. Их зовут Оля (10 лет) и Миша (3 года). Мы живём в квартире в Минске. Мой папа работает в поликлинике. Он - врач. Моя мама - учительница. Оля хорошая спортсменка и любит играть в теннис. Миша ещё не ходит в школу.

Я высокий, у меня тёмные волосы и чёрные глаза. Вы хотите фотографию? Я люблю читать и играть в шахматы, но я больше всего люблю ходить в театр. Зимой я люблю кататься на лыжах. Пожалуйста, напишите. Где вы живёте? Что вы любите делать в свободное время? У вас есть брат или сестра? Вы живёте в квартире или в доме?

Ваш Саша.

▶ Анекдо́т *Anecdote*

У́тром мать говори́т:

– Пора́ идти́ в шко́лу, сын.
– Не хочу́, ма́ма. На́до идти́?
– На́до, сын, ты учи́тель.

And finally, a rhyming toast **тост** to congratulate you on finishing *Teach Yourself Beginner's Russian*.

Пора́ и вы́пить!	*It's time to drink up!*
В до́брый час!	*Good luck!*
За всех госте́й!	*To all the guests!*
За всех за вас!	*To all of you!*

You are now a competent speaker of basic Russian. You should be able to handle most everyday situations on a visit to Russia and to communicate with Russian people sufficiently to make friends. If you would like to extend your ability so that you can develop your confidence, fluency and scope in the language, whether for social or business purposes, why not take your Russian a step further with *Teach Yourself Russian*?

I hope you enjoyed working your way through the course.
I am always keen to receive feedback from people who have used my course, so why not contact me and let me know your reactions?
I'll be particularly pleased to receive your praise, but I should also like to know if you think things could be improved.
I always welcome comments and suggestions and I do my best to incorporate constructive suggestions into later editions.

You can contact me through the publishers at: Teach Yourself Books, Hodder Headline Ltd, 338 Euston Road, London NW1 3BH.
В до́брый час! *Good luck!*

Rachel Farmer

Check how confident you feel with all the material from Units 1–10 by doing this revision test.

1 Choose one appropriate response to each question or remark.

a – Как вас зовут?
   i – Меня зовут Саша. ii – Я живу в Москве.
   iii – Я говорю по-русски.

b – Извините, пожалуйста, это банк?
   i – Идите прямо. ii –Как дела? iii – Нет, это почта.

c – Спасибо.
   i – Плохо. ii – Очень приятно. iii – Не за что!
   iv – Я живу в деревне.

d – Как попасть в цирк?
   i – Аптека вон там. ii – Идите направо.
   iii – Музей закрыт на ремонт.

e – У вас есть сувениры?
   i – Нет, идите налево. ii – Как жаль. iii – Да, вот матрёшки.

f – Сколько стоит?
   i – Семь часов ii – Тысяча рублей. iii – Пятый автобус.

g – Что у вас есть?
   i – Чай и кофе. ii – Я живу в Америке.
   iii – Я – русский.

h – Когда открывается музей?
   i – Фильм начинается в десять часов.
   ii – Я встаю в восемь часов. iii – В три часа.

2   Choose the **least** appropriate phrase from each section.

a   You don't understand, so you say:

i – Извините, я не понимаю. ii – Добрый вечер.
iii – Медленнее, пожалуйста. iv – Повторите,
пожалуйста.

b   You ask what someone does for a job, and they say:

i – Я инженер. ii – Я работаю на фабрике.
iii – Я люблю смотреть телевизор.

c   You ask someone about their hobbies, and they say:

i – Я очень люблю читать. ii – Я люблю спорт.
iii – Я люблю тебя. iv – Я хожу в кино.

3   Choose the correct form of the words below.

a   Какой это город? Это большой/большая город.
b   Я иду в больница/больницу.
c   Вот ваша/ваше комната.
d   Я живу в Магадан/Магадане.
e   Он играет в бадминтон/бадминтоне.
f   Она играет на гитаре/гитара.
g   Сегодня пятый/пятое сентября.

4   How much do you know about Russian life?

a   What would you do with a **папироса?**   i eat it
ii smoke it iii put it in a letter box?

b   In which city would you find **ГУМ**?   i St Petersburg
ii Magadan iii Moscow?

c   If you were at a **вокзал** would you catch   i a train
ii a plane iii a cold?

d   If you were speaking to an **официант** would you be
i showing your passport ii ordering a drink iii paying a fine?

e   Is **каша**   i porridge ii someone's name iii a cash desk?

f   Is **праздник**   i a day of the week ii a shop assistant
iii a holiday?

g   If you are walking along a **набережная** should you look
out for i a runway ii a river iii a hospital?

Numbers in **bold** refer to Units.

1 Choose an appropriate response to the following questions.

a – Э́то ваш бага́ж? **(12)**
   i – Да, э́то мой чемода́н.
   ii – Да, э́то моя́ ба́бушка.
   iii – Да, вокза́л вон там. Иди́те пря́мо.

b – Когда́ ты бу́дешь в Но́вгороде? **(12)**
   i – Я уста́л.
   ii – Я не бу́ду в Москве́.
   iii – В пя́тницу в шесть часо́в.

c – У вас есть свобо́дный но́мер? **(15)**
   i – В но́мере хо́лодно и гря́зно и телефо́н не
       рабо́тает.
   ii – За́втрак начина́ется в во́семь часо́в.
   iii – Да, у нас есть но́мер на двои́х с ва́нной.

d – Каки́е ма́рки вы хоти́те? **(17)**
   i – Я хочу́ позвони́ть в А́нглию.
   ii – Я хочу́ посла́ть э́ту откры́тку в Герма́нию.
   iii – Я хочу́ посла́ть телегра́мму во Фра́нцию.

e – Кака́я сего́дня пого́да? **(18)**
   i – Мой люби́мый сезо́н – о́сень.
   ii – За́втра бу́дет тепло́.
   iii – Идёт дождь.

f – Ско́лько вам лет? **(19)**
   i – Мне два́дцать оди́н год.
   ii – В де́вять часо́в.
   iii – Трина́дцатого ма́рта.

2 Match the questions and answers.
   a – Како́й у неё но́мер телефо́на?
   b – Где мы встре́тимся?

c – Дéвушка, как попáсть на вокзáл?
d – Это далекó?
e – Где мóжно купи́ть проду́кты?
f – Какóй твой люби́мый сезóн
g – Что с вáми?
h – Хóчешь пойти́ на пляж?

  i – Сади́тесь на шестóй трамвáй.
  ii – У меня́ боли́т головá.
  iii – Нет, сегóдня бу́дет снег.
  iv – В гастронóме. Это недалекó.
  v – Нет, три останóвки.
  vi – Три́ста двáдцать пять тринáдцать.
  vii – У меня́ в кварти́ре в четы́ре часá.
  viii – Веснá.

3 What would you say if:
  a you had lost your key? **(15)**
    i – Окнó не закрывáется.
    ii – Вот вам бутербрóд.
    iii – У меня́ пропáл ключ.
  b you wanted tea with lemon and sugar? **(16)**
    i – Дáйте, пожáлуйста, чай с лимóном без сáхара.
    ii – Дáйте, пожáлуйста, чай с молокóм без сáхара.
    iii – Дáйте, пожáлуйста, чай с лимóном и с сáхаром.
  c you loved skiing in your spare time? **(18)**
    i – В свобóдное врéмя я óчень люблю́ катáться на велосипéде.
    ii – В свобóдное врéмя я óчень люблю́ игрáть на гитáре.
    iii – В свобóдное врéмя я óчень люблю́ катáться на лы́жах.
  d you had toothache? **(18)**
    i – У меня́ боли́т гóрло.
    ii – Нáдо вы́звать скóрую пóмощь.
    iii – У меня́ боли́т зуб.
  e you wanted to meet Volodya on Thursday? **(12)**
    i – Встрéтимся в пя́тницу в библиотéке.
    ii – Встрéтимся в понедéльник на стадиóне.
    iii – Встрéтимся в четвéрг в гости́нице.
  f you really liked someone? **(20)**
    i – По-мóему, он симпати́чный и дóбрый.
    ii – Он совсéм неприя́тный и ску́чный.
    iii – К сожалéнию, она глу́пая и проти́вная жéнщина.
  g you were ordering dessert? **(16)**

     i – Я хочу́ грибы́ в смета́не.

     ii – Я хочу́ моро́женое.

     iii – Я хочу́ борщ.

h your friend had flu? **(19)**

     i – На́до отдыха́ть до́ма.

     ii – На́до идти́ в бассе́йн.

     iii – На́до рабо́тать.

i you wanted to know if something was expensive? **(14)**

     i – Э́то далеко́?

     ii – Э́то до́рого?

     iii – Э́то всё?

4 How much do you know about Russian life?

a If you saw a sign saying **В авто́бусе нельзя́ кури́ть**, would you **(13)**

     i – put your sandwiches away?

     ii – get your bus ticket punched?

     iii – put out your cigarette?

b If you dialled 01 for **пожа́р**, what would you get? **(17)**

     i An ambulance.

     ii A fire engine.

     iii The police.

c Where would you meet a **проводни́к**? **(13)**

     i On a train.

     ii In a bath house.

     iii In a restaurant.

d What would you do at a sign saying **Обме́н валю́ты**? **(12)**

     i Buy theatre tickets.

     ii Pick up your left luggage.

     iii Exchange currency.

e If someone said to you **Входи́те, раздева́йтесь**, would you **(16)**

     i come in and take your coat off?

     ii come in and sit down?

     iii shut the door as you leave?

f If you saw **От себя́** on a shop door, would you **(15)**

     i push?

     ii conclude the shop was shut?

     iii pull?

answers

Unit 1

1 a ii b iv c i d v e iii 2 a iii b iv c ii d v e i 3 a iii b i c ii
4 a ii b i c iv d iii 5 snooker, cricket, tennis, stadium, start, knockout,
trainer, record, athletics, sport, sportsman 6 a vi b i c viii d vii e iii
f iv g ix h v i ii 7 visa, tractor, passport, taxi 8 diplomat, tourist,
cosmonaut, chemist, student, administrator, doctor, tractor driver, captain
9 Ivan Nina Alexander Vladimir Ekaterina Liza Lev Irina Valentin Larisa
11 atom, comet, meteor, climate, mechanism, microscope, sputnik, kilo,
litre, planet, moon, kilometre 12 television, cassette, monitor, cinecamera,
lemonade, radio, printer 13 park, kiosk, grocer's, zoo, stadium, café,
sauna, telephone, institute, casino, Internet café, university, antiques
15 lamp, chair, corridor, sofa, mixer, vase, toaster, gas, lift 16 saxophone,
composer, guitar, piano, orchestra, soloist, opera, pianist, compact disc,
heavy metal rock 17 piano 18 omelette, salad, whisky, fruit, coffee,
muesli, cutlet, wine, pepsi-cola, minestrone soup

Unit 2

1 a iii b vi c iv d i e v f ii 2 a stewardess b platform c excursion
d bus e tram f airport g express h signal i Aeroflot j trolleybus
3 football, volleyball, badminton, marathon, arm wrestling, boxing,
gymnastics, ping-pong, surfing, final, rugby, paintball, hockey,
basketball, body building 4 symphony, ballerina, poet, actress,
bestseller, actor, ballet, thriller 5 energy, kilowatt, atmosphere,
kilogram, electronics, experiment 6 America, Mexico, Africa, Pakistan,
Argentina, England, Russia, Ukraine, Canada, India, Australia, Norway
8 a bar b Melody (music shop) c Pizza Hut d museum e circus
f bank g library h Kremlin i post office j Bolshoi Theatre 9 souvenirs,
petshop, militia, driving school, information, pizza, billiard club,
provisions 10 a cheeseburger b banana c cappuccino coffee d pizza
'super supreme' 11 a manager b fax c briefing d marketing e floppy
disk f businessman g know-how h broker i weekend j computer

k notebook (computer) **13 a** Chekhov **b** Tolstoy **c** Pushkin **d** Tchaikovsky **e** Rachmaninov **f** Shostakovich **g** Lenin **h** Gorbachev **i** Yeltsin **j** Putin **14 a** temperature **b** bacterium **c** antibiotic **d** massage **e** tablet **f** diagnosis **g** penicillin **h** infection **15 a** iv **b** iii **c** v **d** ii **e** i **16** Игорь – футболи́ст. Анто́н – тури́ст. Лари́са – студе́нтка. Бори́с – тенниси́ст. Ната́ша – балери́на. **18 a** m **b** f **c** m **d** n **e** f **f** m **g** m **h** f **i** n **j** f **k** m **l** n **19** сестра́/стадио́н/саксофо́н **20** суп омле́т сала́т (masculine) **21 a** сестра́ **b** симфо́ния **c** Аргенти́на **d** библиоте́ка **e** температу́ра

Unit 3

1 a iii **b** i **c** ii **a** i **b** iii **c** ii Vladimir Boris **2 a** до́брое у́тро **b** до́брый день **c** до́брый ве́чер **3** Меня́ зову́т Стю́арт. О́чень прия́тно. **4** e **5 a** iii **b** iv **c** i **d** ii. **6 a** Hello **b** Thank you **c** I speak English **d** Good **e** Where is Boris? **f** I don't know **g** Slower, please **h** Excuse me/Sorry **7 a** iii **b** v **c** ii **d** i **e** iv **8 a** зову́т **b** До́брый **c** не **d** говори́те **e** челове́к **9 a** iii **b** ii **c** iii **10 a** iv **b** v **c** ii **d** iii **e** i

Test yourself
1 Здра́вствуйте. **2** До свида́ния. **3** Извини́те. **4** Как вас зову́т? **5** Вы говори́те по-англи́йски? **6** Я не понима́ю.

Unit 4

Before you start
авто́бус (*m*) о́пера (*f*) пиани́но (*n*) метро́ (*n*) ма́ма (*f*) банк (*m*) **2 a** boulevard **b** avenue **c** campsite **d** taxi rank **e** café-bar **f** tourist hotel **g** botanical garden **h** first-aid post **i** yacht club **j** tourist club **k** canal **l** Red Square **m** swimming pool **n** tourist agency **3 a** он **b** она́ **c** он **d** оно́ **e** она́ **f** он **g** она́ **h** оно́ **5** 2-6, 7-5, 3-4, 8-1, 10-0, 9-10 **6 a** bus no. 5 **b** trolleybus no. 8 **c** tram no. 3 **d** bus no. 9 **7 a** Вот оно́./Оно́ вон там. **b** Извини́те, я не зна́ю. **c** Нет, э́то по́чта. **d** Не́ за что! **8** кра́сное вино́, бе́лая табле́тка, зелёный сала́т, жёлтый бана́н, чёрный кот **9** b d e c a

Test yourself
d c a e b

Unit 5

2 a i **b** ii **c** i **d** i *1* в рестора́н *2* в институ́т *3* в универма́г *4* в бассе́йн *5* в кафе́ *6* в библиоте́ку *7* в шко́лу *8* на пло́щадь *9* в поликли́нику *10* в це́рковь *11* в больни́цу *12* в музе́й *13* в теа́тр *14* в апте́ку *15* в цирк *16* на ста́нцию метро́ *17* на по́чту *18* в парк *19* на стадио́н *20* в кино́ *21* в гастроно́м *22* в банк *23* на фа́брику *24* в спра́вочное бюро́ *25* в гости́ницу *26* на вокза́л **3** Use same endings as Ex. 2, 1-26. **4 a** И́горь хоро́ший футболи́ст. **b** Ле́на краси́вая балери́на. **c** Хард-Рок америка́нское кафе́. **d** Ло́ндон большо́й го́род. **e** Пра́вда ру́сская газе́та. **5** Tick **a** and **d** **6 a** vi

b iii/iv **c** i **d** iii **e** ii **f** v **7** бана́ны фру́кты табле́тки сигаре́ты папиро́сы цветы́ конфе́ты **8 a** 12-24-18 **b** 25-30-17 **c** 14-32-11 **d** 15-03-24 **e** 20-19-12 **9 a** ix **b** xi **c** vii **d** i **e** viii **f** iv **g** vi **h** iii **i** x **j** ii **k** v **10 a** v theatre **b** iv library **c** ii grocer's **d** iii station **e** vi restaurant **f** vii hotel **g** i café

Test yourself
1 ii **2** v **3** iii **4** i **5** iv

Unit 6

1 a Где? **b** Как? **c** Куда́ **d** Что? **e** Кто? **2** *Suggested answers.* **a** Да, ру́сская во́дка и матрёшки. **b** Извини́те, нет. **c** Да, ру́сские папиро́сы и америка́нские сигаре́ты. **d** Да, хоро́шие бана́ны. **3 a** iv **b** v **c** ii **d** iii **e** i **4 a** ii **b** iv **c** vii **d** i **e** iii **f** v **g** vi **5 a** ва́ше моё **b** ва́ша моя́ **c** ва́ши мои́ **d** ваш мой **6** Tick everything. Underline во́дка, пи́цца, смета́на, пепси-ко́ла. **7** Большо́й теа́тр, ма́ленькое ра́дио, краси́вые цветы́, ру́сские папиро́сы, интере́сная кни́га, молодо́й челове́к, ботани́ческий сад, хоро́шие конфе́ты, бе́лое вино́

Test yourself
1 Я хочу́ чай с лимо́ном. **2** Я иду́ в кино́. **3** Э́то ру́сская во́дка. **4** Да, метро́ закры́то. **5** Да, э́то мой биле́т.

Unit 7

2 a ii **b** iv **c** vi **d** i **e** iii **f** v **3 a** Scottish **b** Portuguese **c** Irish **d** Norwegian **4 a** ii/4/C **b** iv/1/B **c** i/2/A **d** iii/3/D **5 a** iii **b** v **c** ii **d** vii **e** i **f** iv **g** vi **6 a** в больни́це в Арха́нгельске **b** на стадио́не **c** В гости́нице **d** в рестора́не **7** Э́та книга, э́тот паспорт, Э́ти сигаре́ты, э́то ра́дио **8 a** vi **b** x **c** vii **d** viii **e** i **f** iv **g** ii **h** ix **i** iii **j** v

Test yourself
4, 5, 2, 7, 8, 1, 6, 3

Unit 8

1 a 8.00 **b** 7.00 **c** 3.00 **d** 1.00 **e** 11.00 **f** 2.00 **g** 10.00 **h** 6.00 **i** 4.00 **2 a** Час **b** Три часа́ **c** Пять часо́в **d** Де́вять часо́в три́дцать мину́т **e** Два часа́ со́рок пять мину́т **f** Оди́ннадцать часо́в де́сять мину́т **g** Двена́дцать часо́в пять мину́т **h** Три часа́ два́дцать пять мину́т **i** Четы́ре часа́ пятьдеся́т мину́т **3 a** семь встаю́ **b** во́семь за́втракаю **c** де́вять иду́ **d** обе́даю **e** во́семь **f** де́вять смотрю́ **g** оди́ннадцать **4 a** Музе́й антрополо́гии и этногра́фии открыва́ется в оди́ннадцать часо́в. Выходно́й день – суббо́та. Телефо́н – две́сти восемна́дцать – четы́рнадцать – двена́дцать. **b** Музе́й музыка́льных инструме́нтов открыва́ется в двена́дцать часо́в. Выходно́й день – вто́рник. Телефо́н – три́ста четы́рнадцать – пятьдеся́т три – пятьдеся́т пять. с Музе́й-кварти́ра А. А. Бло́ка открыва́ется в оди́ннадцать часо́в. Выходно́й день – среда́. Телефо́н – сто трина́дцать – во́семьдесят шесть – три́дцать три. d Музе́й А́рктики и Анта́рктики открыва́ется в де́сять часо́в. Выходно́й день – понеде́льник. Телефо́н – три́ста оди́ннадцать – два́дцать пять – со́рок де́вять. **5 a** Чт. **b** Пн. **c** Вт. **d** Ср. **e** Сб. **f** Вс. **g** Пт. **6 a** 1st (ground floor) **b** 2nd **c** 3rd **d** 5th **e** 5th **f** 6th **g** 4th **h** 5th **i** 2nd **7 a** обе́д **b** за́втрак **c** у́жин **8 a** в теа́тре в Но́вгороде **b** в библиоте́ку **c** в университе́те, в шко́ле **d** в институ́т **e** в поликли́нику **9 a** Wednesday **b** Friday **c** Tuesday **d** Monday **e** Thursday **f** Saturday **g** Sunday **10 a** Mon. **b** 13.00–14.00 **c** Sat. **d** Sun. **e** 16.00 **11** Friday

Test yourself

3 Когда́ открыва́ется банк? **4** Когда́ начина́ется фильм?
5 Встре́тимся в семь часо́в в рестора́не.

Unit 9

Dialogue

George – reading, jazz, languages, travel. Lyudmila – badminton, tennis, walking. George – saxophone. Jazz concert, this evening, 5th October.

1 суббо́та пе́рвое октября́, воскресе́нье второ́е октября́, понеде́льник тре́тье октября́, вто́рник четвёртое октября́, среда́ пя́тое октября́, четве́рг шесто́е октября́, пя́тница седьмо́е октября́. **a** Thurs. **b** Wed. **c** Three sisters **d** Tues. **3 a** Likes library, reading books, newspapers. **b** Plays badminton. Likes sport. Plays guitar. **c** Likes travel. Speaks English and French well. Doesn't like going to opera or drinking champagne. **d** Likes going to theatre and concerts. Likes music, plays balalaika. Likes pizza. **4 a** Пе́рвое января́ **b** Седьмо́е января́ **c** Восьмо́е ма́рта **d** Девя́тое ма́я **g** трина́дцатого ию́ня, два́дцать четвёртого декабря́, три́дцать пе́рвого октября́ **h** шесто́го сентября́, тре́тье октября́, четы́рнадцатого февраля́ **5 a** ix **b** vi **c** xi **d** v/x **e** vii **f** v **g** iv **h** iii **i** ii **j** iii/vi/vii/viii **k** xii **l** i **6 a** 6,000 **b** 14,500 **c** 20,380 **d** 5,346 **e** 19,923 **f** 2,411 **g** 1,298 **h** 10,531 **7 a** рабо́таю **b** говори́те **c** понима́ю **d** люблю́ **e** живёте **f** за́втракаю **g** гуля́ю **8 a** Как вас зову́т? **b** Вы ру́сский? **c** Где вы живёте? **d** Кто вы по профе́ссии? **e** Где вы рабо́таете? **f** У вас есть хо́бби? **g** Вы лю́бите спорт? **9 a** On Saturday 25 May, 6.00 **b** On Thursday 31 July, 9.25 **c** В понеде́льник восьмо́го февраля́, в семь часо́в три́дцать мину́т. **d** В пя́тницу шестна́дцатого ма́рта, в пять часо́в. **10 a** Going to billiards clubs **b** Watching satellite TV **c** Playing snooker and pool **d** Computer games **e** Going to the casino **f** Feng-shui

Test yourself

b e о́чень люблю́ **c f** люблю́ **a** не люблю́ **d** совсе́м не люблю́

Unit 10

Dialogues

1 2 children. Parents live at dacha. **2 a** Бе́лла **b** Серёжа **c** Tim **3** Anna prefers city, concerts, theatre, cinema, shops. Historical. Near metro. Sasha prefers countryside. Peaceful. Walks in forest.

1 a 63 tram or 28 bus **b** 28 bus **c** 28 bus **d** 17 trolleybus **e** 63 tram **f** 63 tram **g** 17 trolleybus **h** 28 bus **2 Anya:** Moscow. Pharmacy. Mum and dad, sister. Cinema. Wants to speak German. **Peter:** Bristol. Teacher, school. Son. Football. Wants to travel. **Leonid:** Yekaterinburg. Train station. Wife. TV and sweets. Doesn't like sport. Wants to live in Moscow. **3** живёт магази́ны ку́хня её лю́бит день хо́дит **4 a** iii **b** iv **c** ii **d** i **5 Boris:** brother, flat. **Nastya:** cat, dacha. **Liza:** car, brother, flat, dacha. **6 a** зна́ю **b** идёте, иду́ **c** хочу́ **d** говори́т **e** рабо́таешь **f** за́втракаю **g** люблю́ **h** игра́ем **i** у́жинают **7** Elite cottage. Prestige district. Electricity, water, gas, climate control. Jacuzzi and sauna. Fireplace. Satellite TV. 250 sq. m. Big garage.

Unit 11

1 Sport: баскетбо́л, футбо́л, бокс, пинг-по́нг, те́ннис, ре́гби, хокке́й. Food: хлеб, бана́н, сала́т, борщ, шокола́д, котле́та. Family: ма́ма, дочь, ба́бушка, дя́дя, па́па, сын, брат, сестра́. **2** гита́ра, инжене́р, больни́ца **3 1** теа́тр **2** студе́нт **3** метро́ **4** рестора́н **5** омле́т **6** кли́мат **7** па́спорт **8** входи́те **9** тра́ктор **10** Амстерда́м **11** октя́брь **12** вто́рник **13** телефо́н **4** кварти́ра **5 Menu: Cold Starters:** Salad / Mushrooms / Caviar / Salami sausage / Cheese; **First Course** (*literally* First Dishes): Borshch (beetroot soup) / Shshee (cabbage soup); **Main course** (*literally* Second Dishes): Fish / Cutlets / Chicken / Omelette / Pizza / Sausages; **Sweet dishes:** Fruits / Ice cream / Sweets; **Drinks:** Mineral water / Fruit juice / Beer / Wine / Vodka. **6 a** восто́к **в** де́душка **с** а́вгуст **d** три́дцать **e** Росси́я

Unit 12

1 a 16«а» **б** white wine, бе́лое вино́ **в** 18:35, восемна́дцать часо́в три́дцать пять мину́т, 15 degrees, пятна́дцать гра́дусов **2 a** Де́вять «б» нале́во. **б** У нас есть лимона́д, фрукто́вый сок и ко́фе с молоко́м. **в** Да́йте, пожа́луйста, фрукто́вый сок. **г** У вас есть ру́сский журна́л? **3 a** 4 «д» **б** 10 «г» **в** 25 «г» **г** 11 «в» **д** 2.08, + 30 **е** 9.43, −5 **ж** 1.00, + 7 **4 a** exit, no exit, boarding gate (exit to embarkation) **б** customs control, luggage reclaim, transit, passport control, flight number **в** check-in (registration), red channel, waiting room, entrance **5** до́ллары, пистоле́т, доро́жные че́ки, фу́нты сте́рлингов, ка́мера, компью́тер. **6 a** Здра́вствуй, Валенти́н? **б** Да, как дела́? **в** В пя́тницу. **г** Да, шесто́го ию́ля. **д** В восемна́дцать часо́в со́рок мину́т. **е** Да, коне́чно. **ж** Но́мер ре́йса SU две́сти со́рок два. **з** До свида́ния, Валенти́н. **7** Но́мер ре́йса ВА восемьсо́т се́мьдесят во́семь. Я бу́ду в Санкт Петербу́рге в девятна́дцать часо́в со́рок минут, два́дцать шесто́го января́. **8 а** Как прия́тно тебя́ ви́деть! **б** Как вы пожива́ете? **в** Я немно́жко уста́л/а. **г** как всегда́ **д** Мы ско́ро бу́дем до́ма. **9 а** шестна́дцатого а́вгуста в два́дцать два часа́ три́дцать мину́т **б** пя́того ноября́ в де́сять часо́в пятна́дцать мину́т **в** два́дцать девя́того ма́я в трина́дцать часо́в пятьдеся́т мину́т **г** деся́того февраля́ в пятна́дцать часо́в два́дцать мину́т. **11 а** 165 **б** 392 **в** 78 **г** 413 **д** 521 **12 а** Что вы хоти́те пить? **б** Как ва́ша фами́лия? **в** Где моё ме́сто? **г** У вас есть фу́нты сте́рлингов? **д** Э́то ваш чемода́н и ва́ша су́мка? **13 а** 5 **б** 7 **в** 1 **г** 2 **д** 3 **е** 4 **ж** 6

Anecdote

1 food, transport, hospitals, schools **2** You mustn't grumble in the Soviet Union, but you can grumble in America.

Unit 13

1 а 14 **б** on the right **в** 20-30 minutes **г** 10 minutes **д** 3 **е** на восьмо́й авто́бус **ж** пря́мо **з** Пешко́м три́дцать – со́рок мину́т. А на авто́бусе пятна́дцать. **и** Че́рез четы́ре остано́вки. **2** Smoke **3 а** «Парк Культу́ры» the park of culture **б** «Университе́т» University **в** 4 **4 а** Алекса́ндровский сад. **б** Пу́шкинская **в** Арба́тская **г** Ботани́ческий сад **д** Пло́щадь Револю́ции. Скажи́те, пожа́луйста, как попа́сть в Кремль, в Ботани́ческий сад, на ры́нок, в Дом Кни́ги, в ГУМ? Дое́дете до ста́нции **5 а** 6 August **б** train no. 7, carriage no. 13 **в** 10.30 **г** seat no. 2 **д** 11.00 **6** По́езд но́мер пятьсо́т оди́ннадцать в Петербу́рг отхо́дит в де́вять часо́в три́дцать шесть. По́езд но́мер девяно́сто шесть в Но́вгород отхо́дит в двена́дцать часо́в пятьдеся́т пять. По́езд но́мер семьсо́т шестьна́дцать в Ивано́во отхо́дит в два́дцать часо́в со́рок семь. По́езд но́мер во́семьдесят два в Ту́лу отхо́дит в два́дцать три часа́ пять. **7 а** 9.40 **б** Yes. **в** На Ки́евский вокза́л, пожа́луйста. В де́сять часо́в. **8 а** ii **б** iii **в** i **9 а** Как попа́сть в Кремль? **б** Где остано́вка авто́буса? **в** Вы сейча́с выхо́дите? **г** Я е́ду в Ботани́ческий сад на метро́. **д** Когда́ отхо́дит по́езд?

Anecdote 1

1 In case he loses the first and second ones. **2** He has a season ticket.

Anecdote 2

1 The train conductor **2** A forest

Unit 14

1 Books about sport. **2 а** Estonia. 200 roubles per kilo **б** Мо́жно посмотре́ть? **в** Ско́лько вы хоти́те? **г** Всё? **д** Напро́тив **3 а** Lemons and mandarins **б** Edam cheese from Holland **в** Ketchup **г** Indian **д** Stolichnaya, Smirnoff, Absolut **4** Underline all except Мя́со **5** Coffee, fruit flavoured water, vodka, fruit-tea, champagne. Luncheon meat, chocolate, caramel, sauces, ketchups, sweets. **б а** У вас есть колбаса́? **б** ... чай? **в** ... торт? **г** ... ры́ба? **д** ... молоко́? **е** ... апельси́ны? **ж** огурцы́? **7** (аспири́н – апте́ка) (ма́сло – моло́чные проду́кты/ гастроно́м /универса́м) (са́хар – гастроно́м /универса́м) (вино́ – гастроно́м /универса́м) (моро́женое – кио́ск) (цветы́ – ры́нок) (хлеб – бу́лочная) (самова́р – сувени́ры) (ша́пка – универма́г/сувени́ры) **8 а** Go round the shops. **б** Books, wooden toys, postcards and samovar. **в** No, not far. 3 stops by bus. **г** Opposite **д** она́ говори́т, что **е** The salesgirl's aunt lives in London, and says they work there. **ж** Red, green, yellow. **9 а** Matryoshka doll. «Сувени́р». Straight ahead, on the left. **б** Books. Tram 31. «Дом Кни́ги». Not far. 2 or 3 stops. **в** Cake. Grocer's on у́лица Ми́ра. Bus. **10 а** О́птика **б** Часы́ **в** Бу́лочная **г** Антиквариа́т **д** Диети́ческие проду́кты **е** Ры́ба **ж** Музыка́льные инструме́нты **з** А́удио-Видеоте́хника **и** Автомоби́ли **11 а** Я хочу́ купи́ть хлеб, сыр, помидо́ры и чай. **б** Где мо́жно купи́ть газе́ту? **в** Всё. **г** Повтори́те, пожа́луйста. **д** У вас есть бе́лое вино́? **е** Ско́лько сто́ит?

Anecdote
Fish is what they haven't got in the shop opposite.

Unit 15

1 а A room for one with bath **б** A big room for two with shower **в** $120 **г** tomorrow **д** 7.00. 9.00. **е** yes **ж** suitcase and big bag **з** straight ahead and right **2 а** midnight **б** downstairs on left **3 а** Room for two with shower. **б** Room for one for 7th January. **в** Room for two for week. **4 а** У вас есть свобо́дный но́мер? **b** Но́мер на двои́х с ва́нной, пожа́луйста. **с** Хорошо́. В кото́ром часу́ начина́ется обе́д? **d** Здесь есть лифт? У меня́ большо́й чемода́н. **е** Да, ви́жу. **f** Спаси́бо. Но́мер три́дцать четы́ре. Пра́вильно? **g** Спаси́бо большо́е. До свида́ния. **7 а** Australia, 61. **б** Breakfast, tea with lemon and fruit. She feels unwell. **в** To the station, 10.00 tomorrow. **8 а** Edna's room is hot. Window shut, because noisy outside on square. **б** Mark is cold. Another blanket required. Room 73. Tap won't turn off and TV works badly. **в** Vanessa says they have lost key. Room 16. Key at administrator's desk. Vanessa delighted. **г** Bill wants the bill. Room for two for week. Very pleasant stay, warm and quiet in room. Very pleased. **д** Gary is not happy. Hot water not on, telephone not working, dirty room. **9** Room 9, TV needs mending. Room 14, telephone not working properly. Room 23, tap won't turn off. Room 31, cold, window won't shut. Room 35, hot, window won't open. Room 40, noisy. Room 52, dirty. Room 55, radio not working. **10** В но́мере хо́лодно, гря́зно, шу́мно, телеви́зор не рабо́тает, кран не закрыва́ется, окно́ выхо́дит на вокза́л. Я недово́лен/недово́льна. **11 а** New, red, American suitcase. **б** Old black bag containing visa and passport. **в** New, green coat. **г** Money:

dollars, sterling and roubles. **12** Ground floor: cloakroom, lost property, restaurant. First floor: director, administrator, service desk, newspaper kiosk, snack bar. Second floor: post office, hairdresser's, bar.

Unit 16

1 a with lemon and sugar **б** sandwich (bread with salami sausage)
2 a Да́йте/покажи́те, пожа́луйста, меню́. **б** Да́йте, пожа́луйста, ко́фе и моро́женое. **в** Нет, ко́фе с молоко́м и с са́харом. **г** Я не понима́ю. Повтори́те, пожа́луйста. **д** Поня́тно. Да́йте, пожа́луйста, вани́льное моро́женое. **е** Спаси́бо. Ско́лько с меня́?
3 First (ground) floor, restaurant. Breakfast, 8.00 – 10.00. За́трак начина́ется в во́семь часо́в и конча́ется в де́сять часо́в. Dinner, 13.00–15.00. Обе́д начина́ется в трина́дцать часо́в и конча́ется в пятна́дцать часо́в. Evening meal, 18.00 – 20.00. У́жин начина́ется в восемна́дцать часо́в и конча́ется в два́дцать часо́в. Second (first) floor grill-bar, where coffee and sandwiches can be ordered. **4 a** Moscow salad and borshsh (beetroot soup). **б** Mushrooms in sour cream, shshee (cabbage soup), kebab (shashlik) with rice, fruit, white wine, tea with lemon but no sugar. **в** Her brother. Asks for extra wine glass and plate.
5 Да́йте, пожа́луйста, ещё ча́шку, ло́жку, нож и стул. **6** Mushrooms in sour cream, cabbage soup, shashlik, rice, red wine, bread. Another fork. Грибы́ в смета́не, щи, шашлы́к, рис и красное вино́. Хлеб. Ещё ви́лка. **7** На столе́ – таре́лка, нож, ви́лка, ло́жка, рю́мка, салфе́тка, вино́, буты́лка хлеб, ку́рица. **8** Да́йте, пожа́луйста, моско́вский сала́т, суп с гриба́ми, беф-стро́ганов, рис, шокола́дное моро́женое, бе́лое вино́ и ко́фе с молоко́м. Да́йте, пожа́луйста, счёт. **9** ж б з а д г и е в **11 Ка́ша ри́совая моло́чная:** рис – **сто** грамм; ма́сло – два́дцать пять грамм; са́хар – два́дцать грамм; соль – пять грамм; молоко́ – две́сти шестьдеся́т миллили́тров; вода́ – две́сти миллили́тров **12 a** Champagne and flowers (roses). **б** Fine. **в** Mushrooms in sour cream and caviar. **г** Yes, very tasty. **д** Vodka. **е** It's late. **13 a** Я о́чень люблю́ шампа́нское. **б** За ва́ше здоро́вье! **в** Каки́е краси́вые рю́мки! **г** Как дела́?

Anecdote
Someone has stolen his bike, so he does not need to avoid alcohol.

Unit 17

1 a iii **б** ii **в** iii **2 a** ii **б** iii **в** v **г** i **д** iv **3 a** Krasnodar. 861-992-54-16. Tomorrow at 10.00. Three minutes. **б** Nottingham, England. 0115-923-44-19. Today at 11.00. Eight minutes. **в** Novgorod. 816-25-13-67. Tomorrow evening at 7.00. Five minutes. **4 a** v **б** ix **в** x **г** i **д** iv **е** iii **ж** vi **з** ii **и** vii **к** viii **5 a** stamps, envelopes, postcards **б** 4 stamps at 500 roubles for letter to UK **в** fill in form **г** books and toys **6 a** три ма́рки по де́сять рубле́й **б** Что на́до де́лать? **в** Коне́чно мо́жно. **г** пра́вильно **д** Спаси́бо вам большо́е. **е** мо́жно **ж** хоти́те з запо́лнить **и** Э́то **к** свида́ния **7 а** Как **б** Где **в** Куда́ **г** Кто **д** Ско́лько **е** Как **ж** Что **з** Когда́ **8** Куда́, кому́ ... Москва́, Проспе́кт Ми́ра, дом 26, кварти́ра 9, Ивано́в, А. Текст ... Я в Москве́ в гости́нице «Росси́я», у́лица Варва́рка, но́мер 331. Фами́лия и а́дрес отправи́теля ... Москва́, гости́ница «Росси́я», у́лица Варва́рка, но́мер 331, your surname and initials in Cyrillic script. **9** сын дочь/соль пе́рец/стол стул/вокза́л по́езд/я́блоки гру́ши/ ма́ма па́па/теа́тр пье́са/де́вушка молодо́й челове́к **10** Росси́я 194358, Санкт Петербу́рг, Проспе́кт Э́нгельса, дом 121 ко́рпус 2 кварти́ра 69, Кузнецо́ва, Т. И.

Unit 18

Holiday advert:

Malta. Aeroflot flights. 3 star hotel, twin rooms, bar, café, discos, tennis, pool, diving, shopping tour, casino, excursions. Staff speak Russian.

1 а Go skiing in forest. **б** Cold, frosty, sunny, minus 10. **в** Sit at home and watch TV. **г** Summer, hot, can walk on beach, eat ice cream. **д** To ring Andrew. **е** 739-15-42. **2 а** 3 **б** 4 **в** 2 **г** 5 **д** 1 **3** Tomorrow: cold, air temperature –7°, northerly wind, snow and frost. **4** На за́паде па́смурно и идёт дождь. На се́вере тума́нно. На восто́ке ми́нус 10 гра́дусов и идёт снег. На ю́ге тепло́, плюс 20 гра́дусов и со́лнце све́тит. **5** Helen is from Lancaster. Likes radio, chess, reading, films and concerts. Yura is from Krasnodar. Plays hockey, skis, walks in country, plays tennis, swims in sea, collects mushrooms. **6** Здесь мо́жно лови́ть ры́бу, купа́ться в мо́ре, загора́ть на пля́же, ката́ться на велосипе́де, ката́ться на ло́дке, игра́ть в те́ннис. **7 i** б **ii** в **iii** а **8** Almost any excuse will do! **9 а** Tomorrow. **б** Eight. **в** 8 a.m. **10 1** Enquiry office **2** tourist complex **3** hotel **4** campsite **5** architectural monument **6** museum **7** archeological monument **8** theatre, concert hall **9** stadium **10** restaurant, café, bar **11** department store **12** market **13** taxi rank **14** petrol station **15** train station **16** beach **17** garden, park. **11 а** Sochi in hotel at beach. **б** Sunny and hot. **в** Eats ice cream and plays volleyball on beach. **12 а** 8.30, 12.30, 16.55, 19.20, 21.00, 23.50 **б** 9.55, 21.40 **в** 14.20, 16.30, 20.40 **г** 11.10, 18.20 **д** 9.20, 14.00, 20.00 **13 а** Б **б** В

Unit 19

1 Vadim has run a marathon, Tanya has fun, Anton has food poisoning **2 1** нос **2** нога́ **3** голова́ **4** се́рдце **5** у́хо **6** живо́т **7** го́рло **8** глаз **9** зу́бы **10** рука́ **11** спина́ **3 а** Brian Wilkinson. **б** Headache, hot and cold, temperature, sore throat. **в** No. **г** To rest at home and take medicine three times a day. **4 а** Broken his right leg. **б** Ambulance. **в** Take an aspirin. **5 а** Hotel Izmailovo **б** Feels bad, heart hurting. **в** Soon, in three minutes. **6 а** Я принима́ю табле́тку. **б** Я иду́ к врачу́. **в** Я е́ду в больни́цу. **г** Я принима́ю лека́рство. **7 а** vii **б** iv **в** i **г** v **д** ii **е** vi

ж iii **8** *Suggested answer*: **Леони́д** **a** ✕ **б** ✓ **в** ✓ **г** ✕ **Ири́на** **a** ✕ **б** ✕
в ✓ **г** ✓ **Арка́дий** **a** ✕ **б** ✓ **в** ✕ **г** ✕ **Мариа́нна** **a** ✕ **б** ✓ **в** ✕ **г** ✕
9 **a** го́да **б** лет **в** го́да **г** лет **д** год **10 1** Nina Andryeyevna. 27. Back
hurts. **2** Nikolay Vladimirovich. 53. Temperature. Feels sick. **3** Sergey
Sergeyevich. Toothache.

Anecdote
Doctor tells her she will live to 90 if she doesn't drink and smoke. She is
already 93.

Unit 20

1 a On a train. **б** Wears spectacles, dressed in coat, boots and hat.
Beautiful. 23 years old. **в** In restaurant 'Vostok' at 7.00. **г** Victor will
wear a suit. 40 years old, smokes cigars. **2** Vanya: ✓ в д ж к. Galya: ✓
а б в д е. **3** Э́то молодо́й челове́к. Ему́ лет девятна́дцать. Да,
высо́кий и худо́й. У него́ коро́ткие, тёмные во́лосы. Он в
джи́нсах и в руба́шке. **4** ску́чный, лени́вый, невысо́кий, то́лстый,
не лю́бит, неприя́тный, глу́пый, дли́нные, тёмные, зелёные глаза́.
5 a ii **б** iv **в** iii **г** i **6 1** б **2** в **3** а **7 a** i **б** iii **в** ii **8 a** vi **б** iii
в v **г** ii **д** iv (e) i **9** Sasha Nikolayevich Ivanov, 18, has sister and
brother. Olya 10, Misha 3. Live in flat, Minsk. Father is doctor, mother is
teacher. Olya likes sport, tennis. Misha not yet at school. Tall, dark hair,
black eyes. Do you want photo? Likes reading and chess, most of all, going
to theatre. Skiing. Please write. Where do you live? What do you like to
do? Brothers or sisters? Do you live in a flat or a house?

Revision test: Units 1–10

1 a i **b** iii **c** iii **d** ii **e** iii **f** ii **g** i **h** iii **2 a** ii **b** iii **c** iii **3 a** большо́й
b больни́цу **c** ва́ша **d** Магада́не **e** бадминто́н **f** гита́ре **g** пя́тое
4 a ii **b** iii **c** i **d** ii **e** i **f** iii **g** ii

Revision test: Units 12–20

1 a i **b** iii **c** iii **d** ii **e** iii **f** i **2 a** vi **b** vii **c** i **d** v **e** iv **f** viii **g** ii **h** iii
3 a ii **b** iii **c** i **d** iii **e** iii **f** i **g** ii **h** i **i** ii **4 a** iii **b** ii **c** i **d** iii **e** i **f** iii

numbers

Cardinal numbers

0	ноль	11	оди́ннадцать
1	оди́н	12	двена́дцать
2	два	13	трина́дцать
3	три	14	четы́рнадцать
4	четы́ре	15	пятна́дцать
5	пять	16	шестна́дцать
6	шесть	17	семна́дцать
7	семь	18	восемна́дцать
8	во́семь	19	девятна́дцать
9	де́вять	20	два́дцать
10	де́сять		

21 два́дцать оди́н

30	три́дцать	200	две́сти
40	со́рок	300	три́ста
50	пятьдеся́т	400	четы́реста
60	шестьдеся́т	500	пятьсо́т
70	се́мьдесят	600	шестьсо́т
80	во́семьдесят	700	семьсо́т
90	девяно́сто	800	восемьсо́т
100	сто	900	девятьсо́т

1,000	ты́сяча
2,000	две ты́сячи
3,000	три ты́сячи
4,000	четы́ре ты́сячи
5,000	пять ты́сяч
6,000	шесть ты́сяч
7,000	семь ты́сяч
8,000	во́семь ты́сяч
9,000	де́вять ты́сяч
10,000	де́сять ты́сяч
20,000	два́дцать ты́сяч

Ordinal numbers

1st	пе́рвый	11th	оди́ннадцатый
2nd	второ́й	12th	двена́дцатый
3rd	тре́тий	13th	трина́дцатый
4th	четвёртый	14th	четы́рнадцатый
5th	пя́тый	15th	пятна́дцатый
6th	шесто́й	16th	шестна́дцатый
7th	седьмо́й	17th	семна́дцатый
8th	восьмо́й	18th	восемна́дцатый
9th	девя́тый	19th	девятна́дцатый
10th	деся́тый	20th	двадца́тый
		21st	два́дцать пе́рвый
		30th	тридца́тый

the/a

There are no words in Russian for *the* and *a*.

to be

The verb *to be* is not used in the present tense.

Spelling rules

1 Do not use ы after г, к, х, ж, ч, ш, щ. Instead, use и.
2 Do not use unstressed о after ж, ч, ш, щ, ц. Instead, use е.

Gender of singular nouns

Masculine nouns end in	**a consonant**	парк
	й	музе́й
	ь	Кремль
	а	па́па
Feminine nouns end in	а	кассе́та
	я	эне́ргия
	ь	дочь
Neuter nouns end in	о	метро́
	е	кафе́

Plural forms of nouns

Masculine

рестора́н/рестора́ны *restaurant/s*
кио́ск/кио́ски *kiosk/s*
рубль/рубли́ *rouble/s*

Feminine

гости́ница/гости́ницы   *hotel/s*
библиоте́ка/библиоте́ки   *library/libraries*
пло́щадь/пло́щади   *square/s*

Neuter

у́тро/у́тра   *morning/s*

Many neuter nouns (бюро́, кака́о, кафе́, кило́, кино́, метро́, пиани́но, ра́дио) do not change.

Adjectives

Masculine singular	Э́то краси́вый парк.	*It's a beautiful park.*
Feminine singular	Э́то краси́вая ва́за.	*It's a beautiful vase.*
Neuter singular	Э́то краси́вое ра́дио.	*It's a beautiful radio.*
Plural	Э́то краси́вые ма́рки.	*They are beautiful stamps.*

Most common endings are **–ый –ий –ой** (*m*), **–ая –яя** (*f*), **–ое –ее** (*n*) and **–ые, –ие** (*pl*).

Possessive pronouns

Мой (*my/mine*), **твой** (*your/yours*), **наш** (*our/ours*), **ваш** (*your/yours*) change form to agree with nouns to which they refer.

Masculine	Feminine	Neuter	Plural
мой па́спорт	моя́ балала́йка	моё пиани́но	мои́ кассе́ты
твой па́спорт	твоя́ балала́йка	твоё пиани́но	твои́ кассе́ты
наш па́спорт	на́ша балала́йка	на́ше пиани́но	на́ши кассе́ты
ваш па́спорт	ва́ша балала́йка	ва́ше пиани́но	ва́ши кассе́ты

Его́ (*his*), **её** (*her/hers*), **их** (*their/theirs*) do not change form.

его́ па́спорт	его́ балала́йка	его́ пиани́но	его́ кассе́ты

Pronouns

Где авто́бус?	*Where is the bus?*	Вот **он**.	There **it** is. (*m*)
Где ва́за?	*Where is the vase?*	Вот **она́**.	There **it** is. (*f*)
Где ра́дио?	*Where is the radio?*	Вот **оно́**.	There **it** is. (*n*)
Где конфе́ты?	*Where are the sweets?*	Вот **они́**.	There **they** are. (*pl*)

Demonstrative pronouns

Да́йте, пожа́луйста, **э́тот** чемода́н.   *Please give me **that** suitcase.*

Эта де́вушка – моя́ дочь.
Покажи́те, пожа́луйста,
  э́то ра́дио.
Эти биле́ты – мои́.

This girl is my daughter.
Please show me that radio.

These tickets are mine.

Personal pronouns

singular		**plural**	
я	*I*	мы	*we*
ты	*you* (informal)	вы	*you* (plural or formal)
он	*he/it*	они́	*they*
она́	*she/it*		
оно́	*it*		

As well as meaning *his*, *her* and *their*, the words **его́**, **её** and **их** mean *him*, *her* and *them* in phrases where personal pronouns are the direct object of the verb.

ты лю́бишь **меня́**	*you love me*	вы лю́бите **нас**	*you love us*
я люблю́ **тебя́**	*I love you*	они́ лю́бят **вас**	*they love you*
она́ лю́бит **его́**	*she loves him*	мы лю́бим **их**	*we love them*
он лю́бит **её**	*he loves her*		

У вас есть ...? *Do you have ...?*

у меня́	*I have*	у нас	*we have*
у тебя́	*you have*	у вас	*you have*
у него́	*he/it has*	у них	*they have*
у неё	*she has*		

Accusative case after *в* and *на* (into/to)

Masculine and neuter singular nouns do not change after **в** and **на** when motion is indicated, but feminine singular nouns change their endings from **-а** to **-у** and **-я** to **-ю**.

Masculine	**Feminine**	**Neuter**
Как попа́сть в теа́тр?	Как попа́сть на по́чту?	Как попа́сть в кафе́?
	Как попа́сть в галере́ю?	

Accusative case with direct objects

The accusative case is used when an inanimate noun is the direct object of a verb. Only the feminine singular ending changes.

(m)	Я люблю́ **спорт**.		*I love sport.*
(f)	Я люблю́ **му́зыку**.		*I love music.*
(n)	Я люблю́ **кино́**.		*I love cinema.*
(pl)	Я люблю́ **кни́ги**.		*I love books.*

Prepositional case after в and на (in)

When **в** and **на** mean *in* or *at* a certain place, they trigger the prepositional case in the following word.

Masculine	**Feminine**	**Neuter**
(институ́т) в институ́те	(шко́ла) в шко́ле	(письмо́) в письме́
(Кремль) в Кремле́		
(музе́й) в музе́е		

Verbs in present tense

Group 1 verbs

рабо́тать   *to work*

я	рабо́таю	мы	рабо́таем
ты	рабо́таешь	вы	рабо́таете
он/она́/оно́	рабо́тает	они́	рабо́тают

идти́   *to go on foot*
  on one occasion

я иду́	мы идём
ты идёшь	вы идёте
он/она́ идёт	они́ иду́т

быть   *to be* (future tense)

я бу́ду	мы бу́дем
ты бу́дешь	вы бу́дете
он/она́ бу́дет	они́ бу́дут

пить   *to drink*

я пью	мы пьём
ты пьёшь	вы пьёте
он/она́ пьёт	они́ пьют

мочь   *to be able*

я могу́	мы мо́жем
ты мо́жешь	вы мо́жете
он/она́ мо́жет	они́ мо́гут

Group 2 verbs

говори́ть   *to speak/talk*

я	говорю́	мы	говори́м
ты	говори́шь	вы	говори́те
он/она́	говори́т	они́	говоря́т

ходи́ть   *to go on foot habitually*

я хожу́	мы хо́дим
ты хо́дишь	вы хо́дите
он/она́ хо́дит	они́ хо́дят

люби́ть   *to love*

я люблю́	мы лю́бим
ты лю́бишь	вы лю́бите
он/она́ лю́бит	они́ лю́бят

Irregular verbs

хотéть *to want*

я	хочý	мы	хоти́м
ты	хо́чешь	вы	хоти́те
он/онá	хо́чет	они́	хотя́т

есть *to eat*

я	ем	мы	еди́м
ты	ешь	вы	еди́те
он/онá	ест	они́	едя́т

vocabulary

1 The English translations apply only to the meaning of the words as used in this book.

2 Nouns ending in a consonant or **-й** are masculine. A few nouns ending in **-a** are also masculine, but this will be clear from their meaning, e.g. **дéдушка** – *grandfather*.
Other nouns ending in **-a** or **-я** are feminine.
Nouns ending in **-ь** may be masculine or feminine. This will be indicated by (*m*) or (*f*).
Nouns ending in **-o** or **-e** are neuter.

3 Adjectives are shown in their masculine singular form, ending **-ый**, **-ий** or **-ой**.

4 Verbs are shown in their infinitive form unless otherwise stated. If they are straightforward verbs it will be shown whether they belong to Group 1 or Group 2.

English–Russian

a little bit немнóжко
a lot мнóго
all right, fine нормáльно
already ужé
also тóже
always всегдá
and и
another ещё
at home дóма
at last наконéц
awful ужáсно

bad плóхо
be быть
be able мочь 1
beautiful красúвый
because потомý, что
better лýчше
big большóй
brother брат
but а, но

closed закрьíт
cold хóлодно

daughter дочь (f)
to do делать 1
do you have? у вас есть?
don't mention it! не за что!
to drink пить 1

each, every каждый
early рано
to eat есть
entrance вход
everything всё
excuse me извините
exit выход
it's expensive дорого

fairly, quite довольно
far, a long way далеко
father отец
favourite любимый
it's fine прекрасно
fine прекрасный
flat квартира
fortunately к счастью
funny смешно

to get to попасть
girl, young woman девушка
give me дайте
go (imperative) идите
to go on foot идти 1
to go on foot (habitually) ходить 2
it's good хорошо
good хороший
good day добрый день
good evening добрый вечер
good morning доброе утро
good night спокойной ночи
goodbye до свидания
grandfather дедушка
grandmother бабушка

to have breakfast завтракать 1
to have dinner обедать 1
to have supper ужинать 1
he, it он
hello здравствуйте
her её

here здесь
his, him его
house, block of flats дом
how как
how is that written? как это пишется?
how much do I owe? сколько с меня?
how much does it cost? сколько стоит?
how much? how many? сколько
how old are you? сколько вам лет?
husband муж

I я
if если
in English по-английски
in my opinion по-моему
in Russian по-русски
in the afternoon днём
in the evening вечером
in the morning утром
in, into в
it's interesting интересно
interesting интересный
it он, она, оно
it is, this (n) это

just so! точно так!

to know знать 1

late поздно
left левый
let's go (by transport) поедем
let's go (on foot) пойдём
let's meet встретимся
to live жить 1
look (imperative) посмотрите
to look, watch смотреть 2
to love любить 2

man мужчина
man, person человек
may I help you? вам помочь?
maybe может быть
me меня
more больше

most of all бо́льше всего́
mother мать
my мой

name и́мя
it's necessary на́до
new но́вый
no нет
it's noisy шу́мно
not не
not allowed, mustn't нельзя́
not far недалеко́
now сейча́с
numbers ци́фры

of course коне́чно
often ча́сто
old ста́рый
only то́лько
open откры́т
opposite напро́тив
or и́ли
our наш

patronymic name о́тчество
it's peaceful споко́йно
pity (what a pity!) жаль (как жаль!)
to play игра́ть 1
please пожа́луйста
it's possible мо́жно
probably наве́рно

it's quiet ти́хо
quite, entirely совсе́м

to read чита́ть 1
repeat (imperative) повтори́те
right пра́вый
rouble рубль
Russian ру́сский, ру́сская

to say, talk говори́ть 2
say, tell me скажи́те
to see ви́деть 2
it seems ка́жется
she, it она́
shop магази́н
show me (imperative) покажи́те

sit down (imperative) сади́тесь
slower ме́дленнее
small ма́ленький
so так
son сын
straight ahead пря́мо
street у́лица
surname фами́лия

thank you спаси́бо
that's nice прия́тно
that's right пра́вильно
to the left нале́во
to the right напра́во
their, them их
then пото́м
there вот, там
there is, there are есть
these э́ти
they они́
to think ду́мать 1
this (m), (f) э́тот, э́та
it's time пора́
today сего́дня
tomorrow за́втра
too, too much сли́шком
town го́род

to understand понима́ть 1
understood поня́тно
unfortunately к сожале́нию
us нас
usually обы́чно

very о́чень

to want хоте́ть (irreg)
it's warm тепло́
we мы
what have you got? что у вас есть?
what is your name? как вас зову́т?
what sort of ...? како́й...?
what time is it? кото́рый час?/ ско́лько сейча́с вре́мени?
what's the matter? в чём де́ло? что с ва́ми?

what, that что	*yes* да
where где	*yesterday* вчера́
where from отку́да	*you (pl. formal)* вы
where to куда́	*you (object)* вас
who кто	*you (sing. informal)* ты
wife жена́	*you (object)* тебя́
with pleasure с удово́льствием	*young* молодо́й
woman же́нщина	*your* ваш, твой
it's wonderful чуде́сно	
to work рабо́тать 1	
worse ху́же	

Russian — English

а *but*
а́вгуст *August*
авиаписьмо́ *airmail letter*
авто́бус *bus*
автомоби́ль (*m*) *car*
автошко́ла *driving school*
администра́тор *administrator*
а́дрес *address*
а́дрес отправи́теля *address of sender*
аккордео́н *accordion*
актёр *actor*
акти́вный *active*
актри́са *actress*
алло́ *hello (on phone)*
альбо́м *album*
Аме́рика *America*
америка́нец, америка́нка *American (m, f)*
америка́нский *American (adj)*
америка́нскйи пул *pool*
англи́йский *English*
А́нглия *England*
англича́нин, англича́нка *Englishman, woman*
анекдо́т *anecdote*
анке́та *questionnaire*
антибио́тик *antibiotic*
антиквариа́т *antiques*
апельси́н *orange*

апте́ка *pharmacy*
а́рмрестлинг *arm wrestling*
аспири́н *aspirin*
атле́тика *athletics*
атмосфе́ра *atmosphere*
а́том *atom*
аэропо́рт *airport*
Аэрофло́т *Aeroflot*

ба́бушка *grandmother*
бага́ж *luggage*
бадминто́н *badminton*
бакте́рия *bacterium*
балала́йка *balalaika*
балери́на *ballerina*
бале́т *ballet*
бана́н *banana*
банк *bank*
ба́нка *tin, jar*
ба́ня *steam bath*
бар *bar*
баскетбо́л *basketball*
бассе́йн *swimming pool*
бато́н *long loaf*
бе́лый *white*
бе́рег *bank, shore*
бери́те *take (imperative)*
(не) беспоко́йтесь *(don't) worry (imperative)*
бестсе́ллер *bestseller*
библиоте́ка *library*
бизнесме́н *businessman*
биле́т *ticket*

билья́рдный клуб *billiard club*
бланк *form*
блонди́н, блонди́нка *blond man, blonde woman*
блу́за *blouse*
блю́до *dish*
бо́дибилдинг *bodybuilding*
бо́же мой! *my God!*
бокс *boxing*
боли́т, боля́т *it hurts, they hurt*
больни́ца *hospital*
бо́льше *more*
бо́льше всего́ *most of all*
большо́й *big*
борода́ beard
борщ *borshsh (beetroot soup)*
ботани́ческий *botanical*
боти́нки *ankle boots*
брат *brother*
бри́финг *briefing*
бро́кер *broker*
брю́ки *trousers*
брюне́т, брюне́тка *brown-haired man, woman*
бу́дет *will be*
бу́лка *sweet bread roll*
бу́лочная *bakery*
бульва́р *boulevard*
бума́жник *wallet*
бутербро́д *sandwich*
буты́лка *bottle*
буфе́т *snack bar*
был *was*
быть *to be*
бюро́ нахо́док *lost property office*
бюро́ обслу́живания *service desk*

в *in, into*
ваго́н *train carriage*
ваго́н-рестора́н *restaurant car*
ва́за *vase*
ва́ленки *felt boots*
вам помо́чь? *may I help you?*
вани́льный *vanilla*
ва́нна *bath*
ва́нная *bathroom*

варе́нье *fruit preserve*
вас *you (object)*
ваш *your*
велосипе́д *bicycle*
вес *weight*
весна́ *spring*
весно́й *in spring*
ве́трено *windy*
ве́чером *in the evening*
вид *view*
ви́деть 2 (ви́жу, ви́дишь) *to see*
ви́за *visa*
ви́лка *fork*
вино́ *wine*
ви́ски *whisky*
вку́сный *tasty*
внизу́ *downstairs*
вода́ *water*
во́дка *vodka*
во́здух *air*
во́зраст *age*
вокза́л (на) *train station*
волейбо́л *volleyball*
во́лосы *hair*
вон там *over there*
воскресе́нье *Sunday*
восто́к (на) *east*
восто́чный *eastern*
вот *there*
врач *doctor*
вре́мя *time*
всегда́ *always*
всё *everything*
встаю́ *I get up*
встре́тимся *let's meet*
вто́рник *Tuesday*
второ́е блю́до *second (main) course*
вход *entrance*
входи́те *come in (imperative)*
в чём де́ло? *what's the matter?*
вчера́ *yesterday*
вы *you*
вы́дача багажа́ *luggage reclaim*
вы́звать *to send for*
высо́кий *tall*

вы́ход   *exit*
вы́ход на поса́дку   *boarding gate*
выходи́ть   *to go out*
выходно́й день   *closing day*

газ   *gas*
газе́та   *newspaper*
газиро́ванный   *sparkling, fizzy*
галере́я   *gallery*
га́лстук   *tie*
гардеро́б   *cloakroom*
гарни́р   *side dishes*
гастроно́м   *grocer's*
где   *where*
Герма́ния   *Germany*
гимна́стика   *gymnastics*
гита́ра   *guitar*
глаз   *eye*
говори́ть 2   *to say, talk*
год   *year*
голова́   *head*
голубо́й   *blue*
гольф   *golf*
гомеопати́ческая апте́ка
   homeopathic chemist
го́рло   *throat*
го́род   *town*
городско́й   *urban*
горя́чий   *hot*
господи́н   *Mr*
госпожа́   *Mrs, Miss*
гости́ная   *lounge*
гости́ница   *hotel*
гото́вить 2 (гото́влю, гото́вишь)
   to prepare, cook
гра́дус   *degree*
гражда́нство   *nationality*
грамм   *gram*
гриб   *mushroom*
грипп   *flu*
гру́ша   *pear*
гря́зный   *dirty*
гуля́ть 1   *to go for a walk*

да   *yes*
да́йвинг   *driving*
да́йте   *give (imperative)*

далеко́   *far, a long way*
да́ча   *dacha (country house)*
дверь (f)   *door*
де́вушка   *girl, young woman*
де́душка   *grandfather*
дежу́рная   *woman on duty*
дека́брь (m)   *December*
деклара́ция   *declaration*
(как) дела́?   *how are things?*
де́лать 1   *to do*
де́ньги   *money*
дере́вня   *village, countryside*
деревя́нный   *wooden*
де́ти   *children*
де́тский сад   *kindergarten*
джаз   *jazz*
джаку́зи   *jacuzzi*
джи́нсы   *jeans*
диа́гноз   *diagnosis*
дива́н   *couch*
диза́йн-сту́дия   *design studio*
диплома́т   *diplomat*
дли́нный   *long*
для куря́щих   *for smokers*
днём   *in the afternoon*
до́брое у́тро   *good morning*
до́брый ве́чер   *good evening*
до́брый день   *good day*
дово́лен   *happy*
дово́льно   *fairly, quite*
дое́дете до   *travel as far as*
дождь (m)   *rain*
до́ктор   *doctor*
докуме́нт   *document*
как вы долете́ли?   *how was your
   flight?*
до́ллар   *dollar*
дом   *house, block of flats*
до́ма   *at home*
Дом Кни́ги   *the Book House (book
   shop)*
домофо́н   *entry phone*
до́рого   *it's expensive*
доро́жный чек   *traveller's cheque*
до свида́ния   *goodbye*
дочь (f)   *daughter*

ду́мать 1   *to think*
дура́к   *fool*
душ   *shower*
ду́шно   *it's humid*
дя́дя   *uncle*

еди́ный биле́т   *season transport ticket*
е́сли   *if*
есть   *there is, there are*
есть   *to eat*
е́хать 1 (е́ду, е́дешь)   *to go by transport*
ещё   *another*
ёлка   *fir tree*

жаль (как жаль!)   *pity (what a pity!)*
жа́рко   *it's hot*
ждать 1 (жду, ждёшь)   *to wait*
жёлтый   *yellow*
жена́   *wife*
же́нщина   *woman*
жёсткий   *hard*
живо́т   *stomach*
жить 1 (живу́, живёшь)   *to live*
журна́л   *magazine*

за ва́ше здоро́вье!   *your health!*
за́втра   *tomorrow*
за́втрак   *breakfast*
за́втракать 1   *to have breakfast*
загора́ть 1   *to sunbathe*
за грани́цей   *abroad*
заказа́ть   *to order*
закрыва́ется, закрыва́ются   *it closes, they close*
закры́т   *closed*
заку́ски   *starters*
зал   *hall*
зал ожида́ния   *waiting room*
за окно́м   *through the window*
за́пад (на)   *west*
запо́лните   *fill in (imperative)*
застегни́те   *fasten (imperative)*
здесь   *here*
здра́вствуйте   *hello*
зелёный   *green*

зе́ркало   *mirror*
зима́   *winter*
зи́мний   *winter (adj)*
зимо́й   *in winter*
знать 1   *to know*
зову́т (как вас зову́т?)   *they call (what are you called?)*
зоологи́ческий   *zoological*
зоомагази́н   *pet shop*
зоопа́рк   *zoo*
зуб   *tooth*

и   *and*
игра́ть 1   *to play*
игру́шка   *toy*
иди́те   *go (imperative)*
идти́ 1 (иду́, идёшь)   *to go on foot*
извини́те   *excuse me (imperative)*
икра́   *caviar*
и́ли   *or*
и́мя   *name*
инжене́р   *engineer*
институ́т   *institute*
интере́сно   *it's interesting*
интере́сный   *interesting*
интерне́т кафе́   *Internet café*
инфе́кция   *infection*
информа́ция   *information*
ирла́ндец, ирла́ндка   *Irish man, woman*
испа́нец, испа́нка   *Spanish man, woman*
Испа́ния   *Spain*
истори́ческий   *historical*
ищу́   *I'm looking for*
ию́ль (m)   *July*
ию́нь (m)   *June*

кабине́т   *study, consulting room*
ка́ждый   *each, every*
ка́жется   *it seems*
казино́   *casino*
как   *how*
кака́о   *cocoa*
како́й   *what sort of*
как э́то мо́жет быть?   *how can this be?*

как э́то пи́шется? *how is that written?*
ка́мера *camera*
ками́н *fireplace*
кана́л *canal*
капита́н *captain*
ка́рий *brown (eyes)*
карто́шка *potato*
ка́сса *cash desk*
кассе́та *cassette*
ката́ться на лы́жах, конька́х, саня́х *to ski, skate, sledge*
кафе́ *café*
ка́ша *porridge*
квадра́тный метр *square metre*
кварти́ра *flat*
ке́мпинг *camping*
кило́ *kilo*
килова́тт *kilowatt*
килогра́мм *kilogram*
киломе́тр *kilometre*
кино́ *cinema*
киноаппара́т *cine-camera*
кинотеа́тр *cinema*
кио́ск *kiosk*
кли́мат *climate*
климатоте́хника *climate control*
ключ *key*
кни́га *book*
кни́жечка *strip of transport tickets*
код *code*
колбаса́ *salami sausage*
коме́та *comet*
ко́мната *room*
компа́кт-ди́ск *compact disk*
компози́тор *composer*
компо́т *stewed fruit*
компью́тер *computer*
компью́терные и́гры *computer games*
кому́ *to whom*
комфо́рт *comfort*
конве́рт *envelope*
коне́чно *of course*
консульта́ция *consultation*
консье́рж *concierge*

конфе́та *sweet*
конча́ется *it finishes*
коридо́р *corridor*
коро́ткий *short*
ко́рпус *section of housing block*
космона́вт *cosmonaut*
костю́м *suit*
кот *cat*
котле́та *cutlet (flat meatball)*
кото́рый час? *what time is it?*
ко́ттедж *cottage*
ко́фе *coffee*
кошелёк *purse*
кошма́р *nightmare*
кран *tap*
краси́вый *beautiful*
Кра́сная пло́щадь *Red Square*
кра́сный *red*
кремль (*m*) *Kremlin*
кре́сло *armchair*
кри́кет *cricket*
крова́ть (*f*) *bed*
к себе́ *pull*
к сожале́нию *unfortunately*
к сча́стью *fortunately*
кто *who*
куда́ *where to*
купа́ться *to swim*
купе́ *compartment*
купи́ть *to buy*
кури́ть *to smoke*
ку́рица *chicken*
курс *exchange rate*
ку́хня *kitchen*

ла́дно *OK*
ла́мпа *lamp*
ле́вый *left*
лека́рство *medicine*
лес *forest*
ле́то *summer*
ле́том *in summer*
лимона́д *lemonade*
литр *litre*
лифт *lift*
лови́ть ры́бу *to catch fish*
ло́дка *boat*

Russian-English vocabulary

ложка *spoon*
ложусь спать *I go to bed*
лошадь (*f*) *horse*
луна *moon*
лучше *better*
лысый *bald*
любимый *favourite*
любить 2 (люблю, любишь) *to love*

магазин *shop*
май *May*
маленький *small*
мальчик *boy*
мама *mum*
марафон *marathon*
марка *stamp*
маркетинг *marketing*
март *March*
маршрут *route*
маршрутное такси *fixed route taxi*
масло *butter*
массаж *massage*
матрёшка *matryoshka doll*
мать (*f*) *mother*
машина *car*
медаль (*f*) *medal*
медленнее *slower*
медпункт *first-aid post*
медсестра *nurse*
междугородный *intercity*
международный *international*
менеджер *manager*
меню *menu*
меня *me*
место *place, seat*
месяц *month*
метеор *meteor*
метр *metre*
метро *metro*
механизм *mechanism*
микроскоп *microscope*
миксер *mixer*
милиция *police*
минеральная вода *mineral water*
минус *minus*

минута *minute*
много *a lot*
может быть *maybe*
можно *it's possible*
мой *my*
молодой *young*
молоко *milk*
молочные продукты *dairy products*
монитор *monitor*
море *sea*
мороженое *ice cream*
мороз *frost*
Москва *Moscow*
москвич, москвичка *Muscovite man, woman*
мост *bridge*
мочь 1 (могу, можешь) *to be able*
мужчина *man*
музей *museum*
музыка *music*
мы *we*
мыло *soap*
мюсли *muesli*
мягкий *soft*
мясо *meat*

на *at, to, on*
набережная *embankment*
наверно *probably*
надо *it's necessary*
наконец *at last*
налево *to the left*
напиток *drink*
напишите *write (imperative)*
направо *to the right*
напротив *opposite*
наркотик *narcotics*
начинается *it starts*
наш *our*
не *not*
неважно *not very well*
невысокий *short, not tall*
недалеко *not far*
неделя *week*
недорого *it's inexpensive*

не́ за что! *don't mention it!*
некраси́вый *ugly*
нельзя́ *it is not allowed, mustn't*
не́мец, не́мка *German man, woman*
немно́жко *a little bit*
нет *no*
но *but*
но́вый *new*
нога́ *leg, foot*
нож *knife*
нока́ут *knock-out*
но́мер *number, hotel room*
норве́жец, норве́жка *Norwegian man, woman*
норма́льно *all right, fine*
нос *nose*
но́утбук *notebook (computer)*
но́чью *at night*
ноя́брь (*m*) *November*

о *about*
обе́д *dinner*
обе́дать 1 *to have dinner*
обме́н валю́ты *currency exchange*
обра́тный биле́т *return ticket*
о́бувь (*f*) *footwear*
обы́чно *usually*
объе́кт *object*
о́вощи *vegetables*
огуре́ц, огу́рчик *cucumber, gherkin*
оде́жда *clothes*
оде́т *dressed*
одея́ло *blanket*
(биле́т в) оди́н коне́ц *one-way ticket*
одну́ мину́точку *wait a minute*
окно́ *window*
октя́брь (*m*) *October*
омле́т *omelette*
он *he, it*
она́ *she, it*
они́ *they*
оно́ *it*
о́пера *opera*

орке́стр *orchestra*
о́сень (*f*) *autumn*
о́сенью *in autumn*
остано́вка *stop (bus)*
осторо́жно *carefully*
отде́л *department*
отдыха́ть 1 *to rest, holiday*
оте́ц *father*
откро́йте *open (imperative)*
открыва́ется *it opens*
откры́т *open*
откры́тка *postcard*
отку́да *where from*
отправле́ние *departure*
о́тпуск *holiday*
от себя́ *push*
отхо́дит (по́езд) *departs (train)*
о́тчество *patronymic name*
официа́нт, официа́нтка *waiter, waitress*
о́чень *very*
о́чередь (*f*) *queue*
очки́ *spectacles*

пальто́ *coat*
па́па *dad*
папиро́са *cigarette with cardboard mouthpiece*
парикма́херская *hairdresser's*
парк *park*
парфюме́рия *perfumery*
па́смурно *it's overcast*
па́спорт *passport*
па́спортный контро́ль *passport control*
пассажи́р *passenger*
пассажи́рский *passenger (adj)*
па́чка *packet*
пеницилли́н *penicillin*
пе́нсия *pension*
пепси-ко́ла *Pepsi-cola*
пе́рвое блю́до *first (soup) course*
переса́дка *change (train)*
перехо́д *crossing*
пе́рец *pepper*
пешко́м *on foot*
пиани́но *piano*

пианист *pianist*
пиво *beer*
пинг-понг *table tennis*
пистолет *pistol*
письмо *letter*
пить 1 (пью, пьёшь) *to drink*
пицца *pizza*
пишу *I write*
план *plan*
планета *planet*
платить *to pay*
платок *shawl*
платформа *platform*
платье *dress*
плохо *it's bad*
площадь (f) (на) *square*
плюс *plus*
по-английски *in English*
повторите *repeat (imperative)*
погода *weather*
подарок *present*
подпись (f) *signature*
подушка *pillow*
поедем *let's go (by transport)*
поезд *train*
пожалуйста *please*
пожар *fire*
(как вы) поживаете? *how are you?*
пожилой *elderly*
позвонить *to telephone*
поздно *it's late*
по-испански *in Spanish*
пойдём *let's go (on foot)*
пойти *to go (on foot)*
покажите *show (imperative)*
полдень (m) *midday*
поликлиника *health centre*
полночь (f) *midnight*
полный *chubby*
полотенце *towel*
помидор *tomato*
помню *I remember*
по-моему *in my opinion*
понедельник *Monday*
по-немецки *in German*

понимать 1 *to understand*
понятно *it's understood*
попасть *to get to*
пора *it's time*
португалец, португалка *Portuguese man, woman*
по-русски *in Russian*
послать *to send*
посмотреть *to have a look*
посмотрите *look (imperative)*
посылка *parcel*
(мы) потеряли *(we) lost*
потом *then*
потому, что *because*
почта (на) *post office*
почтовый ящик *post box*
поэт *poet*
по-японски *in Japanese*
правда *truth (newspaper)*
правильно *that's right*
правый *right*
праздник *public holiday, festive occasion*
прекрасно *it's fine*
прекрасный *fine (adj)*
престижный район *prestige district*
приезжайте к нам в гости *come and visit us (imperative)*
принести *to bring*
принимать 1 (лекарство) *to take (medicine)*
принтер *printer*
приятно *that's nice*
приятного аппетита *bon appétit, enjoy your meal*
пробейте талон *punch ticket (imperative)*
проводник, проводница *conductor, conductress*
прогноз *forecast*
продавец, продавщица *shop assistant (m, f)*
продаётся, продаются *is for sale, are for sale*
продукты *provisions*

(у меня) пропа́л   *(I've) lost*
проспе́кт   *avenue*
профе́ссия   *profession*
прохла́дно   *it's cool*
пря́мо   *straight ahead*
путеше́ствовать   *to travel*
пье́са   *play*
пэйнтбо́л   *paintball*
пя́тница   *Friday*

рабо́та (на)   *work*
рабо́тать 1   *to work*
ра́дио   *radio*
раз   *once, time*
разгово́р   *conversation*
раздева́йтесь   *take coat off*
   (imperative)
ра́но   *early*
расписа́ние   *timetable*
ре́гби   *rugby*
регистра́ция   *registration*
рейс   *flight*
река́   *river*
(вы) рекоменду́ете   *(you)*
   recommend
реко́рд   *record*
ре́мни   *seat belts*
ремо́нт   *repair*
рестора́н   *restaurant*
реце́пт   *prescription, recipe*
рис   *rice*
рисова́ть   *to draw*
рождество́   *Christmas*
ро́за   *rose*
рома́н   *novel*
Росси́я   *Russia*
рот   *mouth*
руба́шка   *shirt*
рубль (m)   *rouble*
рука́   *arm, hand*
ру́сский, ру́сская   *Russian man,*
   woman (adj)
ры́ба   *fish*
ры́жий   *red haired*
ры́нок   *market*
рю́мка   *wine glass*

с   *with*
сад   *garden*
сади́тесь   *sit down (imperative)*
саксофо́н   *saxophone*
сала́т   *salad*
салфе́тка   *napkin*
самова́р   *samovar*
самолёт   *aeroplane*
са́уна   *sauna*
са́хар   *sugar*
све́жий   *fresh*
све́тлый   *light*
сви́тер   *sweater*
свобо́дный   *free*
се́вер (на)   *north*
сего́дня   *today*
сейча́с   *now*
семья́   *family*
сентя́брь (m)   *September*
се́рдце   *heart*
се́рфинг   *surfing*
се́рый   *grey*
серьёзный   *serious*
сестра́   *sister*
сигаре́та   *cigarette*
сигна́л   *signal*
симпто́м   *symptom*
симфо́ния   *symphony*
скажи́те   *say, tell me (imperative)*
ско́лько   *how much, how many*
ско́лько вам лет?   *how old are*
   you?
ско́лько с меня́?   *how much do I*
   owe?
ско́лько сейча́с вре́мени?   *what's*
   the time?
ско́лько сто́ит, стоя́т?   *how much*
   does it, do they cost?
ско́рая медици́нская по́мощь
   ambulance
ско́рый   *fast*
ску́чный   *boring*
сле́дующий   *next*
сли́шком   *too, too much*
сло́во   *word*
слома́ть   *to break*

слу́шать 1 *to listen*
слу́шаю вас *I'm listening*
смета́на *smetana (sour cream)*
смешно́ *it's funny*
смотре́ть 2 *to look, watch*
снег *snow*
сну́кер *snooker*
собира́ть 1 *to collect*
совсе́м *quite, entirely*
сок *juice*
соли́ст *soloist*
со́лнце све́тит *the sun is shining*
соль (f) *salt*
соси́ска *sausage*
спа́льный ваго́н *sleeping car (train)*
спа́льня *bedroom*
спаси́бо *thank you*
спать *to sleep*
спина́ *back*
споко́йно *it's peaceful*
споко́йной но́чи *good night*
спорт *sport*
спортсме́н, спортсме́нка *sportsman, sportswoman*
спра́вочное бюро́ *information bureau*
спу́тник *sputnik*
спу́тниковое ТВ *satellite TV*
среда́ *Wednesday*
стадио́н (на) *stadium*
стака́н *glass*
ста́нция (на) *station (bus, metro)*
старт *start*
ста́рый *old*
стол *table*
столо́вая *dining room*
стоп *stop*
стоя́нка такси́ *taxi rank*
стро́йный *slim*
студе́нт, студе́нтка *student (m, f)*
стул *chair*
суббо́та *Saturday*
сувени́р *souvenir*
стюарде́сса *stewardess*
с удово́льствием *with pleasure*

су́мка *bag*
суп *soup*
суперма́ркет *supermarket*
су́шка *dry ring-shaped biscuit*
счёт *bill*
сын *son*
сыр *cheese*
сюда́ *here (motion)*

таба́к *tobacco*
табле́тка *tablet*
так *so*
такси́ *taxi*
тало́н *ticket (transport)*
там *there*
тамо́женный контро́ль *customs control*
танцева́ть *to dance*
таре́лка *plate*
теа́тр *theatre*
текст *text*
телеви́зор *television*
телегра́мма *telegram*
телефо́н *telephone*
телефо́н-автома́т *public pay phone*
телефонка́рта *phonecard*
тёмный *dark*
температу́ра *temperature*
те́ннис *tennis*
тенниси́ст, тенниси́стка *tennis player (m, f)*
тепло́ *it's warm*
теря́ть *to lose*
тётя *aunt*
ти́хо *it's quiet*
то..., то... *now this, now the other*
това́рищ *comrade*
то́же *also*
то́лстый *fat*
то́лько *only*
торт *cake*
то́стер *toaster*
то́чно так! *just so!*
(меня́) тошни́т *(I) feel sick*
тра́ктор *tractor*
тракори́ст, тракори́стка

tractor driver (m, f)
трамва́й *tram*
трампли́н *ski jump*
транзи́т *transit*
тра́нспорт *transport*
тре́нер *trainer*
три́ллер *thriller*
тролле́йбус *trolleybus*
туале́т *toilet*
тума́нно *it's foggy, misty*
тури́ст, тури́стка *tourist (m, f)*
туристи́ческое аге́тство *tourist agency*
ту́фли *shoes*
ты *you (singular, informal)*

у вас есть? *do you have?*
угоща́йтесь *help yourself (imperative)*
ужа́сно *it's awful*
ужа́сный *awful*
уже́ *already*
у́жин *supper*
у́жинать 1 *to have supper*
у́лица (на) *street*
универма́г *department store*
универса́м *supermarket*
университе́т *university*
уста́л *tired*
у́тром *in the morning*
у́хо, у́ши *ear, ears*
учи́тель, учи́тельница *teacher (m, f)*

фа́брика (на) *factory*
факс *fax*
фами́лия *surname*
февра́ль (m) *February*
фен-шу́й *feng-shui*
фина́л *final*
фотоаппара́т *camera*
Фра́нция *France*
францу́з, францу́женка *French man, woman*
фрукт *fruit*
фунт сте́рлингов *pound sterling*
футбо́л *football*
футболи́ст *footballer*

хе́ви металл-ро́к *heavy metal rock*
хи́мик *chemist*
хлеб *bread*
ходи́ть 2 (хожу́, хо́дишь) *to go on foot (habitually)*
хоккей *ice hockey*
хо́лодно *it's cold*
холо́дный *cold*
хоро́ший *good*
хорошо́ *it's good*
хоте́ть, (хочу́, хо́чешь, хо́чет, хоти́м, хоти́те, хотя́т) *to want*
храм *church*
худо́й *thin*
ху́же *worse*

цветы́ *flowers*
центр *centre*
це́рковь (f) *church*
цирк *circus*
ци́фры *numbers*

чай *tea*
час *hour, o'clock*
ча́сто *often*
часы́ *watch, clock*
ча́шка *cup*
чек *receipt, chit*
челове́к *man, person*
чемода́н *suitcase*
че́рез *after*
чёрный *black*
четве́рг *Thursday*
число́ *number, date*
чита́ть 1 *to read*
что *what, that*
что вы! *what on earth!*
что с ва́ми? *what's the matter?*
что у вас есть? *what have you got?*
я чу́вствую себя́ *I feel*
чуде́сно *it's wonderful*

шампу́нь (m) *shampoo*
ша́пка *hat*
шашлы́к *kebab (shashlik)*

шкаф *cupboard*
шко́ла *school*
шокола́д *chocolate*
шокола́дный *chocolate (adj)*
шотла́ндец, шотла́ндка *Scot (m, f)*
шу́мно *it's noisy*

щи *shshee (cabbage soup)*

экску́рсия *excursion*
экспериме́нт *experiment*
экспре́сс *express*
электри́ческий *electric*
электри́чество *electricity*
электри́чка *suburban train*
электро́ника *electronics*
эли́тная кварти́ра *elite apartment*
энерги́чный *energetic*

эне́ргия *energy*
эта́ж *floor, storey*
э́та *this (f)*
э́ти *these*
э́то *it is, this (n)*
э́тот *this (m)*

ю́бка *skirt*
юг (на) *south*

я *I*
я́блоко *apple*
янва́рь *(m) January*
япо́нец, япо́нка *Japanese man, woman*
Япо́ния *Japan*
я́сли *day nursery*
яхт *yacht*